THIRD EDITION

INSTITUTIONS *and* ORGANIZATIONS

For Joy—who constructs and tends institutions of value to many of us

THIRD EDITION

INSTITUTIONS *and* ORGANIZATIONS
Ideas and Interests

W. RICHARD SCOTT
Stanford University

SAGE Publications

Los Angeles • London • New Delhi • Singapore

For information:

Sage Publications, Inc.
2455 Teller Road
Thousand Oaks,
  California 91320
E-mail: order@sagepub.com

Sage Publications India Pvt. Ltd.
B 1/I 1 Mohan Cooperative
  Industrial Area
Mathura Road, New Delhi 110 044
India

Sage Publications Ltd.
1 Oliver's Yard
55 City Road
London EC1Y 1SP
United Kingdom

Sage Publications Asia-Pacific Pte. Ltd.
33 Pekin Street #02–01
Far East Square
Singapore 048763

Printed in the United States of America

Library of Congress Cataloging-in-Publication Data

Scott, W. Richard.
Institutions and organizations: Ideas and interests/W. Richard Scott.—3rd ed.
    p. cm.
Includes bibliographical references and index.
ISBN 978-1-4129-5090-9 (pbk.)
    1. Organizational sociology. 2. Social institutions. I. Title.

HM786.S3845 2008
302.3'5—dc22   2007020493

Printed on acid-free paper

07   08   09   10   11   10 9 8 7 6 5 4 3 2 1

Acquiring Editor:	Al Bruckner
Editorial Assistant:	MaryAnn Vail
Production Editor:	Sarah K. Quesenberry
Copy Editor:	Heather Jefferson
Proofreader:	Colleen Brennan
Typesetter:	C&M Digitals (P) Ltd.
Marketing Manager:	Nichole Angress

Contents

Preface   vii

Introduction   ix
     Institutional Bridges   x

1. **Early Institutionalists**   1
     Early Institutional Theory in Economics   2
     Early Institutional Theory in Political Science   5
     Early Institutional Theory in Sociology   8
     Concluding Comment   16
     Notes   17

2. **Institutional Theory Meets Organization Studies**   19
     Institutions and Organizations: Early Approaches   20
     Foundations of Neoinstitutional Theory   26
     Concluding Comment   44
     Notes   45

3. **Crafting an Analytic Framework I:**
   Three Pillars of Institutions   47
     Defining Institutions   48
     The Three Pillars of Institutions   50
     The Three Pillars and Legitimacy   59
     Basic Assumptions Associated With the Three Pillars   62
     Concluding Comment   70
     Notes   71

4. **Crafting an Analytic Framework II:**
   Content, Agency, Carriers, and Levels   73
     Institutional Content and Organizations   73
     Agency and Institutions   76
     Varying Carriers   79
     Varying Levels of Analysis   85

Concluding Comment   90
Notes   91

5. **Institutional Construction**   93
    Creating Institutions   94
    Selected Studies of Institutional Construction   106
    Concluding Comment   119
    Notes   119

6. **Institutionalization**   **121**
    Three Conceptions of Institutionalization:
        Underlying Mechanisms   121
    Maintaining and Diffusing Institutions   128
    Carriers and Institutional Mechanisms   140
    Concluding Comment   145
    Notes   146

7. **Institutional Processes and Organizations**   **149**
    Organizations and Institutions: Three Views   150
    Legitimacy and Isomorphism   151
    Institutional Context and Organizational Structure   158
    Strategic Responses   169
    Sources of Divergence   177
    Concluding Comment   178
    Notes   178

8. **Institutional Processes and Organization Fields**   **181**
    Conceptualizing Organization Fields   181
    Field Structuration Processes   190
    Structuration, Destructuration, and Restructuration   195
    Concluding Comment   208
    Notes   209

9. **An Overview and a Caution**   **211**
    Distinctive Features   211
    The Maturation of Institutional Theory and Research   215
    A Cautionary Comment   219
    Notes   220

References   **221**

Index   **259**

About the Author   **265**

Preface

The first edition of this book appeared in 1995. It was developed as part of a larger Sage series, Foundations for Organizational Science, intended to introduce advanced students to core theoretical perspectives in organizational studies. Series editor, David Whetten, invited several of us to review selected central theories and provide an overview of ongoing and needed research to advance the enterprise. Subsequently, I produced an updated and expanded version of this work in 2001. This series is now discontinued, but the basic aim of the current volume remains unchanged.

I see a continuing need for a (relatively) brief, cogent introduction to institutional theory as it relates to organizations. Such a project must acknowledge the strength and variety of early, foundational statements and explain how and why seminal work on institutional forces shaping social forms at the turn of the 19th and 20th centuries was displaced by or subordinated to later scholarly approaches. Equally important, it must explain the ways in which the paths of institutional and organizational studies began to again converge and interact productively in the 1970s.

Most fundamentally, there is a need in this area for theoretical/conceptual coherence. How are we to understand institutions and institutionalization processes? The existing literature is a jungle of conflicting conceptions, divergent underlying assumptions, and discordant voices. Beginning with the 1995 version, I have struggled to craft an inclusive definition of institutions and to develop an "encompassing framework" that both incorporates the major clusters of institutional theories and also indicates the ways in which they differ. With each subsequent edition, I have endeavored to further clarify and elaborate these distinctive traditions while insisting on their underlying commonalities.

In addition to tackling the problem of theoretical incoherence, I have also labored to provide an overview of and guide to recent methodological developments and empirical research on institutional processes as they relate to organizations. It is no exaggeration to say that, beginning around 1990, there has been an explosion of improved methods and research designs in this area. The volume of work produced during the past two decades is such that it is not possible to acknowledge or summarize all of the relevant studies. However, in the present volume, I identify, summarize, and comment on some of the recent, innovative work that has advanced our understanding of how institutional processes relate to organizational structures and behavior.

It is my strong conviction that institutional theory provides the most promising and productive lens for viewing organizations in contemporary society. As a result, it is not surprising to me that institutional work on organizations is currently the most vigorous scholarly arena within organization studies. I attempt to communicate some of this intellectual excitement in this book, and I hope that it serves as an irresistible invitation to beginning and advanced scholars alike to join the conversation.

In preparing this new edition, I received helpful comments from a number of colleagues who read all or parts of the manuscript. I wish to acknowledge, with thanks, the useful comments of Tamar Kricheli-Katz, Ryan Orr, Walter W. (Woody) Powell, and Hayagreeva (Huggy) Rao.

W. Richard (Dick) Scott
Stanford, California

Introduction

Institutional theory, at least in its newest guise, burst on the organizations scene during the mid-1970s and has generated much interest and attention. It has raised provocative questions about the world of organizations:

- Why do organizations of the same type, such as schools and hospitals, located in widely scattered locales so closely resemble one another?
- Institutions of various sorts have existed for thousands of years. What specific types of institutions are associated with the rise of organizations?
- How are we to regard behavior in organizational settings? Does it reflect the pursuit of rational interests and the exercise of conscious choice, or is behavior primarily shaped by conventions, routines, and habits?
- What is the relation between freedom and control in social life?
- Why is organizational participants' behavior often observed to depart from the formal rules and stated goals of the organization?
- Why is it, if formal rules are largely ignored, that resources and energy are expended to maintain these formal structures?
- Why and how do laws, rules, and other types of regulative and normative systems arise? Do individuals voluntarily construct rule systems that then operate to bind their own behavior?
- Where do interests come from? Do they stem from human nature or are they culturally constructed?
- Why do specific structures and practices diffuse through a field of organizations in ways not predicted by the particular characteristics of adopting organizations?
- How do differences in cultural beliefs shape the nature and operation of organizations?

- Why do organizations and individuals conform to institutions? Is it because they are rewarded for doing so, because they think they are morally obliged to obey, or because they can conceive of no other way of behaving?
- What processes relate institutions to organizations? What vehicles or carriers transmit institutional messages to organizations, and how do organizational actions and reactions affect institutions?
- If institutions work to promote stability and order, how does change occur? If institutions control and constitute individuals, how can individuals hope to alter the systems in which they are embedded?

I see the ascendance of institutional theory as simply a continuation and extension of the intellectual revolution begun during the mid-1960s that introduced open systems conceptions into the study of organizations. Open systems theory transformed existing approaches by insisting on the importance of the wider context or environment as it constrains, shapes, penetrates, and renews the organization (see Katz and Kahn 1966; Scott and Davis 2007: chap. 4). First to be recognized was the technical environment—resources and task-related information— as the organization was conceived primarily as an instrumental production system, transforming inputs into outputs. Only later, during the mid-1970s, did investigators begin to recognize the significant effects on organizing of wider social and cultural forces: the institutional environment. Gradually, organizations were seen to be more than production systems; they were also social and cultural systems.

❖ INSTITUTIONAL BRIDGES

The Multiple Meanings of Institutions

Much of the challenge posed by this subject—to the author as well as the readers—resides in the many varying meanings and usage of the concept of *institution*. One of the oldest and most often-employed ideas in social thought, it has continued to take on new and diverse meanings over time, much like barnacles on a ship's hull, without shedding the old. In this book, I attempt to pursue three somewhat contradictory aims.

First, I seek to capture and accurately reflect the richness and diversity of institutional thought, viewed both historically and as a contemporary, ongoing project, drawing on the insights of some of the greatest minds working from the late 19th to the beginning of the 21st centuries. Chapter 1 reviews the principal contributions of influential economists, political scientists, and sociologists working at the turn of the century, a heyday of institutional activity. It appears that, in this early period, institutionalists in economics operated primarily as gadflies and critics, on the margins of the discipline. By contrast, during this same time, institutionalists were regarded as more mainstream in both political science and sociology. Nevertheless, during most of the 20th century, as empiricism and positivism flourished, institutionalists in all disciplines were chased from center stage, persisting primarily in peripheral fields of study such as economic history, industrial relations, and the sociology of work. Hence, when the field of organizations was established as an academic specialty, around the 1940s, institutionalists were hardly to be found. Chapter 2 relates the story of how institutional theory became connected to and developed within the area of organizations.

A second aim of the book is to provide a relatively comprehensive analytic framework so that the different conceptions of institutions and the variety of underlying assumptions and methodological approaches can be better understood. My objective is not to differentiate in order to dismiss or belittle one or another formulation, but to improve our understanding of the many flavors and colors of institutionalism. The construction of the comparative framework commences in chapter 3 and extends into chapter 4, but the exploration of its applications and ramifications continues throughout the remainder of the volume. Although I endeavor to be more, rather than less, inclusive and to be relatively evenhanded in my treatment of the various approaches, I have given more space and attention to those approaches associated with the "new" institutionalism in organizational sociology. This emphasis reflects two motives. First, I am a sociologist by training and temperament and, hence, more comfortable with and, hopefully, better able to describe and assess these perspectives. Second, these newer approaches are, by definition, more recently developed and, as a consequence, more in need of exposition and refinement. I devote considerable energy to interpreting obscure nascent ideas, mediating family disputes, and connecting disparate arguments.

A final objective is to review and assess the burgeoning body of empirical research that has developed in recent years to test and extend institutional arguments. As social scientists, we must be as interested in empirically evaluating theoretical arguments as in generating them. In recent decades, institutional researchers have been both active and highly creative in devising ways to evaluate their assertions. As was the case with the theoretical literature, I have given more coverage to the neoinstitutional sociological studies but have included examples of the wider range of work.

Chapters 5 through 8 present the empirical review. Surveying empirical studies also provides an opportunity to illustrate and further clarify differences in theoretical conceptions. Chapter 5 concentrates on studies concerning the construction of institutional frameworks at diverse levels, ranging from the interpersonal to the international. Chapter 6 examines institutionalization processes more generally, emphasizing the variety of mechanisms involved, both in maintaining and diffusing institutional ideas. Chapter 7 concentrates on the ways in which institutional processes relate to individual organizations, attending to variation in both the unity and complexity of institutional frameworks, as well as to the attributes and strategies of organizations. Chapter 8 assays the concept of organization field, emphasizing its value for pursuing a wide variety of issues regarding the coevolution of organizations and their institutional environments. In chapter 9, I adopt a more individual voice, presenting my personal judgments about the distinctive features associated with an institutional perspective, recent gains in the theoretical and methodological strategies employed, and ending with a cautionary note.

1

Early Institutionalists

No attempt is made here to provide a comprehensive or thorough review of early institutional theory, but to completely neglect these ideas and arguments would be inexcusable. Although much of this work differs from today's institutional agenda, all contemporary scholars draw inspiration from the efforts of the pioneers. In examining this early work, it is important to recognize that contemporary students bring their own interests and concerns to the reading of these texts. As Alexander (1983: vol. 1, 119) observes: "'Reading' is an important part of any theoretical strategy, and if the work in question is in any way open to varied interpretation then it certainly will be so interpreted." Conflicting interpretations are even more likely when the theorists in question change their views over time—so that, for example, there appears to be an "early" Durkheim and a "late" one—or when, like Weber, they simultaneously express contradictory or ambivalent views.

Somewhat arbitrarily, I sort the work into disciplinary categories—although, as soon becomes apparent, greater divisions often exist within than between disciplinary camps—and briefly review leading contributors to institutional thought from the late 19th to the mid-20th centuries in economics, political science, and sociology.

❖ EARLY INSTITUTIONAL THEORY IN ECONOMICS

It is well at the outset to acknowledge the lack of logical coherence in the strands of work to be examined. In many respects, the "old" institutional economics bears a stronger intellectual kinship with the "new" institutional approaches advanced by sociologists and organizational scholars than to the "new" institutional economics. Conversely, the new institutional economics is more indebted to the critics of old institutional economics than to their early namesakes. The earliest institutional arguments arose in Germany and Austria in the late 19th century as one by-product of the famous *Methodenstreit:* the debate over scientific method in the social sciences. Drawing energy and inspiration from the earlier Romantic Movement as well as from the ideas of Kant and Hegel, a collection of economists challenged the conventional cannon that economics could be reduced to a set of universal laws. Led by Gustav Schmoller (1900–1904), this Historical School insisted that economic processes operated within a social framework that was in turn shaped by a set of cultural and historical forces. Historical and comparative research was required to discern the distinctive properties of particular economic systems. Moreover, Schmoller and his associates called for economics to eschew its simplistic assumptions regarding "economic man" and embrace more realistic models of human behavior.

The principal defender of the classical approach in this debate was Carl Menger (1883/1981), the Viennese economist who insisted on the utility of simplifying assumptions and the value of developing economic principles that were both abstract and timeless. Rather than denying the importance of broader societal institutional forces, Menger argued that institutions were themselves social phenomena in need of theoretical explanation. It is for this reason that Langlois (1986a: 5) suggested that Menger "has perhaps more claim to be the patron saint of the new institutional economics than has any of the original institutionalists."

As with many intellectual debates, the warring factions sharpened and perfected their arguments, but neither succeeded in convincing the other. Attempts at reconciliation and synthesis occurred only among scholars of a later generation—principally in the work of Weber, to be discussed later.

Many of the ideas of the Historical School were embraced and further developed by American institutional economists, a number of whom were trained in Germany. An earlier cohort working in the mid-19th century did not receive much attention. However, by the turn of the century, three institutional economists had become quite influential: Thorstein Veblen, John Commons, and Westley Mitchell. Although there were important differences in their views, all three criticized conventional economic models for their unrealistic assumptions and inattention to historical change.

Veblen was highly critical of the underlying economic assumptions regarding individual behavior: He ridiculed "the hedonistic conception of man as that of a lightning calculator of pleasures and pain" (Veblen 1898: 389). Instead, Veblen insisted that much behavior was governed by habit and convention. "Not only is the individual's conduct edged about and directed by his habitual relations to his fellows in the group, but these relations, being of an institutional character, vary as the institutional scene varies" (Veblen 1909: 245). Indeed, Veblen (1919: 239) defined institutions as "settled habits of thought common to the generality of man."

Commons (1924: 7) similarly challenged the conventional emphasis on individual choice behavior, suggesting that a more appropriate unit of economic analysis was the "transaction," a concept borrowed from legal analysis. "The *transaction* is two or more wills giving, taking, persuading, coercing, defrauding, commanding, obeying, competing, governing, in a world of scarcity, mechanisms and rules of conduct" (italics added). The "rules of conduct" to which Commons alluded are social institutions. Institutional rules were necessary to define the limits within which individuals and firms could pursue their objectives (Commons 1950/1970).

> To Commons, the institutions existing at a specific time represent nothing more than imperfect and pragmatic solutions to reconcile past conflicts; they are solutions that consist of a set of rights and duties, an authority for enforcing them, and some degree of adherence to collective norms of prudent reasonable behavior. (Van de Ven 1993: 142)

All three institutional economists emphasized the importance of change and were critical of their colleagues for not making its examination central to their work. Veblen embraced an evolutionary perspective and insisted that a valid economics would emphasize the role of technological change and trace the changing phases of the economy. Commons likewise stressed the centrality of change, viewing the economy as "a moving, changing process" (Commons 1924: 376). Mitchell believed that conventional economics was a hindrance to understanding the nature of the business cycle, and he devoted much energy to studying economic change. Like most institutionalists (except for some varieties of rational choice scholars), he was reluctant to embrace an assumption of economic equilibrium. As one of the founders of the National Bureau of Economic Research and chair of the committee that published the voluminous report, *Recent Social Trends* (President's Research Committee on Social Trends 1934), Mitchell pioneered in the collection of empirical data on the operation of the economy, insisting that economic principles should be grounded in facts as opposed to abstract, deductive theories.

The American institutionalists were influenced not only by the German Historical School, but also by the home-grown philosophy of pragmatism as espoused by Dewey, James, and others. Their work reflected a suspicion of abstract, universal principles; an interest in solving practical problems; and an awareness of the role of chance events and historical contingencies (see chap. 3).

Jaccoby (1990) argues that the approaches offered by the early institutionalists departed from those adopted by their mainstream, neoclassical colleagues in four important respects:

- *Indeterminancy vs. determinancy.* Although the orthodox model assumed "perfect competition and unique equilibria, the institutionalists pointed to pervasive market power and to indeterminacy even under competition" (Jaccoby 1990: 318).
- *Endogenous vs. exogenous determination of preferences.* Neoclassical theorists posited individual preferences or wants, whereas institutionalists argued that such preferences were shaped by social institutions whose operation should be the subject of economic analysis.
- *Behavioral realism vs. simplifying assumptions.* Institutional theorists argued that economists should utilize more pragmatic and psychologically realistic models of economic motivation rather than subscribe to naive utilitarian assumptions.
- *Diachronic vs. synchronic analysis.* Rather than assuming the "timeless and placeless" assumptions of the neoclassical theorists, institutionalists insisted that economists should ascertain "how the economy acquired its features and the conditions that cause these features to vary over time and place" (Jaccoby 1990: 320).[1]

Regardless of whether they were correct in their accusations and assertions, the early institutional economists did not prevail: Neoclassical theory was victorious and continues its dominance up to the present time. Prior to the rise of the new institutional economics in the 1970s, only a few economists attempted to carry forward the institutionalists' agenda, the best known of whom are J. A. Schumpeter, Karl Polanyi, John Kenneth Galbraith, and Gunnar Myrdal (see Swedberg 1991). Arguably, the subfields of economics most affected by the legacy of the institutional theorists are those of labor economics, the field in which Commons specialized; industrial relations, which focuses on broader social and political factors affecting economic structures and processes; and the economics of industry, which examines the varying configurations of industrial structures and their effects on the strategies and performance of individual firms.

Why was the impact of the early institutionalists blunted? Modern-day commentators offer several explanations. The German Historical School no doubt overemphasized the uniqueness of different economic systems and underemphasized the value of analytic theory. Even sympathetic critics acknowledge that Veblen exhibited "an explicit hostility to intellectual 'symmetry and system-building'" (Hodgson 1996: 211) and that Commons' arguments were hampered by his "idiosyncratic terminology and unsystematic style of reasoning" (Vanberg 1989: 343). But a more serious shortcoming was the tendency for the work to degenerate into naive empiricism and historicism. Emphasizing the importance of the particular, of time, place, and historical circumstance, institutional analysis came more and more to underline "the value of largely descriptive work on the nature and function of politico-economic institutions" (Hodgson 1991: 211).

Here then we have the principal reason that the godfather of the "new" institutional economics, Ronald Coase (1983: 230), so cavalierly dismissed the "old" institutional economics: "Without a theory they had nothing to pass on except a mass of descriptive material waiting for a theory, or a fire."

The battle between the particular and the general, between the temporal and the timeless, is one that contemporary institutional theorists continue to confront.

❖ EARLY INSTITUTIONAL THEORY IN POLITICAL SCIENCE

Institutional approaches dominated political science in both Europe and America during the latter half of the 19th and the first two decades of the 20th centuries. I concentrate on the American scene. As carried out by such leading practitioners as J. W. Burgess (1902), Woodrow Wilson (1889), and W. W. Willoughby (1896, 1904), institutional analysis was grounded in constitutional law and moral philosophy. In the heavy tomes produced by these scholars, careful attention was given to the legal framework and administrative arrangements characterizing particular governance (primarily nation-state) structures. Much of the work involved painstaking historical examination of the origins, controversies, and compromises producing specific regimes; some analyses were explicitly comparative, detailing how central problems or functions were variously managed by diverse governance mechanisms. But the underlying tone of the work was normative: "in the mainstream of political science, description was overshadowed by moral philosophy" (Simon 1991: 57).

As depicted by Bill and Hardgrave (1981; see also Peters 1999), the institutional school that developed at the turn of the century exhibited several defining features. First, it was preoccupied with formal structures and legal systems. "Emphasis was placed upon the organized and evident institutions of government, and studies concentrated almost exclusively upon constitutions, cabinets, parliaments, courts, and bureaucracies" (Bill and Hardgrave 1981: 3).

Second, the approach emphasized detailed accounts of particular political systems, resulting in "configurative description"—intricate descriptive accounts of interlinked rules, rights, and procedures (Bill and Hardgrave 1981: 3). Third, the approach was conservative in the sense that it emphasized origins but not ongoing change. "Political institutions were examined in terms of an evolutionary development which found fulfillment in the immediate present. But while these institutions had a past, they apparently had no future" (Bill and Hardgrave 1981: 6). They were regarded as completed products. Fourth, the work was largely nontheoretical, primary attention being given to historical reconstruction of specific institutional forms. Finally, the tone of these studies was more that associated with moral philosophy and less that of empirical science. These scholars devoted more attention to the explication of normative principles than to the formulation of testable propositions.

Although he acknowledged many of the same characteristics, Eckstein (1963) also insists that these early institutionalists ushered in the first crude form of positivism in political science. Unlike their own predecessors, primarily "historicists" who focused their interest on abstracted political systems derived from philosophical principles, they were looking at the real world—at hard facts. Indeed

Primitive, unadulterated positivism insists upon hard facts, indubitable and incontrovertible facts, as well as facts that speak for themselves—and what facts of politics are harder, as well as more self-explanatory than the facts found in formal legal codes? (Eckstein 1963: 10)

In addition, these students attended to the real world in yet another sense: They placed great emphasis on formal political institutions, on charters, legal codes, and administrative rules, in part because "the nineteenth century was a great age of constitution-making" (Eckstein 1963: 10).

Beginning in the mid-1930s and continuing through the 1960s, the institutional perspective was challenged and largely supplanted by the behavioralist approach (not to be confused with "behaviorism" in psychology), which attempted to sever the tie to moral philosophy and rebuild political science as a theoretically guided, empirical science (see Easton 1965). More important for our concerns, the behavioralist persuasion diverted attention away from institutional structures to political behavior.

Behaviorists argued that, in order to understand politics and explain political outcomes, analysts should focus not on the formal attributes of government institutions but instead on informal distributions of power, attitudes and political behavior. (Thelen and Steinmo 1992: 4)

Students of politics focused attention on voting behavior, party formation, and public opinion. Moreover, this reductionist shift in emphasis from rules and structures to behavior was accompanied by a more utilitarian orientation, viewing action as "the product of calculated self-interest," and taking an instrumentalist view of politics regarding the "allocation of resources as the central concern of political life" (March and Olsen 1984: 735). To study politics was to study "Who Gets What, When, and How?" (Lasswell 1936).

These theoretical strands associated with behavioralism were reinforced and deepened by the "rational revolution" arising in the 1970s and 1980s. As I discuss in later chapters, the rational choice approach—based on the application of economic assumptions to political behavior—brought about fundamental changes in political science. Peters (1999) suggests that the attributes characterizing both movements, behavioral and rational, include: (1) an emphasis on more rigorous and deductive theory and methodology; (2) a bias against normative, prescriptive approaches; (3) methodological individualism—the assumptions that individuals are the only actors and that they are motivated by individual utility maximization; and (4) "inputism," a focus on societal inputs to the political system (e.g., votes, interest group pressures, money) to the exclusion of attention to the internal workings of the system—the institutional political structures—as they may affect outcomes.

The "new institutionalism" in political science developed in reaction to the excesses of the behavioralist revolution, although one major variant employs rational choice approaches to account for the building and maintenance of institutions. Current institutionalists do not call for a return to "configurational history," but do seek to reestablish the importance of normative frameworks and rule systems in guiding, constraining, and empowering social and political behavior.

❖ EARLY INSTITUTIONAL THEORY IN SOCIOLOGY

Attention to institutions by sociologists has been more constant than that exhibited by either economists or political scientists. Although there are a number of different discernable strands with their distinctive vocabularies and emphases, we also observe continuity from the early work of Spencer and Sumner through Davis to the recent work of Friedland and Alford; from Cooley and Park through Hughes to the contemporary analyses of Freidson and Abbott; from the early efforts of Marx, Durkheim, and Weber through Parsons to DiMaggio and Powell; and from the early work on the social sources of mind and self in Mead and Schutz to the emphasis on cognitive processes and knowledge systems in Berger and Luckmann and in Meyer and Rowan.

Spencer and Sumner

Without question, the most influential conception of institutions pervading mainstream sociology throughout the 20th century has its origins in the work of Herbert Spencer. Spencer (1876, 1896, 1910) viewed society as an organic system evolving through time. Adaptation of the system to its context was achieved via the functions of specialized "organs" structured as institutional subsystems. Spencer devoted the main body of his work to a comparative study of these institutions, attempting to draw generalizations from comparing and contrasting their operation in different societies.

Spencer's general conceptions were embraced and amplified by William Graham Sumner (1906) in his major treatise, *Folkways*. Teeming with ethnographic and historical materials, the book generated numerous hypotheses concerning the origins, persistence, and change of folkways and mores (albeit many of these have a strong biopsychological basis). For Sumner (1906: 53), "an institution consists of a concept (idea, notion, doctrine, interest) and a structure." The "concept" defines the purposes or functions of the institution, whereas the "structure" embodies the idea of the institution and furnishes the instrumentalities through which the idea is put into action. Societal evolution progresses from individual activities to folkways, to mores, to full-fledged institutions. Such institutions are "crescive"—evolving slowly through instinctive efforts over long periods of time—although institutions can also be "enacted"—the products of rational intention and invention.

Later generations of sociologists discarded the strong biological/ evolutionary analogies and functional arguments devised by Spencer and Sumner, but nevertheless recognized the centrality of institutions as a sociological focus. Thus, in his influential mid-century text, *Human Society,* Kingsley Davis (1949: 71) defined institutions as "a set of interwoven folkways, mores and laws built around one or more functions," adding that, in his opinion, "the concept of institutions seems better than any other to convey the notion of segments or parts of the normative order." Every major sociological text and curriculum of the last 100 years has reflected on not only the important distinction of levels (e.g., individuals, groups, communities, societies), but also the functional division of social life into spheres or arenas—such as kinship, stratification, politics, economics, and religion—governed by varying normative systems. The conception of institutions as functionally specialized arenas persists in contemporary notions of organization "field" or "sector" (DiMaggio and Powell 1983; Scott and Meyer 1983; see chaps. 3 and 8) and is strongly reflected in the work of Friedland and Alford (1991), who stress the role of multiple, differentiated, and partially conflicting institutional spheres in producing social change.

Cooley and Hughes

Cooley and his followers emphasized the interdependence of individuals and institutions, of self and social structure. Although the great institutions—"language, government, the church, laws and customs of property and of the family"—appear to be independent and external to behavior, they are developed and preserved through interactions among individuals and exist "as a habit of mind and of action, largely unconscious because largely common to all the group. . . . The individual is always cause as well as effect of the institution" (Cooley 1902/1956: 313–314).

Hughes shared and developed this interdependent model. Deftly defining institutions as an "establishment of relative permanence of a distinctly social sort" (Hughes 1936: 180), he identified their essential elements as:

(1) a set of mores or formal rules, or both, which can be fulfilled only by (2) people acting collectively, in established complementary capacities or offices. The first element represents consistency; the second concert or organization. (Hughes 1939: 297)

Although institutions represent continuity and persistence, they exist only to the extent that they are carried forward by individuals: "Institutions exist in the integrated and standardized behavior of individuals" (Hughes 1939: 319). In most of his writing, Hughes directed attention to the institutional structures surrounding and supporting work activities: in particular, to occupations and professions. His studies and essays are laced with insights on the myriad ways in which the institutional interacts with the individual—creating identities, shaping the life course ("careers"), providing a "license" to perform otherwise forbidden tasks, and a rationale to account for the inevitable mistakes that occur when one is performing complex work (see Hughes 1958).[2]

Empirical work developing these insights has focused more on occupations—in particular, professions—than on organizations as institutional systems constraining and empowering individual participants (see e.g., Abbott 1988; Becker 1982; Freidson 1970). However, a number of studies examined "strong" organizational contexts, such as mental hospitals and medical schools (Becker et al. 1961; Goffman 1961). These studies emphasized "the microprocesses by which individuals attempt to limit the power of institutions," identifying "the cracks, the loopholes in social structures" that enable patients, students, or other subordinate participants to construct meaningful selves and obtain some freedom even when confronting these "total institutions" (Fine and Ducharme 1995: 125, 126).

As a sociologist studying occupations, Abbott (1992) perceives an unbroken (Midwest/Chicago) tradition linking contemporary with earlier work and wondered what was so "new" about the new institutionalism in sociology. The institutional tradition has indeed been carried forward in an uninterrupted fashion by the Chicago school studying occupations and the sociology of work, but this was much less the case for research on organizations. Over a substantial period during its development, from the 1920s to the 1970s, the sociology of organizations largely lost sight of, defocalized, and gave insufficient attention to the institutional moorings of organizations.

Marx, Durkheim, Weber, and Parsons

The European tradition in institutional analysis was spearheaded by Karl Marx, whose influence permeated economics and political science, as well as sociology. Although Marx inspired a diverse array of theories and political movements, the work of primary importance to institutional theory involved his struggle with, and reinterpretation of, Hegel, the great German idealist philosopher. Hegel viewed history as the self-realization through time of abstract ideas or "spirit" (*Geist*). This self-creative spirit is reflected in the objective world, which most of us mistakenly take to be the true reality. It is the task of man to overcome this alienated state in which the world appears to be other than spirit (Hegel 1807/1967; Tucker 1972). Marx famously turned Hegel's arguments upside down.

For Marx, the materialist world is the true one, and the alienation we experience occurs because humankind is estranged from itself in existing political and economic structures. Marx, working in the early decades of the Industrial Revolution, saw the key realm as economic: Productive activity had been transformed into involuntary "labor." Under a capitalist system, work was no longer an expression of creative productivity, but alienated labor. The nature and meaning of work and work relations were seen to be transformed by structures of oppression and exploitation. These structures—involving the accompanying beliefs, norms, and power relations—are the product of human ideas and activities, but appear to be external and objective to their participants. Ideas and ideologies reflect and attempt to justify material reality, not the other way around (Marx 1844/1972; Marx 1845–1846/1972). Thus, in important (but historically specific) respects, Marx gave early expression to the social construction of reality.

The other two major European figures involved in establishing sociological variants of institutional analysis were Durkheim and Weber. The French sociologist Emile Durkheim was preoccupied with understanding the changing bases of social order that accompanied the Industrial Revolution, but, as previously noted, he appears to have modified his views over time. His early classic, *The Division of Labor in Society* (1893/1949), differentiated between the "mechanical" solidarity based on shared religious and cultural beliefs that integrated traditional societies and the newly emerging "organic" solidarity associated with an advanced division of labor. Initially, Durkheim viewed this new collective order as "based on the belief that action was rational and that order could be successfully negotiated in an individualistic way"—social order as "the unintended aggregate of individual self-interest" (Alexander 1983: 131, 134). However, his revised arguments led him away from an instrumentalist, individualist explanation to a focus on collective, normative frameworks that supply "the noncontractual elements" of contract (Durkheim 1893/1949: book 1, chap. 7).

Durkheim's mature formulation emphasizes the pivotal role played by symbolic systems—systems of belief and "collective representations"—shared cognitive frames, and schemas that, if not explicitly religious, have a moral or spiritual character.

> There is something eternal in religion which is destined to survive all the particular symbols in which religious thought has successively enveloped itself. There can be no society which does not feel the need of upholding and reaffirming at regular intervals, the collective sentiments and the collective ideas which make its unity and its personality. (Durkheim 1912/1961: 474–475)

These systems, although a product of human interaction, are experienced by individuals as objective. Although subjectively formed, they become "crystallized." They are, in Durkheim's (1901/1950) terms, "social facts": phenomena perceived by the individual to be both "external" [to that person] and "coercive" [backed by sanctions]. As is the case with religious systems, ritual and ceremonies play a vital role in expressing and reinforcing belief. Rituals and ceremonies enact beliefs. They "act entirely upon the mind and upon it alone" (Durkheim 1912/1961: 420) so that, to the extent that these activities have an impact on situations, it is through their effects on beliefs held about these situations.

These symbolic systems—systems of knowledge, belief, and "moral authority"—are, for Durkheim, social institutions.

> Institutions, Durkheim writes, are a product of joint activity and association, the effect of which is to "fix," to "institute" outside us certain initially subjective and individual ways of acting and judging. Institutions, then, are the "crystallizations" of Durkheim's earlier writing. (Alexander 1983, vol. 2: 259)

The third major European figure contributing to institutional theory was Max Weber. As I note in more detail in chapter 2, more contemporary analysts of institutions lay claim to Weber as their guiding genius than to any other early theorist. Although Weber did not explicitly employ the concept of "institution," his work is permeated with a concern for understanding the ways in which cultural rules— ranging in nature from customary mores to legally defined constitutions or rule systems—define social structures and govern social behavior, including economic structures and behavior. For example, his justly famous typology of administrative systems—traditional, charismatic, and rational-legal—represents three types of authority systems differing primarily in the kinds of belief or cultural systems that legitimate the exercise of authority (see Bendix 1960; Dornbusch and Scott, 1975, chap. 2; Weber 1924/1968: 215).

There remains much controversy as to how to characterize Weber's theoretical stance because he stood at the crossroads of three major debates raging at the turn of the 19th and 20th centuries: first, that between those who viewed the social sciences as a natural science and those who argued that it was rather a cultural science (the *Methodenstreit*); second, between idealist arguments associated with Durkheim and the materialist emphasis of Marx; and third, between the institutionalist Historical School of economics and the neoclassical interest in developing general theory. More so than any other figure of his time, he wrestled with and attempted to reconcile these apparently conflicting ideas.

Weber argued that the social sciences differ fundamentally from the natural sciences in that, in the former but not the latter, both the researcher and the object of study attach meaning to events. For Weber (1924/1968: 4), action is social "when and in so far as the acting individual attaches a subjective meaning to his behavior." Individuals do not mechanically respond to stimuli; they first interpret them and then determine their response. Researchers cannot expect to understand social behavior without taking into account the meanings that mediate social action. Weber employed his interpretive approach to attempt a synthesis in which both the material conditions and interests stressed by materialists—such as Marx—and the idealist values—emphasized by Durkheim—combined to motivate and guide action (see Alexander 1983, vol. 2; see also chap. 3, this volume). In developing his *Wirtschaftssoziologie* (economic sociology), Weber embraced the institutionalist arguments that economics needs to be historically informed and comparative in its approach, but at the same time he sided with Menger and the classicists in supporting the value of theoretical models that allowed one to abstract from specific, historically embedded systems, in order to formulate and evaluate general arguments. Weber believed that economic sociology could bridge the chasm by attending to both historical circumstance and the development of analytic theory (Swedberg 1991, 1998). Weber suggested that by abstracting from the specificity and complexity of concrete events, researchers could create "ideal types" to guide and inform comparative studies. If researchers were careful not to mistake the ideal types for reality—for example, to insist that individuals under all conditions would behave as rational "economic men"—such models could provide useful maps to guide analysis and increase understanding of the real world (Weber, 1904–1918/1949). More precisely, "Weber views rational behavior as evolving historically, or, to phrase it differently, to Weber— unlike to today's economists—rational behavior is a variable, not an assumption" (Swedberg 1998: 36).

The American sociologist Talcott Parsons also attempted to synthesize the arguments of major early theorists, in particular, Durkheim, Weber, and Freud, in constructing his voluntaristic theory of action (see Parsons, 1937, 1951). Parsons was the most influential social theorist in sociology throughout the mid-20th century, although he is much less in vogue today.[3] Like Weber, he attempted to reconcile a subjective and an objective approach to social action by emphasizing that normative frameworks existed independently of a given social actor, whereas analysts needed to take into account the "orientation" of actors to them. A system of action was said to be institutionalized to the extent that actors in an ongoing relation oriented their actions to a common set of normative standards and value patterns. As such a normative system becomes internalized, "conformity with it becomes a need-disposition in the actor's own personality structure" (1951: 37). In this sense, institutionalized action is motivated by "moral" rather than instrumental concerns: "the primary motive for obedience to an institutional norm lies in the moral authority it exercises over the individual" (Parsons 1934/1990: 326). The actor conforms because of his or her belief in a value standard, not out of expediency or self-interest.

Viewed more objectively, from the standpoint of the social analyst, institutions are appropriately seen as a system of norms that "regulate the relations of individuals to each other," that define "what the relations of individuals ought to be" (Parsons 1934/1990: 327). Also, implicitly following the lead of Spencer and Sumner, Parsons developed his own abstract typology of norms oriented to the solution of the four generic system problems: adaptation, goal attainment, integration, and latency (maintenance of cultural patterns) (see Parsons 1951; Parsons, Bales, and Shils 1953).

Contemporary theorists note several kinds of limitations with Parsons' formulation. Alexander (1983: 242) concluded that, although

Parsons attempted to develop a multidimensional view of social action, his conception of institutionalization put too much weight on cultural patterns, overemphasizing the "control exerted by values over conditions." The importance of interests and instrumental action and rational choice was underemphasized. DiMaggio and Powell (1991) praised Parsons for the contribution he made to the "microfoundations" of institutional theory in his attempt to understand the ways in which culture influences behavior. But they complained that his conception of culture failed to stress its existence as "an object of orientation existing outside the individual." Instead, following Freud, Parsons viewed culture as acting primarily as "an internalized element of the personality system"—thus giving too much weight to a subjective in contrast to an objective view. Additionally, they argued that Parsons' analysis of culture neglected its cognitive dimensions in favor of its evaluative components: Culture was limited to "value-orientations" (DiMaggio and Powell 1991: 17). Each of these emphases drew Parsons away from examining the interplay of the instrumental and the normative in social action.

Mead, Schutz, Bourdieu, Berger, and Luckmann

George Herbert Mead, like Cooley, emphasized the interdependence of self and society, but gave particular attention to the role played by symbolic systems in creating both the human and the social. Meaning is created in interaction as gestures, particularly vocal gestures (language), call out the same response in self as in other. Self arises in interaction as an individual "takes on the attitudes of the other" in arriving at a self-conception (Mead 1934).

Working at about the same time as Mead, but in Vienna, Alfred Schutz also examined in detail the ways in which common meanings are constructed through interactions by individuals. However, Schutz also explored the wider "structure of the social world," noting the great variety of social relations in which we become involved. In addition to intimate, face-to-face, "Thou" and "We" relations with persons thought to be similar to ourselves, we engage in multiple "They" relations with others known only indirectly and impersonally. Such relations are only possible to the extent that we develop an "ideal type" conception that enables us to deal with these others as needed (e.g., to mail a letter or to stand beside someone in an elevator). These relations are based on typifications of the other and taken-for-granted assumptions as to the way the interaction will proceed. In this sense, the meanings are highly institutionalized (Schutz 1932/1967).

Moving closer to the present, the French scholar Pierre Bourdieu (1971, 1973) endeavored to combine the insights of Marx and Durkheim by examining the ways in which class interests express themselves in symbolic struggles: the power of some groups to impose their knowledge frameworks and conceptions of social reality on others. Bourdieu's work reached and began to influence organizational scholars about a decade later (see DiMaggio 1979). In particular, Bourdieu's concept of "field" (a social arena) was usefully appropriated by DiMaggio and Powell (1983) to better situate the locus of institutional processes shaping organizations (see chaps. 2, 3, and 8).

Peter Berger and Thomas Luckmann, working in the United States, also provided a critical link between earlier work and that of later organizational scholars. Influenced by the work of Mead, but even more by that of Schutz,[4] Berger and Luckmann (1967: 15) redirected the sociology of knowledge away from its earlier concerns with epistemological issues or a focus on intellectual history to more mainstream sociological concerns, insisting that: "The sociology of knowledge must concern itself with everything that passes for 'knowledge' in society." The concern is not with the validity of this knowledge, but with its production, with "the social creation of reality." Berger and Luckmann argue that social reality is a human construction, a product of social interaction. They underscore this position in their attention to language (systems of symbols) and cognition mediated by social processes as crucial to the ways in which actions are produced, repeated, and come to evoke stable, similar meanings in the self and other. They define this process as one of *institutionalization*. In contrast to Durkheim and Parsons, Berger and Luckmann emphasized the creation of shared knowledge and belief systems rather than the production of rules and norms. Cognitive frameworks are stressed over normative systems. A focus on the centrality of cognitive systems forms the foundation for the sociological version of the new institutionalism in organizations (see chap. 2).

❖ CONCLUDING COMMENT

This brief review attempts to identify some of the varying interests and emphases of the early institutional theorists—formulations developed between 1880 and the mid-20th century. As we will see, in numerous ways these theorists anticipated distinctions and insights rediscovered by later analysts. Contemporary economists—with the notable exception of economic historians—have rejected the approaches promoted by the German Historical School, but some strands of the new institutionalism in economics reflect the interests of Menger and the Austrian School. Contemporary political scientists have left behind the moral-philosophical roots of their institutional forebears, but a lively subset has rediscovered an interest in the historical and comparative study of political systems. An even larger collection of political scientists has adapted rational choice models devised by economists to better explain the emergence and functioning of political institutions.

Contemporary sociologists continue to pursue and refine the ideas of their numerous and varied predecessors. Some continue to examine the diverse institutional spheres that make up society, others examine the ways in which individuals are empowered and constrained by shared normative systems, and still others explore the ways in which symbolic systems—cultural rules and schemas—shape and support social life.

Although there is continuity, there is also change and perhaps even progress. Most of the early work on institutions shared a common limitation: Little attention was accorded to organizations.[5] Some theorists focused their analyses on wider institutional structures—on constitutions and political systems, language and legal systems, and kinship and religious structures—whereas others emphasized the emergence of common meanings and normative frameworks out of localized social interaction. Few, however, treated organizations as institutional forms or directed attention to the ways in which wider institutions shaped collections of organizations.

Theorists in the 1940s and 1950s began to recognize the existence and importance of particular collectivities—individual organizations— entities distinguishable from both broader social institutions, on the one hand, and the behavior of individuals, on the other hand. Later developments in the 1970s and 1980s called attention to the significance of organizational forms and organizational fields, and the recognition that each of these levels has stimulated much fruitful development of institutional theory and research.

❖ NOTES

1. These generalizations—particularly the first and the fourth—are less applicable to the Austrian branch of economics led by Menger and Hayek. These theorists, while insisting on the importance of theory and of simplifying assumptions, were interested in understanding economic change and so were sympathetic to a more evolutionary approach and the study of economic processes (see Langlois 1986a). Their ideas fueled the development of evolutionary economics (see chap. 2).

2. It is interesting to note the ways in which the ideas of Cooley and Hughes anticipated the later work of Berger and Luckmann and of Giddens, developments discussed in subsequent chapters.

3. Camic (1992) argued that Parsons strategically selected these European predecessors—rather than American institutional scholars, such as Veblen and Mitchell, and his own teachers (Hamilton and Ayres), who shared their interests—because of the tarnished reputation of these institutional economists at the time when Parsons was constructing his theory of action. There is a politics to selecting intellectual forebears that helps to explain why it is that some previous work is "drawn upon, while other work is overlooked."

Ironically, in a parallel fashion, Hall (1992) accused sociological neoinstitutionalists of failing to acknowledge the influence of Parsons (whose reputation until recently has been on the wane) as an important intellectual predecessor.

4. Berger (1992) reports that he and Luckmann were both junior members of the graduate faculty of the New School for Social Research (now the New School University) in the early 1960s. Berger recalls:

> We found ourselves in the lucky situation of being in the company of a small but lively group of young colleagues and graduate students who broadly shared a theoretical orientation, the one that all of us had learned from our teacher Alfred Schutz. One of Schutz's unrealized projects had been to formulate a new theoretical foundation for the sociology of knowledge in terms of his blend of phenomenology and Weberian theory. We intended to realize this project (1992: 1).

5. An essay by Znaniecki (1945) in an influential review volume edited by Gurvitch and Moore is an exception to this generalization. Taking off from Spencer and Sumner's definition of institution, Znaniecki (1945: 208) proposed that research on institutions should focus on "the comparative study of those many and diverse organized groups or associations, small and large, simple and complex" that provide the forms and carry out the specialized purposes of a given institutional arena. This approach anticipates by more than 25 years the concept of organizational field that emerged in the early 1980s (see chaps. 3, 4, and 8), but did not stimulate visible interest or related work at the time.

2

Institutional Theory
Meets Organization Studies

Although, as we have seen, institutions were identified and analyzed quite early by social scientists, organizations, as distinctive types of social forms, did not become a focus of study until relatively recently. March (1965) dates the origins of organization studies to the period 1937–1947, noting the appearance of the influential publications of Gulick and Urwick (1937), Barnard (1938), Roethlisberger and Dickson (1939), and Simon (1945/1997). Sociologists entered just at the end of this period (e.g., Merton et al. 1952; Selznick 1949).

This chapter reviews work connecting organizations and institutional arguments beginning in the 1940s and continuing until the emergence of the "new" institutional approaches in the 1970s. Three streams of work are identifiable among early theorists of organizations. The first was stimulated by the translation into English of Weber's (1906–1924/1946, 1924/1947) work on bureaucracy, which aroused much interest among a collection of sociologists at Columbia University.[1] Talcott Parsons, the reigning American sociological theorist of his time, at Harvard became a second early conduit both as a translator of Weber and because he was encouraged to apply his own "cultural-institutional" theory to organizations by James D. Thompson. Thompson, the founding editor of *Administrative Science Quarterly*, a new interdisciplinary journal devoted to research on organizations, invited Parsons to prepare an article for the inaugural issue in 1956. Third, Herbert Simon's pioneering work at the Carnegie Institute of Technology (now Carnegie-Mellon University) on organizational decision making was expanded, in collaboration with James G. March, into an influential statement of the nature of rationality in organizations.

This early work, carried out during the 1950s, which first connected institutions and organizations, is reviewed in the first section of this chapter. Then, in the following section, I consider the emergence of a complex set of new ideas, during the 1960s and 1970s, that provided the basis for the more recent, somewhat novel, conception of institutions: work that laid the foundations of neoinstitutional organization theory. As in chapter 1, this chapter is organized roughly by disciplinary emphases.

❖ INSTITUTIONS AND ORGANIZATIONS:
EARLY APPROACHES

The Columbia School: Merton's and Selznick's Institutional Models

Shortly after selections from Weber's seminal writings on bureaucracy were translated into English during the late 1940s, a collection of scholars at Columbia University, under the leadership of Robert K. Merton, revived interest in bureaucracy and bureaucratization and its sources and consequences for behavior in organizations (Merton et al. 1952).[2] It is generally acknowledged that a series of empirical studies of diverse organizations carried out by Merton's students—Selznick (1949) of the Tennessee Valley Authority (TVA), Gouldner (1954) of a gypsum plant and mine, Blau (1955) of a federal and a state bureau, and Lipset, Trow, and Coleman (1956) of a typographical union—were instrumental in establishing organizations as a distinctive arena of study (see Scott and Davis 2007: 9). What is less widely recognized is Merton's influence on Selznick's institutional theory of organizations.

Merton: Rules Trump Instrumentalism

As described in the following, Merton's (1936) early work on "unanticipated consequences of purposive action" was helpful to Selznick, but his analysis of bureaucratic behavior was even more directly influential. Although Merton (1940/1957: 199) did not employ the term institutionalization in his well-known essay, "Bureaucratic Structure and Personality," he provided a lucid discussion of processes within organizations leading officials to orient their actions around rules even "to the point where primary concern with conformity to the rules interferes with the achievement of the purposes of the organization."

Merton depicted the multiple forces within bureaucracy producing discipline and orienting officials to a valued normative order. The strength of these pressures is such that officials are prone to follow the rules to the point of rigidity, formalism, and even ritualism. Stimulated by the arguments of Durkheim and Hughes (and Parsons), Merton (1940/1957: 202) spelled out his version of institutional processes within organizations:

> There may ensue, in particular vocations and in particular types of organization, the process of sanctification. . . . (T)hrough sentiment-formation, emotional dependence upon bureaucratic symbols and status, and affective involvement in spheres of competence and authority, there develop prerogatives involving attitudes of moral legitimacy which are established as values in their own right, and are no longer viewed as merely technical means for expediting administration.

Selznick: Means Become Infused With Value

The leading early figure in the institutional analysis of organizations is Philip Selznick, whose conception of institutional processes was strongly influenced by Merton's work.[3] His views have evolved throughout the corpus of his writings. From the beginning, Selznick (1948: 25) was intent on distinguishing between organization as "the structural expression of rational action"—as a mechanistic instrument designed to achieve specified goals—and organization viewed as an adaptive, organic system affected by the social characteristics of its participants as well as by the varied pressures imposed by its environment. "Organizations," created as instrumental mechanisms to achieve specific goals, to a variable extent and over time, are transformed into "institutions."

In his earliest formulation, Selznick borrowed heavily on Merton's (1936) analysis of "the unanticipated consequences of purposive social action." Whereas some consequences of our actions occur as planned, others are unanticipated; social actions are not context-free, but are constrained, and their outcomes are shaped by the setting in which they occur. Especially significant are the constraints on action that arise from commitments enforced by institutionalization. . . . Because organizations are social systems, goals or procedures tend to achieve an established, value-impregnated status. We say that they become institutionalized. (Selznick 1949: 256–257)

In his later work on leadership, Selznick (1957: 16–17; italics original) elaborated on his views:

Institutionalization is a process. It is something that happens to an organization over time, reflecting the organization's own distinctive history, the people who have been in it, the groups it embodies and the vested interests they have created, and the way it has adapted to its environment. . . . In what is perhaps its most significant meaning, "to institutionalize" is to *infuse with value* beyond the technical requirements of the task at hand.

As organizations become infused with value, they are no longer regarded as expendable tools; participants want to see that they are preserved. By embodying a particular set of values, the organization acquires a "character structure," a distinctive identity. Maintaining the organization is no longer simply an instrumental matter of keeping the machinery working, but becomes a struggle to preserve a set of unique values. A vital role of leadership for Selznick, echoing Chester Barnard's (1938) influential message in *The Functions of the Executive*, is to define and defend these values.

In addition to viewing institutionalization as a process, as something "that happens to the organization over time," Selznick also treated institutionalization as a variable: Organizations with more precisely defined goals or with better developed technologies are less subject to institutionalization than those with diffuse goals and weak technologies (Selznick 1957). Organizations vary in their degree of institutionalization.

Contrasting Selznick's conception with Merton's, both emphasized quite similar processes of value commitments to procedures extending beyond instrumental utilities. However, Selznick focused on commitments distinctive to the developing character of a specific organization, whereas Merton stressed commitments associated with characteristics of bureaucratic (rational-legal) organizations generally. Selznick's approach calls for depicting a "natural history" of a specific organization, a description of the processes by which, over time, it develops its distinctive structures, capabilities, and liabilities. He studied the evolution of the TVA, noting how its original structures and goals were transformed over time by the commitments of its participants and the requirements imposed by powerful constituencies in its environment (Selznick 1949; see also chap. 4). Selznick's students conducted similar case studies of the transformation of organizational goals, such as occurred in the Women's Christian Temperance Union (WCTU) (Gusfield 1955), a community college (Clark 1960), a voluntary hospital (Perrow 1961), and the YMCA (Zald and Denton 1963). In all of these studies, the official goals of the organization are shown to differ from—to mask—the "real" objectives, which had been transformed in interaction with interests both within and external to the organization. As Perrow (1986: 159) noted, Selznick's institutional school tends to produce an "expose" view of organizations: Organizations are not the rational creatures they pretend to be, but vehicles for embodying (sometimes surreptitious) values.

Another of Selznick's students, Arthur Stinchcombe (1968: 107), built on Selznick's formulation, making more explicit the role of agency and power. Stinchcombe defined an *institution* as "a structure in which powerful people are committed to some value or interest," emphasizing that values are preserved and interests are protected only if those holding them possess and retain power. Institutionalization connotes stability over time, and Stinchcombe's analysis attempts to identify the ways in which power holders are able to preserve their power. He asserts: "By selection, socialization, controlling conditions of incumbency, and hero worship, succeeding generations of power-holders tend to regenerate the same institutions" (Stinchcombe 1968: 111).

Merton and Selznick laid the basis for a process model of institutions; Merton described processes operating in all or most bureaucratic organizations conducing officials toward overconformity, whereas Selznick focused on processes within particular organizations giving rise to a distinctive set of value commitments. Stinchcombe stressed the role of power and elaborated on the mechanisms utilized by powerful actors to perpetuate their interests and commitments.

Parsons' Institutional Approach

Talcott Parsons applied his general "cultural-institutional" arguments to organizations primarily by examining the relation between an organization and its environment—the ways in which the value system of an organization is legitimated by its connections to "the main institutional patterns" in "different functional contexts" (Parsons 1960a: 20). Although in most of his writing, as noted in chapter 1, Parsons stressed the "subjective" dimension of institutions, whereby individual actors internalize shared norms so they become the basis for the individual's action, in his analysis of organizations he shifted attention to what he termed the "objective" dimension: "a system of norms defining what the relations of individuals [or organizations] ought to be" (Parsons 1934/1990: 327).

Parsons (1960a: 21) argued that these wider normative structures within societies serve to legitimate the existence of organizations, but, "more specifically, they legitimize the main functional patterns of operation which are necessary to implement the values." Schools, for example, receive legitimacy in a society to the extent that their goals are connected to wider cultural values, such as training and education, and to the degree that they conform in their structures and procedures to established "patterns of operation" specified for educational organizations. Note that in some respects this argument replicates at the organizational level Parsons' discussion of institutionalization at the individual level because it focuses on the individual unit's—whether a person's or an organization's—orientation to a normative system. Organizations operating in different functional sectors are legitimated by differing values, exhibit different adaptive patterns, and are governed by different codes and normative frameworks. Moreover, value systems are stratified within a society such that organizations serving more highly esteemed values are thought to be more legitimate and are expected to receive a disproportionate share of societal resources (Parsons 1953).[4]

Parsons finds yet another use for the concept of institution. He argues that organizations tend to become differentiated vertically into three somewhat distinctive levels or layers: the *technical*, concerned with production activities; the *managerial*, concerned with control and coordination activities, procurement of resources, and disposal of products; and the *institutional*, concerned with relating the organization to the norms and conventions of the community and society. Every organization is a subsystem of "a wider social system which is the source of the 'meaning,' legitimation, or higher-level support which makes the implementation of the organization's goals possible" (Parsons 1960b: 63–64). Parsons' typology of organizational levels was subsequently embraced by Thompson (1967/2003) and has been widely employed.[5]

Unlike Selznick's formulation, Parsons' theoretical work on organizations did not stimulate much empirical research. A few students, such as Georgopoulos (1972), employed Parsons' general conceptual scheme and described the importance of institutional underpinnings for specific types of organizations, but in general Parsons' insights were not so much built upon as rediscovered by later theorists.

The Carnegie School

Political scientist Herbert Simon developed his theory of administrative behavior to counteract and correct conventional economic theories that made heroic, unreasonable assumptions about individual rationality. Although Simon retained the assumption that value premises (preferences) are beyond the analyst's purview (are exogenous), he challenged the assumption that actors have complete knowledge of means and their consequences. He was among the first theorists to link the limits of individual cognitive capacity with the features of organizational structure. In his classic book, *Administrative Behavior* (1945/1997), Simon described how organizational structures work to simplify and support decision making of individuals in organizations, allowing them to achieve higher levels of consistent, albeit "boundedly rational," behavior than would otherwise be possible. In accepting organizational membership, individuals are expected to adopt organizational value premises as a guide for their decisions; factual premises—beliefs about means-ends connections—are also commonly supplied to participants in the form of organizational rules, procedures, and routines (Simon 1945/1997: chap. 5). Behavior is rational in organizations because choices are constrained and individuals are guided by rules.

Together with March, Simon developed his arguments concerning the ways in which organizations shape the behavior of participants by developing "performance programs" to guide routine behavior and "search programs" to follow when confronting unusual tasks. March and Simon (1958: 141–142) argued that, in many circumstances, "search and choice processes are very much abridged. . . . Most behavior, and particularly most behavior in organizations, is governed by performance programs"—preset routines that provide guidance to individuals confronted by recurring demands. Such routines greatly reduce the discretion of most participants so that they make fewer choices and are more circumscribed in the choices they do make. Value assumptions, cognitive frames, and rules and routines are the ingredients that conduce individuals to behave rationally. Indeed, "the rational individual is, and must be, an organized and institutionalized individual" (Simon 1945/1997: 111).

March and Simon's arguments, albeit among the earliest, remain among the most influential and clearest statements of the microfeatures and functions of neoinstitutional forms (see DiMaggio and Powell 1991: 15–26).

❖ FOUNDATIONS OF NEOINSTITUTIONAL THEORY

We have arrived at the point in our history when the ideas that have come to be recognized as "neoinstitutional" theory appeared. Although they do not represent a sharp break with the past, there are new emphases and insights. In the following discussion, I review the proximate sources and founding conceptions linking neoinstitutional theory to organizational analysis in economics, political science, and sociology. Then, in chapter 3, I attempt a more analytic synthesis of current conceptual approaches, noting areas of consensus and dispute.

Neoinstitutional Theory in Economics

Many diverse lines of work contribute to the mixture of ideas fueling neoinstitutional theory in economics. It is instructive and rather ironic that the newer economic work "reflects less the ideas of the early institutionalists than it does those of their opponents" (Langlois 1986a: 2). Most neoinstitutional economists do not seek to replace orthodox economic theory with the study of multiple and diverse institutional conditions, but rather to develop an economic theory of institutions.

In his useful review, Langlois (1986a) incorporated within neoinstitutional economics the contributions of Simon (discussed above), a focus on transaction cost and property rights inspired by Coase (1937) (with a slight nod to Commons), the modern Austrian School as influenced by Hayek (1948), the work of Schumpeter on innovation (1926/ 1961), and evolutionary theory as developed by Nelson and Winter (1982). Three more or less common themes underlie and link these contributions (see Knudsen 1993; Langlois 1986a):

1. A broader conception of the economic agent is embraced, replacing the assumption of maximizing within a set of known alternatives.

How broad a view is taken varies greatly among the identified schools. In his work on transaction costs, Williamson embraces Simon's conception of "bounded" rationality, whereas the Austrian and evolutionary theorists utilize an even more expansive view that includes rule-based or "procedural" rationality (behavior is rational if specified procedures are followed, irrespective of outcome).

2. A focus on the study of economic processes rather than on the purely logical study of equilibrium states and a recognition that economic systems evolve over time, reflecting, in part, learning by the agents.

Conventional economics devotes the lion's share of its resources to the study of various types of economic systems that have attained an equilibrium (stable and well-coordinated behavior), but little to the question of how a state of equilibrium came into being or comes apart. Ad hoc "stories" are generated about how stability may have been achieved, but are only "tacked on" to the formal model (see Knudsen 1993). Neoinstitutional economists are interested in developing and testing these process arguments. Rather than treating institutions mainly as exogenous variables affecting economic behavior, the newer scholarship considers how institutions affecting economic transactions arise, are maintained, and are transformed. Game theorists have also become interested in these questions, asking how norms or rules emerge as actors interact to devise "treaties" or regimes to deal with conflicts.

3. The coordination of economic activity is not simply a matter of market-mediated transactions, but involves many other types of institutional structures that are important topics of study.

In addition to the role of governmental systems, the most important of these institutional structures are those embedded in organizations.

It is not possible here to consider in detail all of the specific approaches associated with these themes (for reviews, see Hodgson 1993, 1994; Mäki, Gustafsson, and Knudsen 1993; Silverman 2002; Zajac and Westphal 2002), but two of the more influential contributions are briefly described.

Transaction Cost Economics

One branch of neoinstitutional economics is concerned with the rule and governance systems that develop to regulate or manage economic exchanges. These systems occur at many levels, from macroregimes at the international level to understandings governing microexchanges between individuals. Accounting for the emergence and change of trading regimes among societies has been of primary interest to economic historians (e.g., North 1990), industry systems have been examined by industrial organization economists (e.g., Stigler 1968), and studies of the sources of organizational forms are being conducted by a growing set of organizational economists (see Milgrom and Roberts 1992). Although all of this work is properly regarded as institutional economics, it is the latter work, focusing on firm-level structures, that is especially identified with the new institutionalism in economics.

By consensus, the pioneer theorist inaugurating this approach was Ronald Coase (1937), whose article, "The Nature of the Firm," asks why some economic exchanges are carried out within firms under a governance structure involving rules and hierarchical enforcement mechanisms, rather than being directly subject to the price mechanism in markets. Coase (1937: 389) suggested that the reason must be that "there is a cost of using the price mechanism," namely "the costs of negotiating and concluding a separate contract for each exchange transaction which takes place in a market." It is because of these *transaction costs* that firms arise.

This insight lay fallow—in Coase's (1972: 69) own words, his article was "much cited and little used"—until it was resurrected in the 1970s by Oliver Williamson, who pursued its development by both conditionalizing and elaborating it. Williamson argued that transaction costs increase as a function of two paired conditions: when individual rationality, which is "bounded" (cognitively limited), is confronted by heightened complexity and uncertainty, and when opportunism— some actors' propensity to lie and cheat—is coupled with the absence of alternative exchange partners. Under such conditions, exchanges are likely to be removed from the market and brought within an organizational framework or, if already inside an organization, to stimulate the development of more elaborate controls (Williamson 1975, 1985). Williamson extended Coase's arguments by pushing them beyond the market versus firm comparison to consider a wide variety of alternative "governance systems" ranging from markets, to hybrid organizational forms, such as franchising or alliance arrangements, to various types of hierarchical structures, such as unified firms and multidivisional corporations (Williamson 1985, 1991)[6] In this approach, Williamson built on the previous work of Barnard (1938), who emphasized adaptation as a central problem facing organizations; Simon (1945/1997), with his conception of bounded rationality and organizational strategies for supporting decision making; and Chandler (1962), with his focus on matching a firm's structure to its strategy (Williamson 2005).

Thus, the Williamson (1991: 269) variant of new institutional economics focuses primarily on the mesoanalytic questions of "the comparative efficacy with which alternative generic forms of governance—markets, hybrids, hierarchies—economize on transactions costs," rather than on the more macroquestions regarding the origins and effects of the "institutional rules of the game: customs, laws, politics"—the latter issues being left to economic historians and sociologists (see also Williamson 1994, 2005).

Although Williamson stretched conventional economics to take seriously the effects of varying institutional contexts or governance structures on economic behavior, unlike earlier economic institutionalists, he remained firmly within the neoclassical tradition. Hodgson (1994: 70) underlines the point:

> Like the work of other new institutionalists, Williamson's is constructed in atomistic and individualistic terms because its elemental conceptual building block is the given, "opportunistic" individual. He does not consider the possibility that the preference functions of the individual may be molded by circumstances, such as the structure and culture of the firm, or that this phenomenon may be significant in analyzing or understanding such institutions. (p. 70)

In addition, Williamson showed little interest in the processes by which varying governance structures arise or are transformed. His explanation of structure is more often constructed as a functionalist one, "explaining" the choice of a given form by pointing to its consequences (Knudsen 1993; see also chap. 5).

In contrast, other economists, such as Douglass North, developed approaches that incorporate assumptions much more similar to those embraced by the turn-of-the-century economic institutionalists. As noted, North (1989, 1990) focused on a higher level of analysis, examining the origins of cultural, political, and legal frameworks and their effects on economic forms and processes. As an economic historian, his focus is on development and change, rather than on comparative statics (see also chap. 5). Although he attends to transaction costs in his analysis of economic systems, he is more prone to treat them as dependent variables—subject to the effects of wider institutional frameworks—than as independent variables to explain differences among actors' choice of governance mechanisms (see Hirsch and Lounsbury 1996).

Whereas Williamson (1994: 79) focuses attention on organizations as institutional forms—governance systems devised to reduce transaction costs—that must take into account "background conditions" such as property rights, laws, norms, and conventions, North (1990: 5) directs attention to these wider institutional frameworks—societal "rules of the game"—and views organizations as "players" who are attempting to devise strategies to win the game.

Evolutionary Economics

A second, important addition to neoinstitutional economic theory was developed by Nelson and Winter (1982; Winter 1964). Their evolutionary economics distantly echoes the interests of Veblen, but is more solidly based on Schumpeter's (1934) ideas on innovation and Alchian's (1950) arguments that economic agents such as firms are subject to adaptation and selection processes (Winter 2005). Nelson and Winter embraced an evolutionary theory of the firm analogous to biological models, in which a firm's "routines" are argued to be the equivalent of genes in a plant or an animal. Routines—or "capabilities"—are made up of both the conscious and tacit knowledge and skills held by participants who carry out organizational tasks. To survive, a firm must be able to reproduce and modify its routines in the face of changing situations.

Nelson and Winter (1982) locate their arguments at the industry or organizational population level of analysis to develop a theory of economic change processes. Their concern is to examine the ways in which competitive processes operate among firms so that those whose routines are best adapted to current conditions flourish, whereas those with less adequate routines falter. A dynamic model of accumulating knowledge and capabilities is developed to displace the static model of orthodox economics. Firms are viewed as historical entities, their routines being "the result of an endogenous, experience-based learning process" (Knudsen 1995: 203). Moreover,

> It is quite inappropriate to conceive of firm behavior in terms of deliberate choice from a broad menu of alternatives that some external observer considers to be "available" opportunities for the organization. The menu is not broad, but narrow and idiosyncratic; it is built into the firm's routines, and most of the "choosing" is also accomplished automatically by those routines. (Nelson and Winter 1982: 134)

Nelson and Winter did not employ the term *institution* in their arguments, but it is quite clear that their conception of organizational routines can be treated as one mode of institutionalized behavior. Implicitly, as Langlois (1986a: 19) suggests, their view of institution is one of "regularities of behavior understandable in terms of rules, norms, and routines." Nelson and Winter embrace a much broader conception of factors shaping behavior and structure in organizations than do transaction cost economists. Also, their approach strongly favors a process orientation rather than one of comparative statics.

In summary, there are important differences among contemporary institutional economists in the nature of their assumptions and the focus of their analytic attention. However, it is unquestionably the case that the new institutional economics is dominated currently by scholars who cling to the neoclassical core of the discipline while struggling to broaden its boundaries.

Neoinstitutional Theory in Political Science

As described in chapter 1, neoinstitutionalism in political science may be viewed, at least in part, as a reaction to the behavioralist emphasis that dominated the field up through the mid-20th century. Resembling, to some extent, the situation in economics, the new institutionalists in political science and political sociology have grouped themselves into two quite distinct camps: historical and rational choice theorists.[7] The two perspectives differ along several dimensions.

Historical Institutionalism

The historical institutionalists, in many respects, hearken back to the turn-of-the-century institutional scholars, who devoted themselves to the detailed analysis of regimes and governance mechanisms, but also reflect the influence of Weber and his comparative approach. Members of this camp include March and Olsen (1984, 1989), Katzenstein (1978), Krasner (1988), Hall (1986), Skocpol (1985), and Zysman (1983). Institutions are viewed as including "both formal structures and informal rules and procedures that structure conduct" (Thelen and Steinmo 1992: 2). These scholars began by focusing attention on the state, examining the ways in which these structures shape the character and outcomes of conflicts by the ways in which they distribute power among actors and shape actors' conceptions of their interests (Hall and Taylor 1996). They emphasizes that political institutions are not entirely derivative from other social structures such as class, but have independent effects on social phenomena (Evans, Rueschemeyer, and Skocpol 1985); that social arrangements are not only or even primarily the result of aggregating individual choices and actions; that many structures and outcomes are not those planned or intended, but the consequence of unanticipated effects and constrained choice; and that history is not usually "efficient"—a process "that moves rapidly to a unique solution" (March and Olsen 1984: 737)—but one that is much more indeterminate and context-dependent.

The historical group takes a social-constructionist position that assumes "that capabilities and preferences, that is, the very nature of the actors, cannot be understood except as part of some larger institutional framework" (Krasner 1988: 72; see also chap. 3). Individual preferences are not stable and often result from rather than precede or determine choices. Institutions construct actors and define their available modes of action; they constrain behavior, but they also empower it. Analysis from this perspective is aimed at providing a detailed account of the specifics of institutional forms because they are expected to exert strong effects on individual behavior: structuring agendas, attention, preferences, and modes of acting.

These analysts attempt to show that political systems are not neutral arenas within which "external" interests compete, but rather complex forms and forums that generate independent interests and advantages and whose rules and procedures exert important effects on whatever business is being transacted. In accounting for the origins of these structures, the approach is primarily that of historical reconstruction. Although individuals build these structures, there is no assurance that they will produce what they intend. Current choices and possibilities are constrained and conditioned by past choices (see e.g., Ertman 1996; Karl 1997; Skowronek 1982). Once institutions are established, they have a "continuing effect on subsequent decision-making and institution-building episodes" (Campbell 2004: 25).

These insights have been derived from and applied to a wide variety of political systems, including private associations, nation-states, international organizations, and regimes such as monetary and trade agreements (e.g., Finnemore 1993; Keohane 1989; Schmitter and Lehmbruch 1982; Skowronek 1982). Critics point out that the work is too often historicist, focusing too much on the details of a single, complex case.

Rational Choice Theory

The second camp consists of the rational choice theorists (also termed *positive* theory) and includes such scholars as Moe, Shepsle, and Weingast. These analysts view institutions as governance or rule systems, but argue that they represent deliberately constructed edifices established by individuals seeking to promote or protect their interests. The approach represents an extension of the neoinstitutional work in economics—including the transaction cost approach of Williamson and the work of agency theorists such as Alchian and Demsetz (1972)—and its application to the study of political systems. Tullock (1976: 5), an early advocate of importing economic models to explain political behavior, argued that: "Voters and customers are essentially the same people. Mr. Smith buys and votes; he is the same man in the supermarket and the voting booth" (see also Buchanan and Tullock 1962). Moe (1984: 750) enumerates the major elements making up the paradigm adopted from the economists as including:

> the contractual nature of organizations; markets vs. hierarchies, transactions costs, the rationality of structure, individualistic explanation, and economic methods of analysis. Standard neo-classical notions—optimization, marginality, equilibrium—are often central to work in this new tradition.

Political theorists recognize that economic models developed to account for economic organizations require modification if they are to be applied to political systems (Pierson 2004: 30–48). However, they also insist that many of the basic questions are parallel, including: Why do public organizations exist? How are we to account for their varying forms and governance mechanisms? How can elected political officials, as "principals," control their bureaucratic "agents"? What are the effects of political institutions on political and social behavior? What are the mechanisms by which politicians secure their power positions? As Peters (1999: 45) observes, "Within this approach institutions are conceptualized largely as sets of positive (inducements) and negative (rules) motivations for individuals, with individual utility maximization providing the dynamic for behavior within the models."

Rational choice theorists recognize that, "in the reality of politics social choices are not chaotic. They are quite stable." They are stable because "of the distinctive role that institutions play" (Moe 1990a: 216). Many early scholars argued that much of the stability observed in the law-making process could be explained by the ways in which the rules of procedure and committee structures of legislatures structured the choices available to members (Ferejohn and Fiorina 1975; Riker 1980). Thus, the task becomes to understand the role of institutions and, "more fundamentally, to determine where these institutions come from in the first place" (Moe 1990a: 216). The general argument embraced by these theorists is that "economic organizations and institutions are explained in the same way: they are structures that emerge and take the specific form they do because they solve collective-action problems and thereby facilitate gains from trade" (Moe 1990a: 217–218).

Theorists disagree as to what is distinctive about political institutions. Weingast (1989) argued that politics differs from markets in that, in the former, actors cannot simply engage in market exchange, but must make decisions under some framework such as majority rule. Shepsle (1989) suggested that the most important task of political systems is to "get property rights right": to establish rule systems that promote efficient economic organizations. Moe (1990a: 221) argued that political decisions are distinctive in that they are "fundamentally about the exercise of public authority," which entails access to unique coercive powers. Pierson (2004: 38) added that politics is "a far, far murkier environment" than the economic realm, lacking "the measuring rod of price" and entailing the pursuit of often incommensurable goals with opaque processes. These and related researchers have attempted to account for the distinctive powers and influential procedures of congressional committees (Shepsle and Weingast 1987) and the performance (including the ineffectiveness) of some governmental bureaucracies (Moe 1990a, 1990b) as rational solutions to collective problems (see chap. 5). Hall and Taylor (1996: 945) observe that one of the principal contributions of this approach has been to draw our attention to the crucial "role of strategic interaction in the determination of political outcomes" and to provide a set of tools for understanding how institutions structure such interactions.

An important arena of application for both historical and rational choice theorists has been that of international relations. Rational models view nation-states as self-interested actors attempting to maximize their own advantage in dealing with other nations. Rules are accepted when they lower the transaction costs of a participant and/or decrease the overall level of uncertainty (Hasenclever, Mayer, and Rittberger 1997; Rittberger 1993). By contrast, historical institutionalists, such as Krasner (1983) and Keohane (1989), emphasize the important independent effects of the emergence of cooperative norms among participating nations. In addition, as Keohane (1989: 382) pointed out, "institutions do not merely reflect the preferences and power of the units constituting them; the institutions themselves shape those preferences and that power" (see also Kahn and Zald 1990). As an advocate of a historical perspective, Pierson (2004: 108) identifies some of the limitations of the "institutional design" perspective embraced by rational choice economists and political scientists:

Actors may be instrumental and farsighted but have such multiple and diverse goals that institutional functioning cannot easily be derived from the preference of designers. Alternatively, actors may not be instrumental in the sense implied by this framework. Or they may be instrumental, but not farsighted. Perhaps, most important, they may in fact have a single, instrumental goal and be farsighted, but major institutional effects may be unintended. Finally, actors may make rational design choices, but change in broader social environments and/or in the character of these actors themselves [e.g., their preferences] may markedly worsen the fit between actors and institutional arrangements after they are chosen.

In summary, although both historical institutionalists and rational choice theorists agree on the importance of institutions in political life, important differences in assumptions and perspectives remain. Rational choice theorists are more likely to stress the microfoundations of institutions, asking how institutions are devised to solve collective action problems experienced by individuals. In contrast, historical institutionalists are more likely to emphasize a macroperspective, tracing the evolution of an institutional form and asking how it affects individual preferences and behavior. Preferences are more likely to be treated by rational choice theorists as stable properties of actors, whereas for historical institutionalists preferences are seen to be more problematic, emergent from the situation (endogenous), and context-specific. The two camps are attracted to different sets of problems. Historical institutionalists "begin with empirical puzzles that emerge from observed events or comparisons," whereas rational choice theorists are more likely to be attracted to "situations in which observed behavior appears to deviate from what the general theory predicts" (Thelen 1999: 374). Finally, rational choice theorists give central place to the concept of equilibria and view institutions as central mechanisms in sustaining this condition, whereas historical institutionalists—like their 19th-century counterparts—are more interested in historical change than in equilibrium—the factors producing political and economic change broadly viewed as "structured institutional change" (see Orren and Skowronek 1994).

Thelen (1999) cites evidence of convergence in the perspectives of the two camps in recent years, and Scharpf (1997) suggests that each approach is incomplete and proposed that, in the long run, they can be combined into a more complete explanation. At the present time, however, they remain relatively distinct approaches, more independent than overlapping in perspective and assumptions and more competitive than cooperative in demeanor.

Neoinstitutional Theory in Sociology

Sociological scholars have ranged rather widely in assembling the principal ingredients making up neoinstitutional approaches to organizational sociology. They have drawn on developments in cognitive and cultural theory in the neighboring disciplines of psychology and anthropology, as well as their home-grown subdiscipline, ethnomethodology.

Theoretical Roots

Cognitive Theory. Simon's work on decision making in organizations paralleled developments in social psychology, as this field of study— both its psychological and sociological sides—experienced the "cognitive revolution." During the 1940s and 1950s, the stimulus–response (S–R) approach was revised to include attention to the participation of an active organism (S–O–R) that mediated between the provocation and reaction (see Lewin 1951). Early research concentrated on how the state of the organism, as defined by various motivational and emotional variables, affected perception, selective attention, and memory. An early concern with "hot" cognition (e.g., anger or fear) began to be superseded by attention to the effects of "cool" factors (e.g., attention and background assumptions) influencing everyday information-processing and problem-solving behaviors.

> The idea of the human organism as an information processor became popular. The mind came to be viewed by many as a computerlike apparatus that registered the incoming information and then subjected it to a variety of transformations before ordering a response. (Markus and Zajonc 1985: 141)

The question became, what types of "software" provide the programs and transformation rules for these processes? Such factors ranged from the functioning of the brain and nervous system to the structure of individual cognitive processes. Early social theorists, like Durkheim, insisted that "the framework of the intelligence" was entirely provided by the forms of the society into which an individual was born: Social and cultural forms determine mental models ("collective representations"). This argument, with variations, has been echoed and elaborated by Mead, Parsons, and Bourdieu, among numerous others, up to the present time (Bergesen 2004). However, a large and growing body of psychological theory and research suggests that, rather than providing a blank slate, humans (e.g., unsocialized infants) come equipped with a number of fundamental mental capabilities, such as conceptions of space, number, cause-and-effect relations, and recognition of categories (see Gopnik, Melzoff, and Kuhl 1999; Mehler and Dupoux 1994). In a related development, Chomsky (1986) convinced most linguists that "the principles of language [syntax] are not learned but part of our bio-endowment" (Bergesen 2000: 73).[8]

Yet another debate concerns whether individual thought processes follow a logical axis involving an abstract reasoning ("computational") model or a "pattern-recognition" ("connectionist") model—the noting of similarities and differences in the situations encountered. The latter approach appears to be both more consistent with studies of human learning (Edelman and Tonini 1992) and better suited to explaining the ways in which socioeconomic actors cope with the kinds of uncertainties they encounter (North 2005: 27).

Psychologists have long vacillated between positions that regard individuals as basically competent, rational beings and views emphasizing cognitive biases and limitations. The general impact of recent cognitive theory and research has been to emphasize the shortcomings of individuals as information processors and decision makers. Tversky and Kahneman (1974) pioneered in the identification of a number of specific types of biases likely to cause mistakes in assessing information and reaching conclusions. These and related problems were generalized by Nisbett and Ross (1980: 31) into two common sources of inferential error: (a) a tendency to overutilize simplistic strategies and fail to employ the logical and statistical rules that guide scientific analysis, and (b) a "tendency to attribute behavior exclusively to the actor's dispositions and to ignore powerful situational determinants of the behavior."

Although their views have stressed the intellectual limitations of individuals, cognitive psychologists have recognized that individuals actively participate in perceiving, interpreting, and making sense of their world. By contrast, until fairly recently, sociologists have tended to give primacy to the effects of contextual factors, viewing individuals as more passive, prone to conform to the demands of their social systems and roles. "Identity theory" has emerged as a corrective to this over-socialized view by giving renewed attention to an active and reflexive self that creates, sustains, and changes social structures (see Burke and Reitzes 1981; Rosenberg 1979; Stryker 1980). Similar issues are addressed by "structuration theory," which is discussed in chapter 4.

Culture Theory. These advances by advocates of the "nature" persuasion have forced some retreats by, but have by no means defeated, the "nurture" advocates. Irrespective of capacities and predispositions on the part of individual human actors, all scholars agree that learning occurs in a social context. The groundwork was laid by Franz Boas (1982), a cultural anthropologist working at the turn of the 20th century, who, "by stressing the plasticity of human culture . . . expanded human nature into an infinity of possibilities rather than a prison of constraints" (Ridley 2003: 202). One of the important developments in cultural theory involved a shift away from a more diffuse definition of *culture* as encompassing the entire way of life of a people to focus on its semiotic functions. Worthy successors to Boas, such as Alfred Kroeber and Clyde Kluckholn (1952), carried this tradition forward, concluding that, "Culture consists of explicit and implicit patterns of historically derived and selected ideas and their embodiment in institutions, practices, and artifacts." Their more eloquent protégé, Clifford Geertz (1973: 5, 12) elaborated on the message:

> Believing, with Max Weber, that man is a social animal suspended in webs of significance he himself has spun, I take culture to be these webs. . . . Culture consists of socially established structures of meaning.

Donald (1991) proposed a coevolutionary view, in which the cognitive capacities of our species and the cultures we have developed have advanced in complementary ways. Advancing a "cognitive classification of culture," Donald suggested that human culture has progressed from:

- an *episodic* one, in which lives were experienced as "a series of concrete episodes," to
- a *mimetic* one, resting on visuomotor skills that produced conscious, intentional, representational acts (e.g., tool-making, coordinated hunting), to
- the use of language, which supports a *mythic* culture enabling an oral-narrative system and allowing the creation of more comprehensive models of the nature of the world and our place in it, to
- a *theoretic* culture, involving written language and other forms of symbolic representation (maps, musical notation, architectural drawings), that allows for their externalization in media (books, films, computer memory) that can be preserved, corrected, and transmitted over time and space.

Note that the emergence of theoretic culture supports new types of human enterprise, including the development of the sciences, numerous theoreticians, and a wide range of professions specializing in the production, evaluation, and dissemination of various types of knowledge.

Each of these levels or phases represents not only advances in the complexity of culture, but, simultaneously, improvement in cognitive capacity to the point where some scholars propose that

> Genes are very far from being fixed in their actions. Instead, they are devices for extracting information from the environment. Every minute, every second, the pattern of genes being expressed in your brain changes, often in direct or indirect response to events outside the body. Genes are the mechanisms of experience. (Ridley 2003: 248)

All culture theorists underline the importance of symbolic systems in the ordering of social life, but a growing number also recognize that such systems embody not only content, but also affect. The meanings embedded in systems are emotional as well as substantive. It is no doubt in recognition of this fact that de Tocqueville (1835–1840/1969: 279), the justly famous student of American character and culture, referred to the cultural mores guiding its citizens as the "habits of the heart" (see also Bellah et al. 1985). As D'Andrade (1984: 99) points out, "ideas, feelings, and intentions are all activated by symbols and are thus part of the meaning of symbols." Sociologist David Heise (1979) went even further to assert that the meanings of settings, actors, and behaviors, indeed, of any social category, are primarily affective (see also Thoits 1989). Almost any type of stimulus evokes some sort of affective response, and many types of symbolic expressions—thanks, apologies, and curses—specifically refer to feelings. Much of the motivation that propels action in any situation comes from the feelings evoked by the shifting patterns of meanings.

A limitation long present in the approach to culture taken by many sociologists is the assumption that culture is subordinate in interest and importance to social structure. The distinction between social structure, made up of the "relational system of interaction among individuals and collectivities" and culture, made up "transmitted and created content and patterns of values, ideas, and other symbolic-meaningful systems" of symbolic and normative systems, is one of long standing (Kroeber and Parsons 1958: 583). Although useful, sociologists have tended to privilege social structure over symbolic systems in their accounts of behavior. The new cultural arguments stress the independent effects of cultural systems.

Symbolic systems vary in the extent to which they exhibit uniformity and promote consistency of action. All too often it is assumed that cultures are stable and constraining. However, more recent work stresses that culture can enable change. For example, Swidler (1986: 277–278) argued that in "settled" times "culture accounts for continuities . . . organizing and anchoring patterns of action," whereas in times of change, culture functions more like a 'tool kit,' providing repertoires "from which actors select different pieces for constructing lines of action."[9]

Phenomenology and Ethnomethodology. Phenomenology, which began as a branch of philosophy, was incorporated into social science by scholars such as Schutz and Berger, who "stressed the in-depth exploration of the meanings associated with symbols" (Wuthnow 1987: 42). These scholars clearly embraced a view of culture as primarily a semiotic system. They also distanced themselves from the prevailing focus on shared norms and values, as exemplified in the work of Durkheim and Parsons, to emphasize shared knowledge and belief systems. Behavior is shaped not only by attention to rules and the operation of norms, but also by common definitions of the situation and shared strategies of action. As noted in chapter 1, attention to cognitive frames and cultural frameworks, rather than normative systems, is one of the major distinguishing marks of neoinstitutional theory in sociology (see DiMaggio and Powell 1991: 15–18).

Corresponding to the changing conceptions of culture, in particular, the *theoretic* mode to use Donald's terminology, another important shift in emphasis involves the recognition that symbols exist not only as internalized beliefs, but also as external frameworks. Much work in sociology (e.g., symbolic interactionism and survey methodologies) treats beliefs as primarily internalized and subjective. By contrast, the types of data preferred by the new cultural scholars "are more readily observable kinds of behavior"—such as verbal utterances, rituals, codified bodies of knowledge and cultural artifacts—"rather than [those] locked away in people's private ruminations" (Wuthnow 1987: 56). Such approaches direct attention away from the internalized, subjective nature of culture and treat symbols as external, objective phenomena.[10] This emphasis is particularly apparent in Berger and Luckmann's (1967: 60–61) conceptualization of the construction of common meaning systems. They stressed three moments or phases:

- *externalization*—the production, in social interaction, of symbolic structures whose meaning comes to be shared by the participants;
- *objectification*—the process by which this production "comes to confront him as a facticity outside of himself," as something "out there," as a reality exerienced in common with others; and

- *internalization*—the process by which the objectified world is "retrojected into consciousness in the course of socialization."

As noted in chapter 1, Berger and Luckmann (1967: 58) defined this three-phase process as one of "institutionalization." Institutions are symbolic systems that are "experienced as possessing a reality of their own, a reality that confronts the individual as an external and coercive fact." A more recent manifestation of this recognition of the importance of culture as an external symbolic framework is a concern with the "production of culture"—an examination of the ways in which cultural items are produced, distributed, selected, and institutionalized (see Becker 1982; Caves 2000; Griswold 1992; Hirsch 1972; Lampel, Shamsie, and Lant 2006).

Closely related to phenomenology is the subfield of *ethnomethodology*. In an attempt to combat the prevalent models of social order advanced by Parsons and others, Harold Garfinkel (1974) coined the term "ethnomethodology," corresponding to usage in cultural anthropology, to refer to the "commonsense knowledge" of how to operate within some social arena as developed and acquired by its participants. *Ethno-* stresses the local, indigenous production of meaning, and *-methodology* stresses that the knowledge involves distinctions and rules necessary for carrying on the work at hand.

Researchers within this tradition have primarily studied behavior in work settings or that of other types of actors, such as jurors, engaged in some collective task. The questions posed by these researchers are: How do such individuals "make sense" of the situations they confront? How do they collectively construct the rules and procedures that allow them to cope with everyday demands? Detailed participant observation studies have been conducted—in police stations, welfare agencies, and psychiatric clinics, among other sites—to elicit these shared meanings (see Cicourel 1968; Garfinkel 1967; Zimmerman 1969).

As DiMaggio and Powell (1991: 20) emphasize, ethnomethodologists challenged and supplemented Parsons' model by stressing the cognitive, rather than the evaluative-normative, components of behavior, and they questioned the neoclassical economic model of rational decision making by emphasizing the tacit, routine nature of "choice" in organizational settings.

These then were the mix of ideas and themes that came together beginning in the 1960s to seed the development of neoinstitutional theory in sociology. Although, as noted, some of these ideas were being developed in and applied to organizations by ethnomethodologists, they did not penetrate the mainstream of organizational studies until the 1970s.

Neoinstitutional Theory and Organizations:
Founding Conceptions

An important early attempt to introduce neoinstitutional arguments to the study of organizations was made by David Silverman (1971), who proposed an "action" theory of organization. Silverman attacked prevailing models of organization, including contingency arguments and Parsons' and Selznick's structural-functional views, as being overly concerned with stability, order, and system maintenance. Drawing on the work of Durkheim, Schutz, Berger and Luckmann, and Goffman, Silverman proposed a phenomenological view of organizations that focuses attention on meaning systems and the ways in which they are constructed and reconstructed in social action. Silverman (1971: 141) contrasted his action approach with the prevailing "systems" view:

> The systems approach tends to regard behaviour as a reflection of the characteristics of a social system containing a series of impersonal processes which are external to actors and constrain them. In emphasizing that action derives from the meanings that men attach to their own and each other's actions, the Action frame of references argues that man is constrained by the way in which he socially constructs his reality.

Adopting the insights of Durkheim, Silverman (1971: 19) argued that meanings operate not only in the minds of individuals, but are also objective "social facts" residing in social institutions. The environments of organizations need to be conceptualized not only as a supply house of resources and target of outputs, but also as a "source of meanings for the members of organizations."

Silverman's critique and attempted redirection of organizational theory had more impact in European than U.S. circles (see Burrell and Morgan 1979; Salaman 1978).[11] Another European social theorist, Pierre Bourdieu, employed a general conception of "social field" to refer to social arenas governed by distinctive values and approaches. Bourdieu emphasized the contested nature of social fields and the role of power in resolving these contests (see chap. 8). Fields can be examined as social phenomena external to any particular actor, but also exist as subjective, internalized mental elements. In his analysis of social structures, Bourdieu (1977: 95) placed great importance on the internalization of cultural rules. His concept of *habitus* refers to the existence of a "system of lasting and transposable dispositions which, integrating past experiences, functions at every moment as a matrix of perceptions, appreciations and actions," allowing individuals to structure their behavior within situations (see also Bourdieu and Wacquant 1992: 94–149). Bourdieu's work was also much more influential in Europe than the United States until recently.

A subsequent effort to introduce the new institutional arguments into organizational sociology proved to be much more successful. Two seminal articles appearing in the same year introduced neoinstitutional theory into the sociological study of organizations. Articles by Meyer and Rowan (1977) and Zucker (1977), like Silverman's work, built primarily on Durkheim's and, especially, Berger and Luckmann's conception of institutions.

John Meyer and Brian Rowan (1977) embraced the view of institutions as complexes of cultural rules. However, in their formulation, not any and all cultural rules are supportive of organizations. Following Berger's lead (see Berger, Berger, and Kellner 1973), Meyer and Rowan stressed the importance of beliefs that are "rationalized"—formulated in ways that specify the design of rulelike procedures to attain specific objectives. The engines of rationalization include the professions, nation-states, and mass media, whose efforts support the development of larger numbers and more types of organizations. Organizations are not simply the product of increasing technical sophistication, as long argued, or even of increasingly complex relational patterns, but result from the increasing rationalization of cultural rules, which provide an independent basis for their construction. Meyer and Rowan emphasized the impact on organizational forms of changes in the wider institutional environment.

While Meyer and Rowan developed the macroside of the argument, Lynne Zucker (a student of Meyer) emphasized the microfoundations of institutions (see Zucker 1991). She stressed the power of cognitive beliefs to anchor behavior: "social knowledge, once institutionalized exists as a fact, as part of objective reality, and can be transmitted directly on that basis" (Zucker 1977: 726).

Other influential contributions soon thereafter, by DiMaggio and Powell (1983) and Meyer and Scott (1983b), elaborated on the macro (environmental) perspective, which has become the dominant emphasis in sociological work. DiMaggio and Powell distinguished three important mechanisms—coercive, mimetic, and normative—by which institutional effects are diffused through a field of organizations and emphasized structural isomorphism (similarity) as an important consequence of both competitive and institutional processes. Meyer and Scott proposed that all organizations are shaped by both technical and institutional forces, but that some types of organizations were more strongly influenced by one than the other. Both sets of authors identified the organization "field" or sector as a new level of analysis particularly suited to the study of institutional processes. Organizational fields help to bound the environments within which institutional processes operate (see chaps. 4 and 8).

This early work ushering in "the new institutionalism in organizational analysis" (Powell and DiMaggio 1991) has continued to fuel and guide an expanding set of studies with applications to new problems and fields of inquiry—from studies of micromobilization to globalization processes. Like pioneering work in any arena, it has had an "imprinting" effect on much of the subsequent development of the field. However, such influence has both its positive and negative sides. As I discuss in subsequent chapters, although the pioneering statements provided valuable insights to pursue, they also contained flawed or limiting assumptions that are still in the process of being corrected.

Also active among sociologists is a set of investigators embracing a rational choice approach to social institutions. Their assumptions and approaches are quite similar to those already described as operating in economics and political science. Although their numbers and influence are considerably smaller in sociology than in these other disciplines, they include a number of prominent sociologists, including Coleman (1990), Hechter (1987; see also Hechter, Opp, and Wippler 1990), and Nee (1998). As Coleman (1994: 167) noted, these theorists embrace the "principle of actor maximization"—some in the stronger sense, others in the weaker, bounded rationality sense—as the "source of deductive power of rational choice theory." However, unlike neoclassical economics, they replace the "assumption of a perfect market with social structures, sometimes regarded as endogenous, and other times as exogenous, which carries individual actions into systemic outcomes." At least some of these analysts allow for the effects of "context-bound rationality within which individual interests and group norms develop" (Brinton and Nee 1998: xv).

❖ CONCLUDING COMMENT

Beginning in the 1950s, with the emergence of organizations as a recognized field of study, scholars began to connect institutional arguments to the structure and behavior of organizations. These approaches both built on and departed from the work of earlier institutional theorists. Institutional arguments began to be connected to organizational studies through the work of Merton and his students, particularly Selznick, as well as the efforts of Parsons, and Simon and March.

The work that has come to be labeled *neoinstitutional theory* assumes quite varied guises across the social sciences. The main thrust of economic approaches embraces orthodox or slightly broadened rationality assumptions and seeks to apply economic arguments to account for the existence of organizations and institutions. Williamson's development of transaction cost analysis exemplifies this approach to organizations. Political science remains split into two factions: the one applying rational choice economic models to political systems, and the other embracing a historical view of the nature of institutions, emphasizing their broad effects in constructing interests and actors.

Neoinstitutional approaches in sociology build on a loosely constructed framework of ideas stemming from cognitive psychology, cultural studies, phenomenology, and ethnomethodology. The newer conceptual models emphasize cognitive over normative frameworks and have focused primary attention on the effects of cultural belief systems operating in the environments of organizations rather than on intraorganizational processes.

In the next chapter, I shift from a historical to an analytic approach. I begin with an attempt to develop an integrated model of institutions—drawing on and encompassing much of the contemporary work of the type just reviewed. I then identify several dimensions along which contemporary theories differ as they consider the relation of institutions as they relate to organizations.

❖ NOTES

1. Related work stimulated by Weber was also carried out at this time by Reinhard Bendix, an exile from Nazi Germany. As a young assistant professor at the University of California, Berkeley, Bendix applied Weber's historical-comparative approach to the study of work and authority systems in two matched pairs of societies: England and the United States, and Russia and East Germany. In many respects, his study of diverse managerial ideologies, *Work and Authority in Industry* (Bendix, 1956/2001), was much more in accord with Weberian insights than most other efforts at this time that invoked Weber's name (see Guillén 2001a, 2001b).

2. Translations of some of Weber's important essays were made by Hans H. Gerth and C. Wright Mills (Weber 1906–1924/1946), who were both at Columbia University and connected to the circle of scholars gathered around Merton. The other important early translators were A. M. Henderson and Talcott Parsons (1924/1947).

3. In addition to his mentor, Merton, Selznick was also clearly influenced by the work of Robert Michels (1915/1949), a contemporary of Max Weber, who first examined the ways in which some members of organizations become more concerned with preserving the organization even at the cost of sacrificing its original goals. Michels observed this process in his study of the Social Democratic Party in Germany, which came to power, but at the sacrifice of its original goals. He gloomily concluded: "Thus from a means, organization become an end" (Michels 1915/1949: 390).

4. Values are expressions of goals or, more precisely, the criteria employed in selecting goals; norms are the generalized rules governing behavior that specify appropriate means for pursuing goals.

5. Parsons (1960b: 65–66) noted that the "points of articulation" between the three system levels are characterized by "a qualitative break in the simple continuity of line authority" because "the functions at each level are qualitatively different." His discussion thus anticipated the recognition by later analysts that some structural elements are "loosely coupled" or "decoupled" (see Meyer and Rowan 1977; Weick 1976).

6. A related line of theory and research, *agency theory,* also addresses the proper design of control structures to deal with the motivation and control of "agents"—those hired to assist the "principal"—the person expected to be the prime beneficiary of the collective work (see Alchian and Demsetz 1972; Jensen and Meckling 1976; Pratt and Zeckhauser 1985). Dealing with a problem common to all organizations, this approach focuses on the design of appropriate control and incentive systems to manage various kinds of work.

7. Peters (1999) identified six institutional perspectives existing within political science, including normative, rational choice, historical, empirical, international, and societal. This typology, in my view, gives too much weight to differences in methodology and/or topic. In a useful review, Hall and Taylor (1996) identified three "new institutionalisms": historical, rational choice, and sociological.

8. Paradoxically, as Chomsky has shown, an innate, hard-wired language capacity provides the basis for a "generative grammar" capable of rich and flexible language usage (Bergesen 2000, 2005).

9. Informative reviews of cultural sociology are provided by Wuthnow et al. (1984), Wuthnow (1987), and DiMaggio (1990, 1997).

10. It is for this reason that phenomenologists such as Schutz and Bellah define themselves as "symbolic realists."

11. In his subsequent work, Silverman (1972; Silverman and Jones 1976) shifted his focus toward a more micro, ethnomethodological emphasis, examining the multiple meanings and rationalities associated with participants' phenomenological accounts of their common situation (see Reed 1985).

3

Crafting an
Analytic Framework I

Three Pillars of Institutions

To an institutionalist, knowledge of what has gone before is vital information. The ideas and insights of our predecessors provide the context for current efforts and the platform on which we necessarily craft our own contributions. However, as should be clear even from my brief review, the concepts and arguments advanced by our predecessors have been strikingly diverse, resting on varied assumptions and privileging differing causal processes. A number of theorists have proposed that we can clarify the arguments by boiling them down to a few dominant paradigms (see e.g., Campbell 2004; Hall and Taylor 1996). However, as Campbell observed, these "schools" exhibit as many similarities as differences. Hence, my own approach to bringing some order into the discussion is to propose a broad definition of institutions that can encompass a variety of arguments and then attempt to identify the key analytic elements that give rise to the most important differences observed and debates encountered. This chapter and the next identify and elucidate the three analytical elements that comprise institutions. Each element is important and, sometimes, one or another will dominate, but more often—in robust institutional frameworks—they work in combination. However, because each operates through distinctive mechanisms and sets in motion disparate processes, I emphasize their differences in my initial discussion.

After introducing the principal distinctions around which the analysis is conducted, I bravely but briefly consider their philosophical underpinnings. Varying conceptions of institutions call up somewhat different views of the nature of social reality and social order. Similarly, the institutional elements relate to disparate constructs of how actors make choices: the extent to which actors are rational and what is meant by this concept. These issues, although too complex to fully explore, are too important to ignore.

The companion chapter, chapter 4, completes the presentation of the analytical framework and associated issues. It begins by examining what types of institutional beliefs support the development of organizations. I then describe the concept of "structuration," which can assist us in the effort to reconcile institutional constraints with individual agency. Finally, I describe a set of diverse carriers that transport institutional elements and identify the multiple levels at which institutional analysis takes place.

Chapters 3 and 4 should be taken as a prolegomena to the more problem-focused, empirically based discussions in the chapters to follow. They introduce concepts and definitions that are employed to examine particular topics as well as preview controversies and issues that are encountered as we review, in chapters 5 through 8, developments in institutional theory and research from the 1970s to the present.

❖ DEFINING INSTITUTIONS

Let us begin with the following omnibus conception of institutions:

> *Institutions are comprised of regulative, normative and cultural-cognitive elements that, together with associated activities and resources, provide stability and meaning to social life.*

This is a dense definition containing a number of ideas that I will unpack, describe, and elaborate in this chapter and the next. In this conception, institutions are multifaceted, durable social structures made up of symbolic elements, social activities, and material resources. Institutions exhibit distinctive properties: They are relatively resistant to change (Jepperson 1991). They tend to be transmitted across generations, to be maintained and reproduced (Zucker 1977). As Giddens (1984: 24) states, "Institutions by definition are the more enduring features of social life . . . giving 'solidity' [to social systems] across time and space."

Institutions exhibit these properties because of the processes set in motion by regulative, normative, and cultural-cognitive elements. These elements are the central building blocks of institutional structures, providing the elastic fibers that guide behavior and resist change. I examine the distinctive nature and contribution of each element in a subsequent section of this chapter.

Although rules, norms, and cultural-cognitive beliefs—symbolic systems—are central ingredients of institutions, the concept must also encompass associated behaviors and material resources. An institutional perspective gives heightened attention to the symbolic aspects of social life, yet we must also attend to the activities that produce and reproduce them and to the resources that sustain them. Institutions are, in Hallett and Ventresca's (2006) useful metaphor, "inhabited by people and their interactions." Rules, norms, and meanings arise in interaction, and they are preserved and modified by human behavior. To isolate meaning systems from their related behaviors is, as Geertz (1973: 17) cautioned, to commit the error of

> locking cultural analysis away from its proper object, the informal logic of actual life. . . . Behavior must be attended to, and with some exactness, because it is through the flow of behavior—or, more precisely, social action—that cultural forms find articulation. . . . Whatever, or wherever, symbol systems 'in their own terms' may be, we gain empirical access to them by inspecting events, not by arranging abstracted entities into unified patterns.

Similarly, for Berger and Luckmann (1967: 75), institutions are "dead" if they are only represented in verbal designations and physical objects. All such representations are bereft of subjective reality "unless they are ongoingly 'brought to life' in actual human conduct."

Sociological theorists Giddens (1979, 1984) and Sewell (1992) underline the importance of including material resources—both material and human—in any conception of social structure so as to take into account asymmetries of power. If rules and norms are to be effective, they must be backed with sanctioning power. Conversely, those possessing power in the form of excess resources seek authorization and legitimation for its use. For cultural beliefs, or "schemas" in Sewell's (1992: 13) formulation, to be viable, they must relate to and are often embodied in resources:

Schemas not empowered or regenerated by resources would eventually be abandoned and forgotten, just as resources without cultural schemas to direct their use would eventually dissipate and decay.

The Giddens/Sewell formulation usefully stresses the "duality" of social structure, encompassing both idealist and material features of social life and highlighting their interdependence, an argument we elaborate on in chapter 4.

Many treatments of institutions emphasize their capacity to control and constrain behavior. Institutions impose restrictions by defining legal, moral, and cultural boundaries, setting off legitimate from illegitimate activities. However, it is essential to recognize that institutions also support and empower activities and actors. Institutions provide guidelines and resources for taking action as well as prohibitions and constraints on action.

Although institutions function to provide stability and order, they undergo change, both incremental and revolutionary. Thus, our subject must not only include institutions as a "property" or state of an existing social order, but also institutions as "process," including the processes of institutionalization and deinstitutionalization (see Tolbert and Zucker 1996). Scholars increasingly attend not only to how institutions arise and are maintained, but how they undergo change.

Institutions ride on various conveyances and are instantiated in multiple media. These institutional carriers vary in the processes employed to transmit their messages. In addition, institutions operate at multiple levels—from the world system to interpersonal interaction. I examine these diverse carriers and levels in chapter 4.

Important differences exist among the various schools of institutional scholars, as is apparent from our review of previous work. In my view, the most consequential dispute centers on which institutional elements are accorded priority.

❖ THE THREE PILLARS OF INSTITUTIONS

Regulative, normative, and cultural-cognitive systems have each been identified by one or another social theorist as a vital ingredient of institutions. The three elements form a continuum moving "from the conscious to the unconscious, from the legally enforced to the taken for granted" (Hoffman 1997: 36). One possible approach would be to view all of these facets as contributing, in interdependent and mutually reinforcing ways, to a powerful social framework—one that encapsulates and exhibits the celebrated strength and resilience of these structures. In such an integrated conception, institutions appear, as D'Andrade (1984: 98) observed, to be overdetermined systems: "overdetermined in the sense that social sanctions plus pressure for conformity, plus intrinsic direct reward, plus values, are all likely to act together to give a particular meaning system its directive force."

Although such an inclusive model has its strengths, it also masks important differences. The definition knits together three somewhat divergent conceptions that need to be differentiated. Rather than pursuing the development of a more integrated conception,[1] I believe more progress will be made at this juncture by distinguishing among the several component elements and identifying their different underlying assumptions, mechanisms, and indicators.[2] By employing a more analytical approach to these arguments, we can identify important underlying theoretical fault lines that transect the domain.

Consider Table 3.1. The columns contain the three elements—three "pillars"—identified as making up or supporting institutions. The rows define some of the principal dimensions along which assumptions vary and arguments arise among theorists emphasizing one element over the others. This table serves as a guide as I consider each element.

Table 3.1   Three Pillars of Institutions

	Regulative	Normative	Cultural-Cognitive
Basis of compliance	Expedience	Social obligation	Taken-for-grantedness Shared understanding
Basis of order	Regulative rules	Binding expectations	Constitutive schema
Mechanisms	Coercive	Normative	Mimetic
Logic	Instrumentality	Appropriateness	Orthodoxy
Indicators	Rules Laws Sanctions	Certification Accreditation	Common beliefs Shared logics of action Isomorphism
Affect	Fear Guilt/ Innocence	Shame/Honor	Certainty/ Confusion
Basis of legitimacy	Legally sanctioned	Morally governed	Comprehensible Recognizable Culturally supported

The Regulative Pillar

In the broadest sense, all scholars underscore the regulative aspects of institutions: Institutions constrain and regularize behavior. Scholars more specifically associated with the regulatory pillar are distinguished by the prominence they give to explicit regulatory processes—rule-setting, monitoring, and sanctioning activities. In this conception, regulatory processes involve the capacity to establish rules, inspect others' conformity to them, and, as necessary, manipulate sanctions—rewards or punishments—in an attempt to influence future behavior. These processes may operate through diffuse, informal mechanisms, involving folkways such as shaming or shunning activities, or they may be highly formalized and assigned to specialized actors, such as the police and courts.

Economists, including economic historians, are particularly likely to view institutions as resting primarily on the regulatory pillar. The economic historian Douglass North (1990: 4), for example, featured rule systems and enforcement mechanisms in his conceptualization:[3]

> [Institutions] are perfectly analogous to the rules of the game in a competitive team sport. That is, they consist of formal written rules as well as typically unwritten codes of conduct that underlie and supplement formal rules . . . the rules and informal codes are sometimes violated and punishment is enacted. Therefore, an essential part of the functioning of institutions is the costliness of ascertaining violations and the severity of punishment.

This emphasis may stem, in part, from the character of the customary objects studied by economists and rational choice political scientists. They are likely to focus attention on the behavior of individuals and firms in markets and other competitive situations, such as politics, where contending interests are more common and, hence, explicit rules and referees are more necessary to preserve order. Such economists and political scientists view individuals and organizations that construct rule systems or conform to rules as pursuing their self-interests—as behaving instrumentally and expediently. The primary mechanism of control observed, employing DiMaggio and Powell's (1983) typology, is coercion.

Although the concept of regulation conjures up visions of repression and constraint, many types of regulations enable social actors and action, conferring licenses, special powers, and benefits to some types of actors. Institutions work both to constrain and empower social behavior.

Force, sanctions, and expedience responses are central ingredients of the regulatory pillar, but they are often tempered by the existence of rules, whether in the guise of informal mores or formal rules and laws. As Weber (1924/1968) emphasized, few if any rulers are content to base their regime on force alone; all attempt to cultivate a belief in its legitimacy. Hence, powerful actors may sometimes impose their will on others, based on the use or threat of sanctions. They may provide inducements to secure compliance—for example, firms may supply price breaks to favored customers and many federal programs that lack programmatic authority to impose conformity secure local cooperation by supplying funds to support desired programs. The most common case, however, involves the use of authority, in which coercive power is legitimated by a normative framework that both supports and constrains the exercise of power (see Scott 1987; Dornbusch and Scott 1975: chap. 2). The regulative and normative pillars can be mutually reinforcing.

Much work in economics emphasizes the costs of regulation. Agency theory stresses the expense and difficulty entailed in accurately monitoring performances relevant to contracts, whether implicit or explicit, and in designing appropriate incentives (see Milgrom and Roberts 1992; Pratt and Zeckhauser 1985). Although in some situations agreements can be monitored and mutually enforced by the parties involved, in many circumstances it is necessary to vest the enforcement machinery in a "third party" expected to behave in a neutral fashion. Economic historians view this as an important function of the state. Thus, North (1990: 64) argued:

> Because ultimately a third party must always involve the state as a source of coercion, a theory of institutions also inevitably involves an analysis of the political structure of a society and the degree to which that political structure provides a framework of effective enforcement.

North (1990: 54) also called attention to problems that can arise because "enforcement is undertaken by agents whose own utility functions influence outcomes" (i.e., third parties who are not neutral). This possibility is stressed by many historical institutionalists, such as Skocpol (1985), who argued that the state develops its own interests and operates somewhat autonomously from other societal actors. In this and other ways, attention to the regulative aspects of institutions creates renewed interest in the role of the state: as rule maker, referee, and enforcer.

Law and society theorists, however, point out that analysts should not conflate the coercive functions of law with its normative and cognitive dimensions. Rather than operating in an authoritative and exogenous manner, many laws are sufficiently controversial or ambiguous that they do not provide clear prescriptions for conduct. In such cases, law is better conceived as an occasion for sense-making and collective interpretation, relying more on cognitive and normative than coercive elements for its effects (see Suchman and Edelman 1997; see also chap. 6). In short, institutions supported by one pillar may, as time passes and circumstances change, be sustained by different pillars.

In short, there is much to examine in understanding how regulative institutions function and how they interact with other institutional elements. Through the work of agency and game theorists, at one end of the spectrum, and law and society theorists, at the other, we are reminded that laws do not spring from the head of Zeus or norms from the collective soul of a people; rules must be interpreted and disputes resolved; incentives and sanctions must be designed and will have unintended effects; surveillance mechanisms are required but will prove to be fallible, not foolproof; and conformity is only one of many possible responses by those subject to regulative institutions.

As noted in chapter 2, symbolic systems comprehend not only substance but affect and, hence, stimulate not only interpretive but also emotional reactions. Are their distinctive types of feelings engendered by encounters with the regulative organs of society? We think so and believe that the feelings induced may constitute an important component of the power of this element. To confront a system of rules backed by the machinery of enforcement is to experience, at the one extreme, fear, dread, and guilt, or, at the other, relief, innocence, and vindication. Powerful emotions indeed!

A stable system of rules, whether formal or informal, backed by surveillance and sanctioning power that is accompanied by feelings of fear/guilt or innocence/incorruptibility is one prevailing view of institutions.

The Normative Pillar

A second group of theorists sees institutions as resting primarily on a normative pillar (again, see table 3.1). Emphasis here is placed on normative rules that introduce a prescriptive, evaluative, and obligatory dimension into social life. Normative systems include both values and norms. *Values* are conceptions of the preferred or the desirable, together with the construction of standards to which existing structures or behaviors can be compared and assessed. *Norms* specify how things should be done; they define legitimate means to pursue valued ends. Normative systems define goals or objectives (e.g., winning the game, making a profit), but also designate appropriate ways to pursue them (e.g., rules specifying how the game is to be played, conceptions of fair business practices).

Some values and norms are applicable to all members of the collectivity, whereas others apply only to selected types of actors or positions. The latter give rise to *roles*: conceptions of appropriate goals and activities for particular individuals or specified social positions. These beliefs are not simply anticipations or predictions, but prescriptions— normative expectations—of how specified actors are supposed to behave. The expectations are held by other salient actors in the situation, and so are experienced by the focal actor as external pressures. Also, and to varying degrees, they become internalized by the actor. Roles can be formally constructed. For example, in an organizational context, particular positions are defined to carry specified rights and responsibilities and to have varying access to material resources. Roles can also emerge informally as, over time through interaction, differentiated expectations develop to guide behavior.[4]

Normative systems are typically viewed as imposing constraints on social behavior, and so they do. At the same time, they empower and enable social action. They confer rights as well as responsibilities; privileges as well as duties; licenses as well as mandates. In his essays on the professions, Hughes (1958) reminded us how much of the power and mystique associated with these types of roles comes from the "license" they are given to engage in "forbidden" or fateful activities— conducting intimate physical examinations or sentencing individuals to prison or death.

The normative conception of institutions was embraced by most early sociologists—from Durkheim through Parsons and Selznick— perhaps because sociologists are more likely to examine those types of institutions, such as kinship groups, social classes, religious systems, and voluntary associations, where common beliefs and values are more likely to exist and constitute an important basis for order. Moreover, it continues to guide and inform much contemporary work by sociologists and political scientists on organizations. For example, March and Olsen (1989: 21) embraced a primarily normative conception of institutions:

> The proposition that organizations follow rules, that much of the behavior in an organization is specified by standard operating procedures, is a common one in the bureaucratic and organizational literature. . . . It can be extended to the institutions of politics.

Much of the behavior we observe in political institutions reflects the routine way in which people do what they are supposed to do.

Although their conception of rules is quite broad, including cultural-cognitive as well as normative elements—"routines, procedures, conventions, roles, strategies, organizational forms, and technologies . . . beliefs, paradigms, codes, cultures, and knowledge" (March and Olsen: 22)—their focus remains on social obligations:

> To describe behavior as driven by rules is to see action as a matching of a situation to the demands of a position. Rules define relationships among roles in terms of what an incumbent of one role owes to incumbents of other roles. (March and Olsen 1989: 23)

Norms can also evoke strong feelings, but these are somewhat different from those that accompany the violation of rules and regulations. Feelings associated with the trespassing of norms include principally a sense of shame or disgrace or, for those who exhibit exemplary behavior, feelings of pride and honor. The conformity to or violation of norms typically involves a large measure of self-evaluation: heightened remorse and/or effects on self-respect. Such emotions provide powerful inducements to compliance with prevailing norms.

Theorists embracing a normative conception of institutions emphasize the stabilizing influence of social beliefs and norms that are both internalized and imposed by others. For early normative theorists such as Parsons, shared norms and values were regarded as the primary basis of a stable social order. As Stinchcombe (1997: 18) eloquently reaffirmed, institutions are widely viewed as having moral roots:

> The guts of institutions is that somebody somewhere really cares to hold an organization to the standards and is often paid to do that. Sometimes that somebody is inside the organization, maintaining its competence. Sometimes it is an accrediting body, sending out volunteers to see if there is really any algebra in the algebra course. And sometimes that somebody, or his or her commitment is lacking, in which case the center cannot hold, and mere anarchy is loosed upon the world.

The Cultural-Cognitive Pillar

A third set of institutionalists—principally anthropologists like Geertz and Douglas; sociologists like Berger, Goffman, and Meyer; and organizational scholars such as DiMaggio, Powell, and Scott—stress the centrality of cultural-cognitive elements of institutions: the shared conceptions that constitute the nature of social reality and the frames through which meaning is made (again, see table 3.1). Attention to the cultural-cognitive dimension of institutions is the major distinguishing feature of neoinstitutionalism within sociology and organizational studies.

These institutionalists take seriously the cognitive dimensions of human existence: mediating between the external world of stimuli and the response of the individual organism is a collection of internalized symbolic representations of the world. "In the cognitive paradigm, what a creature does is, in large part, a function of the creature's internal representation of its environment" (D'Andrade 1984: 88). Symbols— words, signs, and gestures—shape the meanings we attribute to objects and activities. Meanings arise in interaction and are maintained and transformed as they are employed to make sense of the ongoing stream of happenings. Emphasizing the importance of symbols and meanings returns us to Max Weber's central premise. As noted in chapter 1, Weber regarded action as social only to the extent that the actor attaches meaning to the behavior. To understand or explain any action, the analyst must take into account not only the objective conditions, but the actor's subjective interpretation of them. Extensive research by psychologists over the past three decades has shown that cognitive frames enter into the full range of information-processing activities, from determining what information will receive attention, how it will be in encoded, how it will be retained, retrieved, and organized into memory, to how it will be interpreted, thus affecting evaluations, judgments, predictions, and inferences (for an extensive review, see Markus and Zajonc 1985).

As discussed in chapter 2, the new cultural perspective focuses on the semiotic facets of culture, treating them not simply as subjective beliefs, but also as symbolic systems perceived to be objective and external to individual actors. As Berger and Kellner (1981: 31) summarize: "Every human institution is, as it were, a sedimentation of meanings or, to vary the image, a crystallization of meanings in objective form." My use of the hyphenated label *cognitive-cultural* recognizes that "internal" interpretive processes are shaped by "external" cultural frameworks. As Douglas (1982: 12) proposed: We should "treat cultural categories as the cognitive containers in which social interests are defined and classified, argued, negotiated, and fought out." In Hofstede's (1991: 4) graphic metaphor, culture provides patterns of thinking, feeling, and acting: mental programs or the "software of the mind."[5] Culture indeed exhibits these aggregate features—in conceptions of situations shared by collections of individuals. However, culture also exists at a more global level (e.g., in the form of collective symbols like flags, national anthems, and prevailing ideologies regarding preferred political or economic systems).

Of course cultural elements vary in their degree of institutionalization—the extent of their linkage to other elements and the degree to which they are embodied in routines or organizing schema. When we talk about cognitive-cultural elements of institutions, we call attention to these more embedded cultural forms: "culture congealed in forms that require less by way of maintenance, ritual reinforcement, and symbolic elaboration than the softer (or more 'living') realms we usually think of as cultural" (Jepperson and Swidler 1994: 363).

Cultures are often conceived of as unitary systems, internally consistent across groups and situations. I believe it is important to recognize that cultural conceptions often vary: Beliefs are held by some, but not by others. People in the same situation can perceive the situation quite differently—both in terms of what is and what should be. Cultural beliefs vary and are frequently contested, particularly in times of social disorganization and change (see DiMaggio 1997; Martin 1992; Swidler 1986).

For cultural-cognitive theorists, compliance occurs in many circumstances because other types of behavior are inconceivable; routines are followed because they are taken for granted as "the way we do these things." Social roles are given a somewhat different interpretation by cultural than by normative theorists. Rather than stressing the force of mutually reinforcing obligations, cultural theorists point to the power of templates for particular types of actors and scripts for action. For Berger and Luckmann (1967: 73–75), roles arise as common understandings develop that particular actions are associated with particular actors.[6]

> We can properly begin to speak of roles when this kind of typification occurs in the context of an objectified stock of knowledge common to a collectivity of actors. . . . Institutions are embodied in individual experience by means of roles. . . . The institution, with its assemblage of "programmed" actions, is like the unwritten libretto of a drama. The realization of the drama depends upon the reiterated performance of its prescribed roles by living actors. . . . Neither drama nor institution exists empirically apart from this recurrent realization.

Differentiated roles can and do develop in localized contexts as repetitive patterns of action gradually become habitualized and objectified, but it is also important to recognize the operation of wider institutional frameworks that provide prefabricated organizing models and scripts (see Goffman 1974, 1983). Meyer and Rowan (1977) and DiMaggio and Powell (1983) emphasized the extent to which wider belief systems and cultural frames are imposed on or adopted by individual actors and organizations.

The affective dimension of this pillar is expressed in feelings ranging from the positive affect of certitude and confidence, on the one hand, to the negative feelings of confusion or disorientation, on the other hand. Actors who align themselves with prevailing cultural beliefs are likely to feel competent and connected, whereas those who are at odds are regarded, at best, as "clueless" and, at worst, as "crazy."

A cultural-cognitive conception of institutions stresses the central role played by the socially mediated construction of a common framework of meaning.

❖ THE THREE PILLARS AND LEGITIMACY

"Organizations require more than material resources and technical information if they are to survive and thrive in their social environments. They also need social acceptability and credibility" (Scott et al. 2000: 237). Sociologists employ the concept of legitimacy to refer to these conditions. Suchman (1995b: 574) provides a helpful definition of this central concept: "*Legitimacy* is a generalized perception or assumption that the actions of an entity are desirable, proper, or appropriate within some socially constructed system of norms, values, beliefs, and definitions." Legitimacy is a generalized rather than an event-specific evaluation and is "possessed objectively, yet created subjectively" (574). The "socially constructed systems" to which Suchman referred are, of course, institutional frameworks. Consistent with the preceding discussion, each of the three pillars provides a basis for legitimacy, albeit a different one.

In a resource-dependent or social-exchange approach to organizations, legitimacy is typically treated as simply another kind of resource that organizations extract from their institutional environment (e.g., Dowling and Pfeffer 1975; Suchman 1995a). However, from an institutional perspective, legitimacy is not a commodity to be possessed or exchanged, but rather a condition reflecting perceived consonance with relevant rules and laws, normative support, or alignment with cultural-cognitive frameworks. Moreover, unlike material resources or technical information, legitimacy is not an input to be combined or transformed to produce some new and different output, but a symbolic value to be displayed in a manner such that it is visible to outsiders (see Scott 2003b: 213–214).

Berger and Luckmann (1967) described legitimacy as evoking a "second order" of meaning. In their early stages, institutionalized activities develop as repeated patterns of behavior that evoke shared meanings among the participants. The legitimation of this order involves connecting it to wider cultural frames, norms, or rules. "Legitimation 'explains' the institutional order by ascribing cognitive validity to its objectified meanings. Legitimation justifies the institutional order by giving a normative dignity to its practical imperatives" (Berger and Luckman 1967: 92–93). In a parallel vein, Weber (1924/1968) argued that power becomes legitimated as authority to the extent that its exercise is supported by prevailing social norms, whether traditional, charismatic, or bureaucratic (see also Dornbusch and Scott 1975: chap. 2). Emphasizing the cultural-cognitive dimension, Meyer and I proposed that "organizational legitimacy refers to the degree of cultural support for an organization" (Meyer and Scott 1983a: 201).

This vertical dimension entails the support of significant others: various types of "authorities"—cultural as well as political—empowered to confer legitimacy. Who these authorities are varies from time to time and place to place, but, in our time, agents of the state and professional and trade associations are often critical for organizations. Certification or accreditation by these bodies is frequently employed as a prime indicator of legitimacy (Dowling and Pfeffer 1975; Ruef and Scott 1998). In complex situations, individuals or organizations may be confronted by competing sovereigns. Actors confronting conflicting normative requirements and standards typically find it difficult to take action because conformity to one undermines the normative support of other bodies. "The legitimacy of a given organization is negatively affected by the number of different authorities sovereign over it and by the diversity or inconsistency of their accounts of how it is to function" (Meyer and Scott 1983a: 202).

There is always the question as to whose assessments count in determining the legitimacy of a set of arrangements. Many structures persist and spread because they are regarded as "appropriate" by entrenched authorities, although their legitimacy is challenged by other, less powerful constituencies. Martin (1994), for example, noted that salary inequities between men and women are institutionalized in American society, although the disadvantaged groups perceive them to be unjust and press for reforms. "Legitimate" structures may, at the same time, be contested structures.

Stinchcombe (1968: 162) asserts that, in the end, whose values define legitimacy is a matter of concerted social power:

> A power is legitimate to the degree that, by virtue of the doctrines and norms by which it is justified, the power-holder can call upon sufficient other centers of power, as reserves in case of need, to make his power effective.

Although power certainly matters in supporting legitimacy processes as in other social activities, power is not the absolute arbiter. Entrenched power is, in the long run, hapless against the onslaught of opposing power allied with more persuasive ideas or stronger commitments.

The three pillars elicit three related, but distinguishable bases of legitimacy (see table 3.1).[7] The regulatory emphasis is on conformity to rules: Legitimate organizations are those established by and operating in accordance with relevant legal or quasilegal requirements. A normative conception stresses a deeper, moral base for assessing legitimacy. Normative controls are much more likely to be internalized than are regulative controls, and the incentives for conformity are hence likely to include intrinsic as well as extrinsic rewards. A cultural-cognitive view points to the legitimacy that comes from conforming to a common definition of the situation, frame of reference, or a recognizable role or structural template. To adopt an orthodox structure or identity in order to relate to a specific situation is to seek the legitimacy that comes from cognitive consistency. The cultural-cognitive mode is the "deepest" level because it rests on preconscious, taken-for-granted understandings.

The bases of legitimacy associated with the three elements are decidedly different and may, sometimes, be in conflict. A regulative view would ascertain whether the organization is legally established and whether it is acting in accord with relevant laws and regulations. A normative orientation, stressing moral obligations, may countenance actions departing from "mere" legal requirements. Many professionals adhere to normative standards that motivate them to depart from the rule-based requirements of bureaucratic organizations. Whistle-blowers claim that they are acting on the basis of a "higher authority" when they contest organizational rules or superiors' orders. An organization such as the Mafia may be widely recognized, signifying that it exhibits a culturally constituted mode of organizing to achieve specified ends, and it is regarded as a legitimate way of organizing by its members. Nevertheless, it is treated as an illegal form by police and other regulative bodies, and it lacks the normative endorsement of most citizens.

What is taken as evidence of legitimacy varies by which elements of institutions are privileged as well as which audiences or authorities are consulted.

Combinations of Elements

Having introduced the three basic elements and emphasized their distinctive features and modes of working, it is important to restate the truth that, in most empirically observed institutional forms, we observe not one, single element at work, but varying combinations of elements. In stable social systems, we observe practices that persist and are reinforced because they are taken for granted, normatively endorsed, and backed by authorized powers. When the pillars are aligned, the strength of their combined forces can be formidable.

In some situations, however, one or another pillar will operate virtually alone in supporting the social order, and in many situations, a given pillar will assume primacy.

Equally important, the pillars may be misaligned: They may support and motivate differing choices and behaviors. As Strang and Sine (2002: 499) point out: "where cognitive, normative, and regulative supports are not well aligned, they provide resources that different actors can employ for different ends." Such situations exhibit both confusion and conflict, and provide conditions that are highly likely to give rise to institutional change (Caronna 2004; Hoffman 1997; see also chap. 8).

❖ BASIC ASSUMPTIONS ASSOCIATED
WITH THE THREE PILLARS

Although the differences among analysts emphasizing one or another element are partly a matter of substantive focus—what types of social systems are being examined—they are also associated with more profound differences in underlying philosophical assumptions. It is not possible to do full justice to the complexity and subtlety of these issues, but I attempt to depict the differences in broad outline. Two matters are particularly significant: differences among analysts in their ontological assumptions—assumptions concerning the nature of social reality—and differences among them in the extent and type of rationality invoked in explaining behavior.

Regulative and Constitutive Rules

Truth and Reality

To examine the ontological assumptions underlying the varying conceptions of institutional elements, I believe it is necessary to begin by clarifying one's epistemological assumptions: How do we understand the nature of scientific knowledge? My position on these debates has been greatly influenced by the formulation advanced by Jeffrey C. Alexander (1983, vol. 1), who provides a broad, synthetic examination of the nature and development of theoretical logic in modern sociological thought. Following Kuhn (1970), Alexander adopted a "postpositivist" perspective, viewing science as operating along a continuum stretching from the empirical environment, on the one hand, to the metaphysical environment, on the other (see fig. 3.1).

At the metaphysical end, the most abstract general presuppositions and models associated with more "theoretical" activity reside. At the empirical end, one finds observations, correlations, and propositions. The continuum obviously incorporates numerous types of statements, ranging from the more abstract and general to the more specific and particular. More importantly, however, the framework emphasizes that, although the mix of empirical and metaphysical elements varies, every point on the continuum is an admixture of both elements. "What appears, concretely, to be a difference in types of scientific statements—models, definitions, propositions—simply reflects the different emphasis within a given statement on generality or specificity" (Alexander 1983: vol. 1, 4).

Figure 3.1   The Scientific Continuum and Its Components

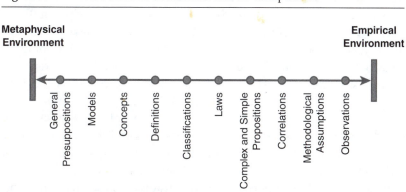

SOURCE: Alexander (1983, Volume 1, p. 3). Reprinted with permission of the author.

The postpostivist conception of science emphasizes the fundamental similarity of the social and physical sciences—both are human attempts to develop and test general statements about the behavior of the empirical world. It rejects both a radical materialist view that espouses that the only reality is a physical one and also the idealist (and postmodernist) view that the only reality exists in the human mind. It also usefully differentiates reality from truth, as Rorty (1989: 4–5) observed:

> We need to make a distinction between the claim that the world is out there and the claim that truth is out there. To say that the world is out there, that it is not our creation, is to say, with common sense, that most things in space and time are the effects of causes which do not include human mental states. To say that truth is not out there is simply to say that where there are no sentences there is no truth, that sentences are elements of human languages, and that human languages are human creations.

Social Reality

Although the physical and social sciences share important basic features, it is essential to recognize that the subject matter of the social sciences is distinctive. In John Searle's (1995: 1, 11, 13) terminology, portions of the real world, although treated as "epistemically objective" facts in the world, "are facts only by human agreement." Their existence is "observer-relative": dependent on observers who share a common conception of a given social fact. Social reality is an important subclass of reality.[8]

Social institutions refer to types of social reality that involve the collective development and use of both regulative and constitutive rules. *Regulative* rules involve attempts to influence "antecedently existing activities," and *constitutive* rules "create the very possibility of certain activities" (Searle, 1995: 27). Constitutive rules take the general form: X counts as Y in context C (e.g., an American dollar bill counts as legal currency in the United States). "Institutional facts exist only within systems of constitutive rules" (28). In general, as the label implies, scholars embracing the regulative view of institutions focus primary attention on regulative rules; for example, they assume the existence of actors with a given set of interests and then ask how various rule systems, manipulating sanctions and incentives, can affect the behavior of these actors as they pursue their interests. Cultural-cognitive scholars stress the importance of constitutive rules: They ask what types of actors are present, how their interests are shaped by these definitions, and what types of actions they are allowed to take. Thus, they thus differ in their ontological assumptions or, at least, in the ontological level at which they work.

Constitutive rules operate at a deeper level of reality creation, involving the devising of categories and the construction of typifications: processes by which "concrete and subjectively unique experiences . . . are ongoingly subsumed under general orders of meaning that are both objectively and subjectively real" (Berger and Luckmann 1967: 39). Such processes are variously applied to things, ideas, events, and actors. Games provide a ready illustration. Constitutive rules construct the game of "football" as consisting of things such as "goal posts" and the "gridiron" and events such as "first downs" and "off-sides" (see D'Andrade 1984). Similarly, other types of constitutive rules result in the social construction of actors and associated capacities and roles; in the football context, the creation of "quarterbacks," "coaches," and "referees." Regulative rules define how the ball may legitimately be advanced or what penalties are associated with what rule infractions. Thus, cultural-cognitive theorists amend and augment the portrait of institutions crafted by regulative theorists. Cultural-cognitive theorists insist that games involve more than rules and enforcement mechanisms: They consist of socially constructed players endowed with differing capacities for action and parts to play. Constitutive rules construct the social objects and events to which regulative rules are applied.

Such processes, although most visible in games, are not limited to these relatively artificial situations. Constitutive rules are so basic to social structure, so fundamental to social life, that they are often overlooked. In our liberal democracies, we take for granted that individual persons have interests and capacities for action. It seems natural that there are "citizens" with opinions and rights (as opposed to "subjects" with no or limited rights), "students" with a capacity to learn, "fathers" with rights and responsibilities, and "employees" with aptitudes and skills. Yet all of these types of actors—and a multitude of others—are social constructions; all depend for their existence on constitutive frameworks, which, although they arose in particular interaction contexts, have become reified in cultural rules that can be imported as guidelines into new situations (see Berger and Luckmann 1967; Gergen and Davis 1985).

Moreover, recognition of the existence of such constitutive processes provides a view of social behavior that differs greatly from lay interpretations or even from those found in much of social science. As Meyer, Boli, and Thomas (1987: 13) argued:

Most social theory takes actors (from individuals to states) and their actions as real, a priori, elements. . . . [In contrast] we see the "existence" and characteristics of actors as socially constructed and highly problematic, and action as the enactment of broad institutional scripts rather than a matter of internally generated and autonomous choice, motivation and purpose.

In short, as constitutive rules are recognized, individual behavior is seen to often reflect external definitions rather than (or as a source of) internal intentions. The difference is nicely captured in the anecdote reported by Peter Hay (1993: 70):

Gertrude Lawrence and Noel Coward were starring in one of the latter's plays when the production was honored with a royal visit. As Queen Elizabeth entered the Royal Box, the entire audience rose to its feet. Miss Lawrence, watching from the wings, murmured: "What an entrance!" Noel Coward, peeking on tip-toe behind her, added "What a part!"

The social construction of actors also defines what they consider to be their interests. The stereotypic "economic man," which rests at the heart of much economic theorizing, is not a reflection of human nature, but a social construct that arose under specific historical circumstances and is maintained by particular institutional logics associated with the rise of capitalism (see Heilbroner 1985).[9] From the cultural-cognitive perspective, interests are not assumed to be "natural" or outside the scope of investigation: They are not treated as exogenous to the theoretical framework. Rather, they are recognized as varying by institutional context and requiring explanation.

The social construction of actors and their associated activities is not limited to persons. Collective actors are similarly constituted and come in a wide variety of forms. Naturally, we are particularly interested in the nature of those institutional processes at work in the constitution of organizations, processes considered in chapters 4 and 5.

Parsing Rationality

Theorists make different assumptions regarding how actors make choices: what logics determine social action. As discussed earlier in this chapter and in chapter 1, Weber defined social action so as to emphasize the importance of the meanings individuals attach to their own and other's behavior. For Weber and many other social theorists, "the central question that every social theory addresses in defining the nature of action is whether or not—or to what degree—action is rational"

(Alexander 1983: vol. 1, 72). A more basic question, however, is how ratio-nality is to be defined. Institutional theorists propose a wide range of answers.

At one end of the spectrum, a neoclassical economic perspective embraces an "atomist" view that focuses on an individual actor engaged in maximizing behavior, guided by stable preferences and possessing complete knowledge of the possible alternatives and their consequences. Game-theoretic analysts typically adhere rather closely to this "lean" model of the rational actor (see e.g., Schotter 1986). Embracing a some-what broader set of assumptions, neoinstitutional analysts in economics and rational-choice theorists in political science (e.g., Moe 1990a; Williamson 1985) utilize Simon's (1945/1997) model of bounded ratio-nality, which presumes that actors are "intendedly rational, but only boundedly so." These versions relax the assumptions regarding com-plete information and utility maximization as the criterion of choice, while retaining the premise that actors seek "to do the best they can to satisfy whatever their wants might be" (Abell 1995:7). Institutional theo-rists employing these and related models of individual rational actors are more likely to view institutions primarily as regulative frameworks. Actors construct institutions to deal with collective action problems—to regulate their own and others' behaviors—and they respond to institu-tions because the regulations are backed by incentives and sanctions.

A strength of these models is that rational-choice theorists have "an explicit theory of individual behavior in mind" when they examine motives for developing and consequences attendant to the formation of institutional structures (Peters 1999: 45; see also Abell 1995). Economic theorists argue that, although their assumptions may not be completely accurate, "many institutions and business practices are designed as if people were entirely motivated by narrow, selfish concerns and were quite clever and largely unprincipled in their pursuit of their goals" (Milgrom and Roberts 1992: 42).

From a sociological perspective, a limitation of employing an overly narrow rational framework is that it "portrays action as simply an adap-tation to material conditions"—a calculus of costs and benefits—rather than allowing for the "internal subjective reference of action" that opens up potential for the "multidimensional alternation of freedom and con-straint" (Alexander 1983: vol. 1, 74). Another limitation involves the rigid distinction in rational-choice models made between ends, which are pre-sumed to be fixed, and means. Alternative models variously propose that ends are modified by means, that ends emerge in ongoing activities, and even that means can become ends (March and Olsen 1989; Selznick 1949; Weick 1979). In addition, rather than positing a lone individual decision maker, the sociological version embraces an "organicist rather than an atomist view," such that "the essential characteristics of any element are seen as outcomes of relations with other entities" (Hodgson 1994: 61). Actors in interaction constitute social structures, which in turn constitute actors. The products of prior interactions—norms, rules, beliefs, and resources—provide the situational elements that enter into individual decision making (see the discussion of "structuration" in chap. 4).

A number of terms have been proposed for this broadened view of rationality. As usual, Weber anticipated much of the current debate by distinguishing among several variants of rationality, including *Zweckrationalität*—action that is rational in the instrumental, calculative sense—and *Wertrationalität*—action that is inspired by and directed toward the realization of substantive values (Weber 1924/1968: 24; see also Swedberg 1998: 36). The former focuses on means-ends connections, whereas the latter focuses on the types of ends pursued. Although Weber was inconsistent in his usage of these ideal types, Alexander suggests that they are best treated as analytic distinctions, with actual rational behavior being seen as involving an admixture of the two types. All social action involves some combination of calculation (in selection of means) and orientation toward socially defined values.[10]

A related distinction has been proposed by March (1981), who differentiated between a logic of "instrumentalism" and a logic of "appropriateness" (see also March 1994; March and Olsen 1989). An instrumental logic asks, "What are my interests in this situation?" A logic of appropriateness asks, "Given my role in this situation, what is expected of me?" The latter conception stresses the normative pillar, where choice is seen to be grounded in a social context and oriented by a moral framework that takes into account one's relations and obligations to others in the situation. A logic of appropriateness replaces or sets limits on individualistic instrumental behavior.

Cultural-cognitive theorists emphasize the extent to which behavior is informed and constrained by the ways in which knowledge is constructed and codified. Underlying all decisions and choices are socially constructed models, assumptions, and schemas. All decisions are admixtures of rational calculations and nonrational premises. At the microlevel, DiMaggio and Powell (1991: 22) propose that a recognition of these conditions provides the basis for what they term a theory of *practical* action. This conception departs from a "preoccupation with the rational, calculative aspect of cognition to focus on preconscious processes and schema as they enter into routine, taken-for-granted behavior." At the same time, it eschews the individualistic, asocial assumptions associated with the narrow rational perspective to emphasize the extent to which individual choices are governed by normative rules and embedded in networks of mutual social obligations.

Langlois (1986b: 237) proposed that the model of an intendedly rational actor needs to be supplemented by a model of the actor's "situation," which includes, importantly, relevant social institutions. Institutions provide an informational-support function, serving as "interpersonal stores of coordinative knowledge." Such common conceptions enable the routine accomplishment of highly complex and interdependent tasks, often with a minimum of conscious deliberation or decision making. Analysts are enjoined to "pay attention to the existence of social institutions of various kinds as bounds to and definitions of the agent's situation" (252). Langlois encouraged us to broaden the neoclassical conception of rational action to encompass reasonable action, a conception that allows actors to "prefer more to less [of] all things considered," but also that allows for "other kinds of reasonable action in certain situations," including rule-following behavior (252). Social action is always grounded in social contexts that specify valued ends and appropriate means; action acquires its very reasonableness from taking into account these social rules and guidelines for behavior.

Emerging work involves an attempt to resurrect and update pragmatism, a theory promulgated during the late 19th and early 20th centuries by some of America's most ingenuous social philosophers and social scientists, including Oliver Wendell Holmes, William James, Charles Peirce, and John Dewey. Among their central tenants were that (a) "ideas are not 'out there,' waiting to be discovered, but are tools . . . that people devise to cope with the world in which they find themselves"; and (b) ideas are produced "not by individuals, but by groups of individuals—that ideas are social, . . . dependent . . . on their human carriers and the environment" (Menand 2001: xi). Indeed, as Strauss (1993: 72) reminds us:

> In the writings of the Pragmatists we can see a constant battle again the separating, dichotomizing, or opposition of what Pragmatists argued should be joined together: knowledge and practice, environment and actor, biology and culture, means and ends, body and mind, matter and mind, object and subject, logic and inquiry, lay thought and scientific thought, necessity and chance, cognitive and noncognitive, art and science, values and action.

Ansell (2005) suggests that pragmatists favored a model of decision making that could be characterized as "practical reason"—recognizing that people make decisions in "situationally specific contexts," drawing on their past experiences and influenced by their emotions as well as their reason. Reflecting on the insights of the pragmatists, Cohen (2007) criticizes Simon for his rigid separation of fact and values and for building his model of bounded rationality by privileging the role of cognition while neglecting the importance of habit and emotion.

In summary, contemporary theorists not only select different pillars to support their versions of institutional structure, but these pillars are constructed from varying types of ontological rules and make different assumptions about how best to account for social behavior.

❖ CONCLUDING COMMENT

Although it is possible to combine the insights of economic, political, and sociological analysts into a single, complex, integrated model of an institution, I believe it is more useful at this point to recognize the differing assumptions and emphases that accompany the models currently guiding inquiry into these phenomena. Three contrasting models of institutions are identified—the regulative, normative, and cultural-cognitive—although it is not possible to associate any of the disciplines uniquely with any of these proposed models. We find researchers in each discipline emphasizing one or another of the pillars. The models are differentiated such that each identifies a distinctive basis of compliance, mechanism of diffusion, type of logic, cluster of indicators, affective response, and foundation for legitimacy claims.

Although at a superficial level it appears that social analysts are merely emphasizing one or another of the multiple facets of institutional arrangements, a closer examination suggests that the models are aligned with quite profound differences in the assumptions made about the nature of social reality and the ways in which actors make choices in social situations. Two sources of continuing controversy are identified. First, analysts disagree as to whether to attend primarily to regulative rules as helping to structure action among a given set of actors with established interests or to instead give primacy to constitutive rules, which create distinctive types of actors and related modes of action. Second, institutions have become an important combat zone in the broader, ongoing disputation within the social sciences centering on the utility of rational-choice theory for explaining human behavior. Are we to employ a more restricted, instrumental logic in accounting for the determinants and consequences of institutions or is it preferable to posit a broader, more socially embedded logic? There is no sign of a quick or easy resolution to either of these debates.

❖ NOTES

1. This integrated model of institutions is elaborated in Scott (1994b).

2. Not all analysts share this belief. In a rather abrasive critique of an earlier presentation of this argument [*Institutions and Organizations*, 1st ed., 1995], Hirsch (1997: 1704) pointed out that my approach runs the risk of enforcing a "forced-choice" selection of one element as against another, rather than recognizing the reality that all institutional forms are composed of multiple elements. Such is not my intent. I willingly accede to the multiplex nature of institutional reality while insisting on the value of identifying analytic concepts, which, I believe, will aid us as we attempt to sort out the contending theories and interrelated processes. Far from wishing to "rule out" or "discourage interpillar communication" or to make the "cross-fertilization of ideas unusual and unlikely," as Hirsch (1997: 1709) alleged, my intent in constructing this analytic scheme is to encourage and inform such efforts.

3. In his most recent work, however, North (2005: chap. 3) greatly expands his interest in and attention to cultural-cognitive facets of institutions.

4. For an extended discussion, see Scott and Davis (2007: 22–24 and chaps. 2 and 3).

5. Note the similarity of these conceptions to Bourdieu's concept of "habitus," discussed in chapter 2.

6. Schutz (1932/1967: 176–207) analyzed this process at length in his discussion of "the world of contemporaries as a structure of ideal types."

7. Related typologies of the varying bases of legitimacy have been developed by Stryker (1994, 2000) and Suchman (1995b).

8. Searle's framework is, hence, a moderate version of social constructionism. This more conservative stance is signaled by the title of his book, *The Construction of Social Reality*, which differs markedly from the broader interpretation implied by the title of Berger and Luckmann, *The Social Construction of Reality*.

9. As succinctly phrased by the economic historian, Shonfield (1965: 71): "Classical economics, which was largely a British invention, converted the British experience . . . into something very like the Platonic idea of capitalism."

10. Famously, Weber (1906–1924/1946: 280) captured this combination of ideas and interests in his "switchman" metaphor:

> Not ideas, but material and ideal interests directly govern men's conduct. Yet very frequently the "world images" that have been created by "ideas" have, like switchmen, determined the tracks along which action has been pushed by the dynamics of interests.

4

Crafting an Analytic Framework II

Content, Agency, Carriers, and Levels

I n chapter 3, three institutional elements were defined and differences
described related to each in motivation for compliance, enforcement
mechanisms, logic, types of indicators, affect, and bases of legitimacy
and social order. Building on this framework, the present chapter
examines the content of institutional rules conducive to organizational
development, considers the relation of agency to institutions, and describes varying types of carriers employed and levels of analysis utilized
by institutional analysts.

❖ INSTITUTIONAL CONTENT AND ORGANIZATIONS

Institutions of one type or another can be traced back to the earliest stages
of the history of humankind, whereas organizations as we know them are
a relatively recent development. Clearly then not any and all institutional
frameworks are conducive to organizational growth and sustenance.

Numerous social theorists have attempted to specify what types of institutional forms are likely to give rise to formal organizations.[1]

Early views placed more emphasis on regulatory and normative structures. Weber (1924/1968: 24, 953–954) stressed the emergence of a "legal order" consisting of a "system of consciously made rational rules" that support "instrumentally rational" action. Parsons (1951; Parsons, Bales, and Shils 1953) devoted much attention to detailing the value orientations and normative systems that support the development of more instrumental and impersonal social forms. His typology of "pattern variables"—basic value dimensions giving rise to different kinds of action orientations and supporting structures—identified universalism (vs. particularism), affective neutrality (vs. affectivity), achievement (vs. ascription), and specificity (vs. diffuseness) as normative orientations conducive to the rise of organizations.

Later theorists emphasized the cultural-cognitive systems supporting organizations. Ellul (1954/1964) noted the emergence of a "technicist" mentality, which encourages analytic approaches and the development of systematic, instrumental rules to pursue specific objectives. Berger and colleagues (Berger, Berger, and Kellner 1973) described the novel states of consciousness that accompany the emergence of technology and bureaucracy, including "mechanisticity," "reproducibility," "orderliness," and "predictability." Meyer (1983: 265–267) depicted the cultural elements ("rational myths") that underlie the creation of formal organizations as including "definable purposes," "culturally defined means-ends relationships or technologies," viewing things and people as "resources," and presuming the existence of a "unified sovereign" that gives coherence to collective actors.

What all of these arguments have in common is that they embody a rationalized conception of the world. Purposes are specified and then rulelike principles are devised to govern activities aimed at their pursuit. *Rationalization* involves "the creation of cultural schemes defining means-ends relationships and standardizing systems of control over activities and actors" (Scott and Meyer 1994: 3). Some of the principles, as in the "laws of mechanics," have an empirical base, whereas others, as in legal frameworks, are rooted in a consistent logical or philosophical structure. All such rationalized beliefs support the rise of organizations.

Institutional scholars argue that rationalization also entails the creation of entities—identifiable social units—endowed with interests and having the capacity to take action. These are the constitutive aspects of institutions that were discussed in the previous chapter. In the modern world commencing with social processes associated with the Enlightenment, three primary categories of actors have been accorded primacy: individuals, organizations, and societies, the latter in the guise of the nation-state (see Meyer, Boli, and Thomas 1987). James S. Coleman (1974, 1990: chap. 20) provided a valuable historical-analytical account of the emergence of organizations as significant collective actors accorded legal rights, capacities, and resources independent of those held by their individual participants.[2] Coleman views changes in the law not as causal factors, but as significant indicators of the growing independence of these new corporate forms as they became recognized as legal persons in the eyes of the law. Pedersen and Dobbin (1997) suggest that this process was fueled primarily by the growth of a scientific ethos that created abstract and general categories to classify and enumerate first the biological and physical universe and subsequently the social world. The rapid advance of commensuration—"the measurement of characteristics normally represented by different units according to a common metric" (Espeland and Stevens 1998: 315)—allowed the categorization and counting of all manner of material and social objects.

Professionals, initially from the engineering sciences (Shenhav 1995, 1999), attempted to tame the exotic, multiple, idiosyncratic instances of enterprise and fostered the emergence of, on the one hand, the generic category "organization" accompanied by its universal handmaiden "management" and, on the other hand, the differentiation of recognizable subtypes (e.g., schools, hospitals, public agencies, and nonprofit and for-profit corporations). The development of such templates or archetypes and the specification of their structural characteristics, utilities, capabilities, and identities take place over many years, but once established provide cultural models for the rapid molding of other similar forms. This professional project—treating all manner of collectivities as part of a more generic form "organization" and identifying meaningful subtypes—was later embraced and, necessarily, reinforced by the emergence in mid-20th century of an academic discipline devoted to the pursuit of organizational studies. (In short, you and I are part of this process!)

The socially constructed characteristics of both persons and collective actors, such as firms, vary over time and place (see Hall and Soskice 2001a, 2001b; Hollingsworth and Boyer 1997). Institutional rules in the West have accorded greater individual autonomy and independence to social actors—both persons and firms—than have related rules in East Asian societies. Thus, although "the United States has institutionalized competitive individualism in its market structure," and most European countries have developed a somewhat more "concerted" version of industry structures, Asian economies "are organized through networks of [interdependent and less autonomous] economic actors that are believed to be natural and appropriate to economic development" (Biggart and Hamilton 1992: 472). Relations among persons or firms that Western eyes view as involving nepotism or collusion seem, by Eastern observers, normal, inevitable, and beneficial.

In general, regulative and normative theorists give more attention to the examination of regulative rules, treating constitutive rules as background conditions. Thus, for example, neoinstitutionalist economists and rational-choice political scientists inquire into the activities of a firm or agency and consider what kinds of structural arrangements or procedures are associated with specified behaviors, such as improved productivity or the passage of legislation. By contrast, economic historians and historical political scientists give much more attention to the origin of general types of social actors (e.g., "jobber, importer, factor, broker, and the commission agent"; Chandler 1977: 27), organizational archetypes (e.g., joint-stock companies, multidivisional and conglomerant firms), or changes in property or political rights. Similarly, neoinstitutional sociologists are more apt to focus on changes over time in the types of actors involved or the cultural rules establishing the logics of practice within a particular organizational context (e.g., Fligstein 1990; Schneiberg 2002; Scott et al. 2000). Scholars attending to constitutive rules insist that much of the coherence of social life is due to the creation of categories of social actors, both individual and collective, and associated ways of acting.[3]

❖ AGENCY AND INSTITUTIONS

Throughout the history of social science, there has existed a tension between those theorists who emphasize structural and cultural constraints on action and those who emphasize the ability of individual actors to "make a difference" in the flow of events. This is a version of the ancient antinomy between freedom and control. Obviously, the thrust of institutional theory is to privilege continuity and constraint in social structure, but that need not preclude attention to the ways in which individual actors take action to create, maintain, and transform institutions.

Early neoinstitutional scholars, such as Meyer and Rowan (1977), DiMaggio and Powell (1983), and Meyer and Scott (1983b), tended to emphasize the ways in which institutional mechanisms constrained organizational structures and activities. However, more recent work, which I review in subsequent chapters—including that of DiMaggio (1988, 1991), Powell (1991), and Scott (Scott et al. 2000)—gives more attention to the ways in which both individuals and organizations innovate, act strategically, and contribute to institutional change (see Christensen et al. 1997; Oliver 1991).

Many theoretical frameworks treat freedom and constraint as opposing ideas, requiring us to "take sides"—to privilege one social value or the other. Fortunately, recent developments in sociological theory allow us to see the two thrusts as interrelated, compatible processes. In particular, the work of Anthony Giddens (1979, 1984) on "structuration" provided a productive framework for examining the interplay between these forces.

Although *structuration* is a rather infelicitous word, the term, coined by Giddens, reminds us that social structure involves the patterning of social activities and relations through time and across space. Social structures only exist as patterned social activities, incorporating rules, relations, and resources reproduced over time. Giddens (1984: 25) envisioned what he termed the "duality of social structure," recognizing it to be both product and platform of social action. Social structures exhibit a dual role in that they are "both the medium and the outcome of the practices they recursively organize." Individual actors carry out practices that are simultaneously constrained (in some directions) and empowered (in others) by the existing social structure. In Giddens' (1984: 21) model, social structures are made up of rules—"generalized procedures applied in the enactment/reproduction of social life"—and resources—both human and nonhuman, "that can be used to enhance or maintain power" (Sewell 1992: 9). Institutions are those types of social structures that involve more strongly held rules supported by stronger relations and more entrenched resources. Institutional practices are "those deeply embedded in time and space" (Giddens 1984: 13).

Structuration theory views actors as creating and following rules and utilizing resources as they engage in the ongoing production and reproduction of social structures. Actors are viewed as knowledgeable and reflexive, capable of understanding and taking account of everyday situations and routinely monitoring the results of their own and others' actions. *Agency* refers to an actor's ability to have some effect on the social world—altering the rules, relational ties, or distribution of resources. The presence of agency presumes a nondeterminant, "voluntaristic" theory of action: "to be able to 'act otherwise' means being able to intervene in the world, or to refrain from such intervention, with the effect of influencing a specific process or state of affairs"

(Giddens 1984: 14). Agency provides for a consideration of the role of power in institutional processes.[4]

> Actors, under both stable and unstable institutional conditions, are not just captured by shared meanings in their fields. . . . Instead, they operate with a certain amount of social skill to reproduce or contest systems of power and privilege. (Fligstein 2001b: 111)

Such actors may be conceived either from a rational-choice model, as pursuing fixed preferences, or as individuals, whose interests and tastes are changing or being discovered as action proceeds. In either case, there is the possibility of change in institutional arrangements.

The basic theoretical premise underlying the concept of agency is strongly aligned with the phenomenological assumptions that undergird sociological versions of neoinstitutional thought. Between the context and response is the interpreting actor. Agency resides in "the interpretive processes whereby choices are imagined, evaluated, and contingently reconstructed by actors in ongoing dialogue with unfolding situations" (Emirbayer and Mische 1998: 966).

Structuration theory joins with numerous other theoretical arguments to support a more proactive role for individual and organizational actors, and a more interactive and reciprocal view of institutional processes. For example, to view behavior as oriented toward and governed by rules need not imply either that behavior is "unreasoned" or automatic. March and Olsen (1989) point out that rules must be both selected—often more than one rule may be applicable—and interpreted—adapted to the demands of the particular situation. Weick (1979, 1995) emphasized that understandings and scripts emerge out of actions as well as guide them, and that collective symbols are as likely to be used to justify past behaviors as to guide current ones. As noted in chapter 3, newer versions of culture theory view individuals as playing an active part, using existing rules and social resources as a repertory of possibilities for constructing strategies of action. Analysts have posited a "politics of identity," in which individuals or organized groups create goals, identities, and solidarities that provide meaning and generate ongoing social commitments (Aronowitz 1992; Calhoun 1991; Somers and Gibson 1994). They increasingly recognize the extent to which organizational participants do not always conform to conventional patterns, but respond variably, sometimes creating new ways of acting and organizing.

All actors, both individual and collective, possess some degree of agency, but the amount of agency varies greatly among actors as well as among types of social structures. Agency itself is socially and institutionally structured.

❖   VARYING CARRIERS

Institutions, whether regulative, normative, or cultural-cognitive elements are stressed, are conveyed by various types of vehicles or "carriers" (Jepperson 1991: 150). I identify four types: symbolic systems, relational systems, routines, and artifacts.[5] These distinctions are largely orthogonal to the three pillars, permitting us to cross-classify them (see table 4.1). Theorists vary not only in which elements they favor, but in which carriers they emphasize, just as institutional frameworks differ in which elements are central and what type of carriers are utilized. It is readily apparent that carriers are of fundamental importance in considering the ways in which institutions change, whether in convergent or divergent ways. They point to a set of fundamental mechanisms that allow us to account for how ideas move through space and time, and who or what is transporting them.

A substantial literature exists that deals with the subject of carriers, but it is illusive because it is associated with a variety of labels, including diffusion of innovation, technology transfer, organizational learning,

Table 4.1   Institutional Pillars and Carriers

	Pillars		
	Regulative	*Normative*	*Cultural-Cognitive*
Symbolic systems	Rules Laws	Values Expectations	Categories Typifications Schema
Relational systems	Governance systems Power systems	Regimes Authority systems	Structural isomorphism Identities
Routines	Protocols Standard operating procedures	Jobs Roles Obedience to duty	Scripts
Artifacts	Objects complying with mandated specifications	Objects meeting conventions, standards	Objects possessing symbolic value

adoption of reforms, intermediaries, management fads and fashions, and processes of modernization. An emerging theme recognized by observers across all of these areas is that carriers are never neutral modes of transmission, but affect the nature of the message and the ways in which it is received. Thus, although analysts often employ what Reddy (1979) termed "conduit metaphors," such as delivering and circulating messages, how a message arrives affects its interpretation and reception. Thus, it makes a difference, as Abernethy (2000) detailed in his survey of European colonization efforts, whether Western ideas arrived in the guise of missionaries seeking to make converts, merchants looking for trading partners, or armies bent on the acquisition of booty and territorial conquest.

As ideas and artifacts move from time to time and place to place, they are altered, modified, combined with other ideas or objects, and transformed. In Sahlin-Andersson's (1996: 82) terms, they are *edited*: "the models are told and retold in various situations and told differently in each situation." How and how much they are edited varies, however, by the type of carrier. The entries in Table 4.1 describe the content of the message—what is being transported. Carriers emphasize the features of the medium.

Symbolic Systems

As noted in chapter 2, most recent students of culture treat it as a semiotic system: as collections of symbols. For institutionalists, the symbols of interest include the full range of rules, values and norms, classifications, representations, frames, schemas, prototypes, and scripts used to guide behavior. As the entries in Table 4.1 suggest, which aspects of symbolic systems are emphasized vary depending on which elements of institutions are accorded prominence. Cognitive theorists stress the importance of common categories, distinctions, and typifications as shaping perceptions and interpretations; normative theorists accent shared values and normative expectations that guide behavior; and regulative theorists point to the role played by conventions, rules, and laws.

The emergence of language as a human capacity greatly facilitated the transmission of symbols over time and place. As discussed in chapter 2, spoken language provided the foundation for localized mythic cultures, but the power and mobility of words advanced immeasurably with the creation of a theoretic culture involving written language and its externalization in various media ranging from books to digital information. In his admirable survey of media and empire, economic historian Harold Innis (1972, 1995: 332) described differences between reliance on an oral tradition versus all forms of writing:

Introduction of the alphabet meant a concern with sound rather than with sight or with the ear rather than the eye. Empires had been built up on communication based on sight in contrast with [the more geographically restricted] Greek political organization which emphasized oral discussion.

With the invention of writing, the nature of medium employed to carry the words greatly affected transmission possibilities. Innis (1995: 325) observed how writing on stone or clay, for example, functioned to preserve knowledge over time, whereas writing on papyrus or paper was better suited to transport ideas over space. The later appearance of the printing press opened up the possibility of mass dissemination of identical texts. Anderson (1983: 44–45) argued that the use of print languages created unified fields of exchange and communication employing languages "below Latin and above the spoken vernaculars" and the convergence of "capitalism and print technology" provided the basis for the systematic construction of nationalism.

Shifting to the present era, developments in information/ communication technology have played a powerful role in broadcasting images and ideas worldwide, increasing the size of markets, lengthening supply chains by connecting and transforming organizations, and generally moving us more completely into a global economy and more interdependent political community. As Appadurai (1996) observed, the cinema and TV place a premium on the image, whereas the computer and cell phone privilege the word; however, the Web can accommodate both in transcending distance. Myths, stories, song, and images have long provided a repertory of models for living, but today's global media provide a richer mix of imagined possibilities: "More persons in more parts of the world consider a wider set of possible lives than they ever did before" (Appadurai 1996: 53). At the same time that the new ideas arrive, however, they are translated, fused, and blended with local knowledge in a process termed *indigenization*. Schemas are "transposable": "they can be applied to a wide and not fully predictable range of cases outside the context in which they are initially learned" (Sewell 1992: 17). Symbols are transportable, versatile, and malleable.

Relational System Carriers

Institutions can also be carried by relational systems. Such systems are carriers that rely on patterned interactions connected to networks of social positions: role systems. Flows of immigrants bring new ideas, modes of behavior, and relational commitments across societal boundaries. Many robust relational systems transcend and intersect with the boundaries of organizations, as is the case with occupational and professional connections and communities of practice.

Rules and belief systems are coded into positional distinctions and roles; relational systems incorporate—instantiate—institutional elements. As with symbolic systems, some relational arrangements are widely shared across many organizations, creating structural isomorphism (similar forms) or structural equivalence (similar relations among forms). Other forms may be distinctive to a particular organization, embodying localized belief systems and creating what Selznick (1957) termed a unique organizational "character structure."

Which aspects of relational structures are emphasized depends on which elements of institutions are featured. Cognitive theorists stress structural models. Classifications and typifications are often coded into organizational structures as differentiated departments and roles. For example, codified knowledge systems support the development of differentiated academic departments in universities. Normative and regulatory theorists are apt to view relational systems as "governance systems," emphasizing either the normative (authority) or the coercive (power) aspects of these structures. Such governance systems are viewed as creating and enforcing codes, norms, and rules, and as monitoring and sanctioning the activities of participants. The new institutional economists, such as Williamson, emphasize relational systems erected to exercise governance as the principal carriers of institutional forces.

Routines as Carriers

Institutions may also be embodied in—carried by—structured activities in the form of habitualized behavior and routines. Routines are carriers that rely on patterned actions that reflect the tacit knowledge of actors—deeply ingrained habits and procedures based on unarticulated knowledge and beliefs. Rather than privileging symbolic systems, many early institutionalists, such as Veblen, viewed habitualized action, routines, standard operating procedures, and similar patterned activities as the central features of institutions.

March and Simon (1958) identified repetitive "performance programs" as the central ingredient accounting for the reliability of organizations. More recently, evolutionary theorists, such as Nelson and Winter (1982), emphasize the stabilizing role played by participants' skills and organizational routines: activities involving little or no conscious choice and behavior governed by tacit knowledge and skills of which the actor may be unaware. Viewing routines as the "genes" of organizations, Winter (1990: 274–275) point out that they range from "hard"—activities encoded into technologies—to "soft"—organizational routines such as airplane inspection or fast-food procedures—but all involve "repetitive patterns of activity." These patterns include a broad range of behaviors, extending from standard operating procedures and skill sets of individual employees to "organizational activity bundles such as jobs, assembly lines, airline reservations systems, accounting principles or rules of war" (Miner 1991: 773). Such routines involve more than acquiring a "system of rules or representations"; it entails the "learning of modes of acting and problem-solving" (Hanks 1991: 20). These types of skills underlie much of the stability of organizational behavior—accounting for both their reliable performance as well as for their rigidities.

Routines are typically learned within and sustained and renewed by relational systems. Experiential learning and on-the-job training often take place in situations, allowing novices to engage in what Lave and Wenger (1991: 29) termed "legitimate peripheral participation":

> By this we mean to draw attention to the point that learners inevitably participate in communities of practitioners and that the mastery of knowledge and skill requires newcomers to move toward full participation in the sociocultural practices of a community.

The fact that they are learned in and sustained by a community means that routines are not readily transportable to new and different settings involving new actors and relationships.

Artifacts as Carriers

Anthropologists have long recognized the importance of "material culture" or artifacts created by human ingenuity to assist in the performance of various tasks. We adopt Suchman's (2003: 98) definition: "An artifact is a discrete material object, consciously produced or transformed by human activity, under the influence of the physical and/or cultural environment." Earlier forms were often as primitive as shaped rocks and sticks, but more recent artifacts include complex technologies embodied in both hardware and software. Organizational students of technology earlier treated these features as a unidirectional and deterministic influence impacting organizational structure and behavior (see e.g., Blau et al. 1976; Woodward 1958). Later theorists reacted by emphasizing the socially constructed nature of technology and the extent to which its effects are mediated by situational factors and interpretive processes (Bijker, Hughes, and Pinch 1987). In any case, the most important characteristic of artifacts is that they "all embody both technical and symbolic elements" (Suchman 2003: 99; see also Gagliardi 1990).

Orlikowski (1992) usefully proposed that artifacts and technology can be examined within the same theoretical framework devised by Giddens (1984) to accommodate social structure and human agency. Viewing artifacts as an instance of structuration allows analysts to recognize that such inventions are, on the one hand, products of human action, but also that, "once developed and deployed," they become reified and appear "to be part of the objective, structural properties" of the situation (Orlikowski 1992: 406). This perspective is often obscured from participants and analysts because the actors and actions that create the new instruments may be removed in time and space from those that employ them to accomplish work. Analysts focusing on artifact creation are better able to see the multiple possibilities: the path selected versus the "roads not taken"; analysts focusing on artifact use see primarily the constraints imposed by the design selected on those who employ it. Although such differences do exist, they should not obscure the extent to which users interact with and modify the meaning and use of artifacts. As Orlikowski (1992: 408) observes:

> While we can expect a greater engagement of human agents during the initial development of a technology, this does not discount the ongoing potential for users to change it (physically and socially) throughout their interaction with it. In using a technology, users interpret, appropriate, and manipulate it in various ways.

Barley (1986) provided an instructive empirical study of the adoption of "identical" technologies, CT scanners, by radiological departments in two community hospitals, examining the ways and extent to which the technologies were associated with somewhat divergent changes in the decision making and power structure of the departments (see chap. 8).

Artifacts, like other carriers, can be viewed as associated with, and affected by, each of the three pillars. The design and construction of some artifacts and technologies is mandated by regulative authorities often in the interests of safety. Modern societies contain a wide range of agencies—ranging from those that attempt to ensure the reliability of atomic plants to those that set performance and safety standards for commercial aircraft and passenger cars—which oversee product quality. Social contracts, existing in the shadow if not the substance of law, can be examined as social artifacts, as Suchman (2003) demonstrated. Technologies are also shaped by and embody normative processes. Trade and industrial groups often convene to set standards for a wide range of machines and technical equipment, as discussed previously. Such agreements serve to ensure compatibility and can create added value for participants to the extent that many players adopt the standard (Katz and Shapiro 1985). Artifacts can embody and represent particular constellations of ideas. Indeed, the symbolic freight of some objects can outweigh their material essence (e.g., the significance of the bread and wine in the communion service or the goal posts in the football match).

These arguments and distinctions suggest some of the many ways in which organizations are deeply embedded in institutional contexts. A given organization is supported and constrained by institutional forces. Also, a given organization incorporates a multitude of institutionalized features in the form of symbolic systems, relational systems, routines, and artifacts within their own boundaries. Hence, it is appropriate to speak of the extent to which organizational components or features are institutionalized. These views are shared by all or the great majority of institutional theorists. That subset endorsing a cultural-cognitive perspective adds an additional, even more fateful, assertion: The very concept of an organization as a special-purpose, instrumental entity is a product of institutional processes—constitutive processes that define the capacities of collective actors, both generally and as specialized subtypes. This version of institutional theory, in particular, tends to subvert or undermine the conventional distinction between organization and environment. Organizations are penetrated by environments in ways not envisioned by many theoretical models.

❖ VARYING LEVELS OF ANALYSIS

One of the principal ways in which the several varieties of institutional theory differ is in the level at which they are applied. Levels identified differ greatly in terms of whether the investigator is focusing on micro- or macrophenomena. The key underlying dimension is the scope of the phenomena encompassed, whether measured in terms of space, time, or numbers of persons affected. For institutions, level may be usefully operationalized as the range of jurisdiction of the institutional form. Given the complexity and variety of social phenomena, any particular set of distinctions is somewhat arbitrary. Nevertheless, for our purposes, it is useful to identify six categories: the levels of world system, society, organizational field, organizational population, organization, and organizational subsystem (see fig. 4.1).

Most of these levels are widely employed and recognizable to social analysts; all are of interest to students of organizations. Perhaps the least familiar, yet the level of most significance to institutional theory, is that of the organizational field. Following DiMaggio and Powell (1983: 143), an *organization field* refers to

> those organizations that, in the aggregate, constitute a recognized area of institutional life: key suppliers, resource and product consumers, regulatory agencies, and other organizations that produce similar services or products.

Hirsch (1985) proposed the closely related concept of "industry system," and Meyer and I (Scott and Meyer 1983) offered that of "societal sector." All of these conceptions build on the more conventional concept of "industry"—a population of organizations operating in the same domain as indicated by the similarity of their services of products—but adds to this focal population those other and different organizations that critically influence their performance, including exchange partners, competitors, funding sources, and regulators. Fields are bounded by the presence of shared cultural-cognitive or normative frameworks or a common regulatory system so as to "constitute a recognized area of institutional life":

> The notion of field connotes the existence of a community of organizations that partakes of a common meaning system and whose participants interact more frequently and fatefully with one another than with actors outside of the field. (Scott 1994a: 207–208)

An example of an organizational field would be an educational system comprised of a set of schools (focal population) and related organizations such as district offices, state and federal funding agencies, parent-teacher associations, and teacher unions. Given the definition of *field*, it is apparent that this conception provides a level at which institutional forces are likely to be particularly salient (see chap. 8).

The other level of analysis somewhat distinctive to organizational research and often employed in institutional studies is that of the population. *Organizational populations* are defined as a collection or aggregate of organizations that are "alike in some respect," in particular, to "classes of organizations that are relatively homogeneous in terms of environmental vulnerability" (Hannan and Freeman 1977: 166) Newspaper companies or trade unions are examples of organizational populations.

Nevertheless, to reiterate, all six levels are of interest to those who study organizations. As with the notion of carriers, the levels distinction is orthogonal to and can be cross-classified with the set of institutional elements.

Levels and Pillars: Illustrative Studies

Beginning with scholars examining the operation of regulative processes at differing levels, North and Thomas (1973) examined how the institution of property rights and associated state regulatory apparatus developed in the Western world during the 15th through the 17th centuries. Skocpol (1979) examined differences in the organization and operation of the state as it affected the course of revolutions occurring in France, Russia, and China. Analysts such as Schmitter (1990) and Campbell and Lindberg (1991) examined the varying governance mechanisms—particularly, the regulatory structures—at work in different societal sectors or industries. Barnett and Carroll (1993) studied the effects on the development of the population of early telephone companies of various regulatory policies pursued by state and federal authorities. Williamson (1975, 1985, 1991) developed his markets and hierarchies framework to explain the emergence of varying types of organizational forms to govern and reduce the costs of economic transactions at the level of the firm. Shepsle and Weingast (1987) studied the institutional foundations of committee power in Congress.

Turning to theorists emphasizing normative elements, Brunsson and Jacobson (2000) examined the construction of a "standards" (normative frameworks) at the transnational level by professional associations and international nongovernmental organization, while Tate (2001) detailed the continuing persistence of standards at the national level. Parsons (1953) described differences in value systems and normative frameworks at the societal level and their consequences for organizations. Mezias (1990) studied changes in normative beliefs regarding financial reporting requirements for corporations occasioned by the actions of state agents and professional accounting societies, and Stern (1979) and Starr (1982) examined the effects of the rules and conventions promulgated by trade and professional associations on organization fields such as college athletics and the practice of medicine. Singh, Tucker, and House (1986) examined the effects on survival rates in a population of voluntary social service organizations of being certified by public agencies. Selznick (1949) studied the ways in which procedural requirements became "infused with value" in the Tennessee Valley Authority. Roy (1952) and Burawoy (1979) examined the institutionalization of normative frameworks regarding production and restriction of output among workers in a machine shop of a manufacturing plant.

Among those scholars examining cultural-cognitive conceptions of institutional processes, Meyer (1994; see also Drori, Meyer, and Hwang 2006) examined cultural processes operating at the level of the world system giving rise to organizations in a wide variety of contexts. Dobbin (1994b) studied the varying cultural belief systems that undergirded societal policies affecting the construction of railway systems in the United States, England, and France. Working at the level of the organization field, researchers such as Deephouse (1996) and Hoffman (1997) employed discourse analysis and other types of content analytic techniques to assess meaning systems in banking and corporate environmentalism. Carroll and Hannan (1989) employed data on the density or prevalence of newspapers—viewed as an indicator of the taken-for-grantedness of this form—to examine its effects on the growth rates of newspapers in selected U.S. cities. At the organization level, Clark (1970) examined the distinctive cultural values cultivated by a set of elite colleges and their effects on organizational viability, whereas Kunda (1992) studied the "engineering culture" of a high-tech company. Zimmerman (1969), working at the subsystem level, described the development of typifications and shared interpretations among intake work in a social welfare agency.

Levels and Pillars: Illustrative Schools

More generally, as illustrated in Figure 4.1, it is possible to associate various schools or types of work with different locations in the property space created by the cross-classification of pillars and levels. Most of the neoinstitutional work conducted by sociologists in the recent period is guided by the combination of a cultural-cognitive emphasis and attention to the macrolevels: processes operating at a transorganizational level. Moreover, this work stresses cultural elements—widespread beliefs, conventions, and professional knowledge systems—but also attends to the impact of macrostructural carriers such as international organizations, the state, and trade and professional associations.

Organizational ecologists have directed attention to the organizational population level of analysis, and in their recent work have appropriated institutional arguments to account for important features

Figure 4.1   Institutional Pillars and Varying Levels: Illustrative Schools

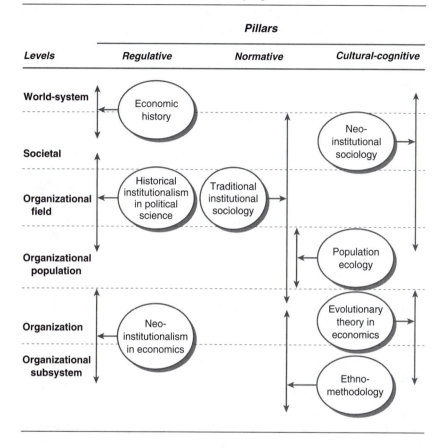

of the density dynamics of organizational populations. The familiar slow take-off and then more rapid growth rate of a specified organization population has been interpreted by Carroll and Hannan (1989) as reflecting the increasing cognitive legitimacy of a particular template or archetype for organizing this type of work (see chap. 6).

Attention to cognitive elements at the organization or organizational subsystem level has largely been provided by ethnomethodologists and students of corporate culture (see Martin 1992; Trice and Beyer 1993). Ethnomethodologists, along with some evolutionary economists, focus on habits and skills and so attend more closely to routines as carriers of institutions at the organizational and suborganizational levels (see Turner 1974). Those who examine corporate culture, of course, give primacy to carriers of symbolic systems.

The traditional institutional approach in sociology—work associated with Becker, Hughes, Parsons, and Selznick—is defined by a focus on normative elements and attention to levels ranging from the individual organization to the society. This mode of analysis is very much alive and well and continues to be emphasized by such scholars as Brint and Karabel (1991) and Pagett and Ansell (1993). Both symbolic and relational carriers are emphasized in this approach.

Economists and (rational-choice) political scientists are most likely to emphasize the regulative view of institutions. Economic historians focus on the macrolevels, examining the origins and functions of transnational and national rules and enforcement mechanisms that are developed to regulate economic behavior of firms and individuals. Historical institutionalists in both sociology and political science emphasize the study of regulatory regimes and governance mechanisms that operate at the societal and industry levels. The new institutionalists in economics, along with the rational-choice theorists in political science, focus primarily on regulatory processes operating at the organizational or suborganizational level. The economic historians and historical institutionalists emphasize symbolic and relational carriers, whereas the new institutional economists emphasize primarily relational carriers.

We discover, then, substantial differences among current schools aligned with the "new" institutionalism. Organizational sociologists pursuing this line of work emphasize a cultural-cognitive conception, symbolic carriers, and macrolevel forces. By contrast, neoinstitutional economists and most political scientists stress a regulative conception, relational carriers, and a microfocus. Rather different perspectives to be sharing the same label!

❖ CONCLUDING COMMENT

Organizations have arisen and gained prominence in part because of the development of distinctive cultural logics that endeavor to rationalize the nature of the physical and social worlds. Valued ends are to be pursued systematically by codified, formalized means, and organizations are viewed as providing appropriate social entities to promote and oversee such projects. As such beliefs become more widespread and invade ever more arenas of social life, organizations become ubiquitous vehicles of collective action.

Although institutional conceptions underline the sources of social stability and order, the structuration framework advanced by Giddens enables us to simultaneously theorize and examine the sources of both social order and social change. These and related conceptions increasingly guide developments in institutional theory and research. To complement the concept of elements or pillars, two other distinctions are introduced in an attempt to recognize the variety of forms and processes exhibited by institutions as well as the great variety of scholarly approaches currently in use. First, institutions are viewed as varying in their mode of carrier. Institutions may be borne by symbols, relational structures, routines, and artifacts. Second, institutions are described as capable of operating—having jurisdiction over—differing levels. Some are restricted to operating within an organizational subunit, whereas others function at levels as broad as that of world systems. The variety of possible carriers through which institutions work together with the multiple levels at which they operate help to account both for why they receive so much attention and why they generate so much confusion and inconsistency among their observers.

❖ NOTES

1. Other theorists have called attention to the role played by technological innovations and associated developments such as labor specialization in the role of organizational forms (see Kerr et al. 1964; Rosenberg and Birdzell 1986; for a review, see Scott 2003b: 154–163).

2. Krasner (1988) and Meyer and colleagues (Meyer et al. 1997; Meyer, Drori, and Hwang 2006) provide an institutional perspective on the emergence of nation-states.

3. Note that one methodological consequence of this different focus is that scholars focusing on regulative processes are more apt to examine similar types of organizations cross-sectionally or over shorter time periods (often assuming equilibrium conditions), whereas scholars focusing on more constitutive processes embrace longer time periods or utilize comparative designs.

4. In addition to Giddens, the other major social theorist at this time emphasizing the role of power processes in the construction and reconstruction of stable social systems was Pierre Bourdieu (1977; Bourdieu and Wacquant 1992).

5. Jepperson (1991) identified a somewhat different set of carriers: cultures, regimes, and organizations.

5

Institutional
Construction

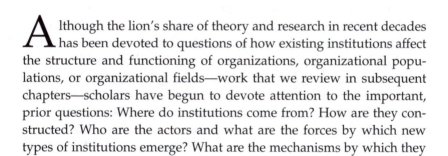

Although the lion's share of theory and research in recent decades
has been devoted to questions of how existing institutions affect
the structure and functioning of organizations, organizational populations, or organizational fields—work that we review in subsequent
chapters—scholars have begun to devote attention to the important,
prior questions: Where do institutions come from? How are they constructed? Who are the actors and what are the forces by which new
types of institutions emerge? What are the mechanisms by which they
are crafted?

Not surprisingly, most of the early statements were primarily theoretical, employing evidence in only a casual and illustrative manner.
It was not long, however, before various types of empirical investiga-
tions began to appear. Their numbers have steadily increased, so that
by now a substantial amount of research relevant to the testing and
elaboration of institutional arguments has been produced. Most of this
work treats institutional frameworks as given and asks how they affect
organizational structures and functions. That is, in most of the empirical literature, institutions are treated as independent variables, and the
studies are directed to examining their effects on some organizational

entity or process, the units ranging from transsocietal systems to organizational subunits. This focus is understandable because students of organizations are primarily interested in assessing whether and to what extent institutional systems affect individual organizations or collections of organizations. If such influences cannot be demonstrated, there would be little incentive for organizational analysts to pursue the related questions regarding the sources of institutions and the causes of institutional change and persistence.

Chapters 6, 7, and 8 describe and discuss the more extensive literature on institutional consequences: the ways in which institutional systems relate to organizational fields, populations, and organizations. The current chapter considers the question of institutional determinants—how institutions arise and achieve stability, legitimacy, and adherents. Later chapters examine how institutions are maintained and diffused (chap. 6) and how institutions lose credibility and undergo change (chap. 8).

❖ CREATING INSTITUTIONS

It is somewhat arbitrary to distinguish the processes involved in creating institutions from those employed to change them. Institutions do not emerge in a vacuum; they always challenge, borrow from, and, to varying degrees, displace prior institutions. The difference lies largely in the investigator's focus. If attention is directed primarily to the processes and conditions giving rise to new rules, understandings, and associated practices, then we have a study of institutional creation. As Greif (2006: 17) pointed out: "Beliefs, norms, and organizations inherited from the past will constitute part of the initial conditions in the processes leading to new institutions." However, if the analyst examines how an existing set of beliefs, norms, and practices comes under attack, undergoes delegitimation, or falls into disuse, to be replaced by new rules, forms, and scripts, we have a study of institutional change. The former interests are reviewed here, whereas the latter are reviewed in chapter 8.

Naturalistic Versus Agent-Based Accounts

Views concerning institutional construction vary greatly, but can roughly be grouped into two categories: naturalistic and agent-based. Building on the work of Schutz (1932/1967) and Berger and Luckmann (1967), who stressed the unconscious ways in which "activities are habitualized and reciprocally interpreted" during social interaction, naturalistic accounts treat institutionalization as a "natural and undirected process" (Strang and Sine 2002: 502). Ecological studies (e.g., Carroll and Hannan 1989) that view increasing organizational density as an indicator of increasing legitimacy, or work regarding embeddedness in community networks as a hallmark of increasing institutionalization (Baum and Oliver 1992), employ a naturalistic conception. Studies of diffusion processes of institutional reforms, first initiated by Tolbert and Zucker (1983), which we review in chapter 6, also depict institutionalization as an unconscious process. In these accounts, institutions are not created by the purposeful actions of interest-based agents, but rather emerge from the collective sense-making and problem-solving behavior of actors confronting similar situations.

By contrast, analysts embracing an agent-based view stress the importance of identifying particular actors as causal agents, emphasizing the extent to which intentionality and self-interest are at work. DiMaggio (1988) was among the earliest theorist to insist on the importance of "bringing agency back in" to accounts of institutional processes. He noted that studies of highly institutionalized organizations or organization fields can easily overlook the role of self-interest and power processes because opposing interests have been suppressed and dissenters silenced. The play of power is more visible during times of institutional change and, especially, institutional construction (DiMaggio 1991).

> Put simply . . . institutionalization is a product of the political efforts of actors to accomplish their ends . . . the success of an institutionalization project and the form that the resulting institution takes depends on the relative power of the actors who support, oppose, or otherwise strive to influence it. . . . Central to this line of argument is an apparent paradox rooted in the two senses in which the term *institutionalization* is used. Institutionalization as an *outcome* places organizational structures and practices beyond the reach of interest and politics. By contrast, institutionalization as a *process* is profoundly political and reflects the relative power of organized interests and the actors who mobilize around them. (DiMaggio 1988: 13; italics original)

Limits of Institutional Design

Although it is appropriate to recognize the role of agency in institutional construction, it is important that we not attribute heroic attributes to those who are seeking to create new frameworks of meaning and governance. It is certainly the case that actors frequently work to create institutions that will reflect, protect, and advance their interests, that "parties often need institutions to help capture gains from cooperation" (Weingast 2002: 670). However, numerous considerations undermine the ability of actors to achieve their intended ends.

Paul Pierson (2004) provides a useful synthesis and summary of the kinds of limitations that beset attempts to design institutions:

- "Specific institutional arrangements invariably have multiple effects" (109), many of which are unexpected, unintended, and may be unwelcome.
- "Institutional designers may not act instrumentally" (110), but be guided by norms of "appropriateness," by fads, or by misguided attempts to apply ready-made solutions that do not fit current circumstances.
- "Institutional designers may have short time horizons" (112), whereas the institutions they develop have long-term effects that frequently differ from those originally sought.
- The plans of institutional designers may lead to unexpected effects because the situations to which they apply have undergone change.
- Institutional designs presume that actors and their interests will remain unchanged, whereas over time actors come and go and interests change.

Such concerns should make us mindful of the assumptions we make when assessing the role of agency, interest, and rationality in the design of institutions.

Accounts and Pillars

Whether a naturalistic or an agent-based approach is employed appears to vary significantly by what types of elements—whether regulative, normative, or cultural-cognitive pillars—are invoked. Those examining regulative elements are more likely to be methodological individualists and assume that individuals function as agents, constructing rules and requirements by some kind of deliberative, strategic, or calculative process. Pros and cons are weighed, causes and effects evaluated and argued, and considered choices are made. Majorities or authorities rule. Analysts examining institutions made up of normative elements are more likely to posit a more naturalistic process, as moral imperatives evolve and obligatory expectations develop in the course of repeated interactions. Cultural-cognitive institutions seem to emerge from the operation of even more ephemeral processes. Particularly in early accounts, shared understandings, common meanings, and taken-for-granted truths seem to have no parents, no obvious sources, no obvious winners or losers.

Although there are differences in the processes associated with each pillar, these characterizations, on reflection, appear to be oversimplified and can be misleading. Consider regulative rules. If they appear rational and transparent, this reflects the extent to which certain types of social settings and procedures have been constructed to be—are institutionalized to serve as—seats of collective authority or as variously constituted forums for decision making. A full analysis of regulatory rule-making would examine the constitutive roots of the specific governance apparatus—how the forums developed, the rules for decision making and for selecting participants evolved—as well as all the backstage activities (the fodder of historical institutionalists) that enter into the creation of laws and legal rulings. Conversely, norms often evolve through interaction, but they can also be rationally crafted. Professional bodies and trade associations act to create and amend their normative frameworks and standards via more conscious and deliberative processes. As with regulatory authorities, some social groups are endowed with special prerogatives allowing them to exercise moral leadership in selected arenas, whether they are environmental scientists dealing with global warming or medical scientists dealing with the control of contagious diseases. Cognitive elements also result from both more and less rational choice processes; they may evolve from inchoate collective interactions or be consciously designed and disseminated by highly institutionalized cultural authorities. Folkways are produced by the former; scientific truths and legal rulings, by the latter.

Types of Agents

Institutional agents come in a variety of guises and include both individual and collective actors. Some of the types of agents we consider—nation-states, professions, and associations—participate in the construction of new institutional forms, but also exercise many kinds of influence on existing forms and processes. We emphasize here their constitutive powers, but also note other ways in which they exert effects on existing organizations and fields.

Following DiMaggio's lead, numerous scholars have pursued the question as to what types of actors are likely to participate in the creation of new types of institutions: the ability to serve in the capacity of "institutional entrepreneurs." In the business literature, entrepreneurs are individuals willing to bear risk to create new organizations (see Aldrich 2005). By contrast, *institutional entrepreneurs* are people (or organizations) who participate in the creation of new types of organizations or new industries, tasks that require marshalling new technologies, designing new organization forms and routines, creating new supply chains and markets, and gaining cognitive, normative, and regulative legitimacy (Aldrich and Ruef 2006, chap. 9). Clearly, we are not talking about a single actor, but a variety of roles and functions distributed across diverse players.

DiMaggio and Powell (1983: 147) astutely observed that the nation-state and the professions "have become the great rationalizers of the second half of the twentieth century," but other types of actors also play important roles.

The Nation-State

From some perspectives, the state is simply another organizational actor: a bureaucratically organized administrative structure empowered to govern a geographically delimited territory. However, such a view is limited and misleading. In our own time, and since the dawn of the modern era, the nation-state has been allocated—is constituted in such a way as to exercise—special powers and prerogatives (Krasner 1993). As Streeck and Schmitter (1985a: 20) pointed out, the state is not simply another actor in the environment of an organization: Its "ability to rely on legitimate coercion" make it a quite distinctive type of actor. All organizations are correctly viewed as "governance structures," but the state is set apart. Lindblom (1977: 21) notes: "the special character of government as an organization is simply . . . that governments exercise authority over other organizations."

In terms of institutional construction, states (in collaboration with legal professionals) possess extraordinary powers to define the nature, capacity, and rights enjoyed by political and economic actors, including collective actors. For example, during the past three centuries, states have worked to shape the powers and rights of the joint stock, limited liability corporate actor that has long since become the preferred form for organizing economic activity (see Coleman 1974, 1990; Seavoy 1982; Micklethwait and Wooldridge 2003).

More generally, Campbell and Lindberg (1990) detail the ways in which, by defining and enforcing property rights, the state influences the economic behavior of organizations. Property rights are "the rules that determine the conditions of ownership and control of the means of production" (Campbell and Lindberg 1990: 635), including labor laws defining the power of workers to organize, antitrust laws that limit ties between competitors, and patent laws that limit access to new technologies.

> The state provides the legal framework within which contracts are written and enforced. . . . The state's influence, quite apart from sporadic interventions, is always present in the economy insofar as it provides an institutional and legal framework that influences the selection of different governance regimes and thereby permanently shapes the economy. (Campbell and Lindberg 1990: 637)

Even the regulatory powers of the state can lead to the creation of new institutional forms. Fligstein (1990) underlined the role of antitrust legislation, including the Sherman Act of 1890, which prevented the development of the cartel-like forms that emerged in Europe at this time—unlike the United States, the German (as well as other European) states emphasized "the benefits of industrial cooperation" (Chandler 1990: 395)—and the Celler-Kefauver Act of 1950, which encouraged diversification as a growth strategy for U.S. corporations after World War II.

States also exert highly significant effects not only on individual firm structures and behaviors, but also on the structuration of organizational fields. Baron, Dobbin, and Jennings (1986) provided a historical account of the powers of the state to shape industry (field) and firm structure in their study of the evolution of modern personnel systems in the United States. The high water mark of state influence occurred in connection with the mobilization for World War II, when the federal government intervened to stabilize employment. Agencies such as the War Production Board, the War Labor Board, and the War Manpower Commission "engaged in unprecedented government manipulation of labor markets, union activities, and personnel practices. These interventions . . . fueled the development of bureaucratic controls by creating models of employment and incentives to formalize and expand personnel functions" (Baron et al. 1986: 369). In short, the pressures created were cultural-cognitive and normative, inducing conformity among professional managers, as well as regulative controls involving coercion.

Later chapters detail other ways in which states influence the structure and behavior of firms and fields.

The Professions

In modern societies, professional occupations have come to play a unique and distinctive role. They have displaced the seers and wise men of earlier times to serve in a variety of capacities as institutional agents. We emphasize here their role as creators of new institutional frameworks.

Employing the pillars framework, we observe that different types of professionals make use of differing combinations of elements (see Scott 2005a, forthcoming-b). Some professionals operate primarily within the cultural-cognitive sphere by creating new conceptual systems:

> Their primary weapons are ideas. They exercise control by defining reality—by devising ontological frameworks, proposing distinctions, creating typifications, and fabricating principles or guidelines for action. (Scott and Backman 1990: 290)

The knowledge systems vary greatly in their content and in the extent of their empirical grounding, with physical and biological scientists working at the more empirically constrained end and philosophers and literary critics operating in less confined arenas. Strang and Meyer (1993: 492) stress the importance of the role of *theorization*—"the development and specification of abstract categories, and the formulation of patterned relationships such as chains of cause and effect" in the construction and diffusion of new institutions.

The types of professionals who emphasize the construction of normative frameworks include theologians and ethicists, many legal scholars, and accountants. However, in addition to these specialists, a great many other professional groups work within their associations to create and promulgate "standards" in their areas of expertise, which range from the threading of screws to the education of children and the control of AIDS (Brunsson and Jacobsson 2000).

Other professionals, including many legal experts, military officers, and managers, exercise substantial influence on the construction of regulatory frameworks. Lawyers in many countries (especially the United States) have a near monopoly on positions within policy-setting and state regulatory bodies: authorities empowered to create and enforce new kinds of institutional regimes. Managerial professionals increasingly are in a position to craft new governance structures for overseeing their enterprises. Institutional economists are ready to supply design criteria to executives seeking to craft more effective and efficient governance systems to reduce production and transaction costs.

Associations

Joining nation-states and professions as important classes of institutional actors exercising authority in cultural-cognitive, normative, and regulative domains are an increasingly diverse array of organizations and associations operating at national and international levels. At the national level, for example, Greenwood, Suddaby, and Hinings (2002) described the role of the Canadian accounting association in legitimating changes in the functions of accountants and the structure of accounting firms as they adopted a new organizational archetype to accommodate multidisciplinary practice. Associations, both trade and professional, vary significantly across countries and over time in their ability to establish and enforce standards of practice (Tate 2001). Their efforts are historically situated and follow distinctive trajectories influenced in particular by the closeness of their connection to the state. Those in liberal regimes are more likely to pursue voluntary and cooperative approaches, whereas those working within more coordinated economies are more likely to seek and receive the backing of the coercive power of the state.

As globalization proceeds apace, associations of all sorts now operate at the transnational level, organized as international nongovernmental organizations (INGOs). Such organizations have existed throughout the 20th century, but have grown rapidly in numbers and influence since World War II. For example, in 1900 about 200 INGOs were active, whereas by 1980 over 4,000 were in existence (Boli and Thomas 1997).

How do INGOs obtain and exercise their influence? Boli and Thomas (1997, 1999) point out that, at the present time, they do not presume to displace or replace nation-states, and, unlike states, they cannot make or enforce law. Unlike global corporations, they are not able to exercise coercive power and lack economic resources. Rather, "INGOs are more or less authoritative transnational bodies employing limited resources to make rules, set standards, propagate principles, and broadly represent 'humanity' vis-à-vis states and other actors" (Boli and Thomas 1997: 172; see also Brunsson and Jacobsson 2000).

Other Elites

Fligstein (1990, 1991) stressed the role of corporate elites who are in a position to negotiate—with their competitors and within constraints imposed by the state—an institutional framework working to curb cutthroat competition and allow multiple firms to operate within a given field or arena, albeit with differing advantages. The ability of elites to manage these negotiations depends "on the resources that organizations command and the types of network and dependency relations the organization has to other organizations" (Fligstein 1991: 314).

Elite organizations can also mobilize politically to advance their collective interests (Cawson 1985). Vogus and Davis (2005) described the efforts of corporate elites to defend themselves against state legislation favorable to takeover attempts. The better organized the local corporate elite—assessed in terms of number of board interlocks—the more likely was the state to adopt management-friendly legislation regulating hostile takeovers.

Marginal Players

It is sometimes the case that institutional innovations arrive from actors who are at the periphery of a field. Organizations differ in their social location, centrality, or connections to existing networks. Such differences are typically associated with varying levels of commitment to extant institutional logics and norms and, sometimes, to increased exposure to new ideas from neighboring fields. In their study of the U.S. radio broadcasting industry, Leblebici and colleagues (1991) described changes occurring between 1920 and 1965. Three stages are identified, differing in terms of who the dominant players were, what served as the medium of exchange, and which institutionalized practices governed these exchanges. The problem posed by the investigators is, "Why do those who occupy the positions of power in the existing institutions willingly change its practices?" (337). The analysis suggests that, at least in this industry and during the period under study, change was primarily endogenous, involving innovations introduced by marginal players that were subsequently adopted by leading members, driven to do so by increased competition. These new practices became conventions when used recurrently and subsequently became "institutional practices by acquiring a normative character when sustained through some form of legitimacy" (342).

Network theorists stress the importance of marginality to innovation and learning processes. Those who locate gaps or missing connections in social networks—"structural holes"—(Burt 1992) or who are associated with persons or organizations unlike themselves—"weak ties"—(Granovetter 1973) are likely to garner influence and be exposed to ideas different from their own. Just as the locations where sea water meets fresh water are particularly supportive of varied forms of marine life, so the areas of overlap and confluence between institutional spheres generate rich possibilities for new forms. Morrill (forthcoming) depicted the emergence of a new organization field staffed by new types of actors at the boundary where conventional legal structures overlap with social welfare forms. The field of alternative dispute resolution (ADR) emerged between 1965 and 1995 in response to a growing number of minor disputes that were clogging the law courts. A community-mediation model, championed by the social work community, and a multidoor-courthouse model, supported by lawyers, competed for the jurisdiction of this interstitial arena. Morrill detailed the processes by which new roles and practices were created (innovation), legitimation and resources were acquired from day players in the existing fields (mobilization), and a stable uncontested institutional settlement achieved (structuration). Morrill concluded:

> In the interstices created by overlapping resource networks across organizational fields, rules, identities, and conventional practices are loosened from their taken-for-granted moorings and alternative practices can emerge, particularly in the face of perceived institutional failure.

Social Movements

Suppressed interests, as well as elite groups, can give rise to new kinds of institutional forms. Such groups lack the resources available to established powers and must use their energies to challenge and disrupt existing routines in order to attract attention. They often are denied conventional modes of exercising voice or influence and, as a consequence, are forced to employ unconventional approaches. Such a case is described by Clemens (1993, 1997) in her well-documented account of the women's movement in the United States at the beginning of the 20th century. Prohibited from the ballot box and from mainstream electoral politics, activist women borrowed from the tactics employed by disreputable lobbyists, only to perfect them into a repertoire of actions now used by all interest groups. They embraced conventional organizing forms (e.g., women's clubs), but used them to advance the political education of their members, mobilize public opinion, gain procedural mastery of the legislative process, and devise ways to intervene in shaping policy and hold political officers accountable for their votes and decisions.

Rank-and-File Participants

Agency is not restricted to professionals, elites, or even social movements. The structuration perspective reminds us that all actors participate, wittingly or not, in the reproduction and reconstruction of the social systems they inhabit. Throughout our discussion of institutional processes, we emphasize that institutions are not only constructed from the top down, but from the bottom up.[1]

Demand- and Supply-Side Explanations

Mark Suchman (1995a) provides an illuminating general discussion of conditions giving rise to new institutional arrangements. He suggests that the impetus for institutional creation is the development, recognition, and naming of a recurrent problem to which no preexisting institution provides a satisfactory repertoire of responses (see fig. 5.1). These cognitive processes can be viewed as giving rise to collective sense-making activities (Weick 1995), as actors attempt to interpret and diagnosis the problem and, subsequently, propose what are, at the outset, various ad hoc solutions. Once these responses have been "generalized into solutions," it may be possible for the participants to engage in "a more thoroughgoing 'theorization' of the situation—in other words, to formulate general accounts of how the system works and, in particular, of which solutions are appropriate in which contexts" (Suchman 1995a: 43). Solutions generated in one context may then diffuse to other situations regarded as similar. Note the extent to which Suchman's discussion maps onto and builds from Berger and Luckmann's (1967) general formulation of institutionalization.

The foregoing description is meant to be sufficiently abstract to be applicable to any level of analysis—from the organizational subsystem to the world system. Suchman (1995a: 41) proposed that the question of where institutions arise—at what level—is determined by "where in the social structure particular shared understandings arise." That is, this question is to be settled empirically by observing the locus of the social processes at work. At a broader level, Suchman's general model embodies a "demand-side" argument: Institutions are crafted by actors in response to recurrent problems for which no existing "off-the-shelf" solutions are available.

A contrasting view of institutional construction offered by John Meyer (1994) is that institutional creation can also be driven by "supply-side" processes. His arguments are developed primarily at the world-system level, but are applicable to other levels. He suggests, as noted earlier, that certain types of actors—particularly those in the sciences and professions—occupy institutionalized roles that enable and encourage them to devise and promote new schemas, rules, models, routines, and artifacts. They see themselves as engaged in the great project of rationalization, whereby more and more arenas of social life are brought under the "rubric of ideologies that claim universal applicability" (42). The adoption of these generalized principles and procedures is promoted as evidence of "modernization," irrespective of whether local circumstances warrant or local actors "need" or want

Figure 5.1   A Multistage Model of Institutionalization

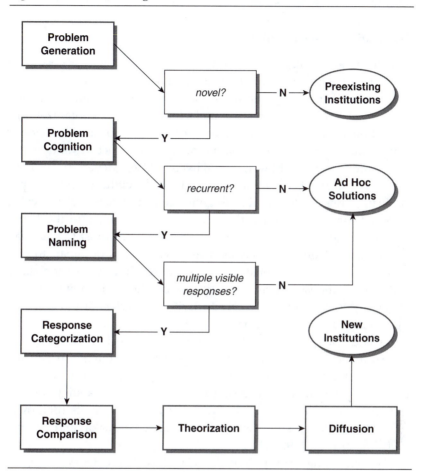

SOURCE: From "Localism and Globalism in Institutional Analysis," by Mark Suchman. In W. R. Scott and S. Christensen (eds.), The Institutional Construction of Organization. Copyright © 1995 by Sage Publications, Inc. (p. 44).

these developments. At the international and societal levels, general rules and principles are promulgated by professional associations and a wide range of nongovernmental organizations. At the level of the organizational field, organizational population, and individual organization, the carriers and promoters include foundations, management schools, accounting and auditing firms, and consulting companies (see DiMaggio and Powell 1983; Sahlin-Andersson and Engwall 2002). These purveyors of solutions must often begin their work by convincing potential adopters that they have a problem.

❖ SELECTED STUDIES OF INSTITUTIONAL CONSTRUCTION

Transnational-Level Studies

Meyer and colleagues developed a theory of the processes by which rational models of organization and organizing have developed during the past several centuries—since the Enlightenment—giving rise to a collection of nation-states and a limited range of organizational forms that are, despite enormous disparities in technical and economic development, remarkably similar in their formal structures and modes of operation (Drori, Meyer, and Hwang 2006; Meyer et al. 1997; Thomas et al. 1987). The approach builds on the cultural-cognitive pillar: Institutions are "cultural rules giving collective meaning and value to particular entities and activities, integrating them into the larger schemes" (Meyer, Boli, and Thomas 1987: 13). In contrast to the "realist" account of organizations as distinctive entities designed to efficiently pursue specific objectives, the approach views nation-states and organizations as being constituted by the wider environment. Organization is not just about productivity and exchange, but serves to signal rationality and legitimacy.

A wide-ranging series of empirical studies document the world-wide diffusion of models for organizing—ranging from the structuring of nation-states, to educational systems, to procedures for protecting the natural environment, advancing women's rights, husbanding "human resources," and ensuring transparency of governing units (Berkovitz 1999; Drori, Meyer, and Hwang 2006; Frank, Hironaka, and Schofer 2000; Meyer et al. 1997).

A contrasting approach is associated with the work of Djelic, Quack, and colleagues, who focus attention on the recent emergence of a wide range of governance mechanisms to manage economic and political activities at the international level. In their view, recent developments in globalization are not "only about adaptation and change of national institutions. [They are] also about institution building in the transnational arena—a space traditionally and typically pictured and described as anomic and adversarial" (Djelic and Quack 2003c: 3). These scholars examined institution-building in such varied realms as the regulation of competition, central banking, control of carbon emissions, and business education (Djelic and Quack 2003b; Djelic and Sahlin-Andersson 2006). The scenario developed is not one of increasing global uniformity—the dominance of a single model—but a more interesting "multilevel and multilayered historical process" marked by "competing and conflicting actors and logics" (Djelic and Quack 2003a: 303) involving both negotiation and the emergence of novel forms. They point out that, at the transnational level at the current time, we are witnessing a period of vibrant institution-building.

Societal-Level Studies

An early influential study of institution-building at the societal level is the historical account provided by North and Thomas (1973) of "the rise of the Western world." These economic historians argued that economic growth does not occur unless there are mechanisms that closely align social and private rates of return. Individuals are motivated to undertake socially desirable activities only if they provide private benefits that exceed private costs. This situation, in turn, requires that appropriate property rights be established and enforced. The need for such regulatory institutions, however, does not guarantee their development. Creating such structures is costly. Since the rise of the nation-state, governments have assumed responsibility for enforcing property rights. However, the interests and fiscal needs of rulers may encourage them to establish and enforce agreements that do not promote economic growth. Hence, "we have no guarantee that productive institutional arrangements will emerge" (North and Thomas 1973: 8).

North and Thomas reviewed historical evidence from the high Middle Ages to the beginning of the 18th century, noting developments in the political economy of Europe that advanced or depressed economic growth. They examined a number of cases and drew on a variety of historical materials, but their most detailed discussion contrasted political and economic developments during the period 1500–1700 in England, The Netherlands, Spain, and France. They concluded that, by the beginning of the 18th century, "a structure of property rights had developed in the Netherlands and England which provided the incentives necessary for sustained growth" (North and Thomas 1973: 157). In England, for example, Tudor kings became dependent on political support from the House of Commons, increasingly dominated by the rising merchant class, and political compromises pressed on the rulers resulted in expanded markets, both internal and colonial. By contrast, French kings developed methods of taxation that did not require them to extend markets, eliminate hereditary land tenure, or challenge the power of guilds and monopolies in order to secure adequate revenue to support army and court. The interests of the fledgling bourgeoisie were not recognized or protected.

Although their particular interpretation of history has not gone unchallenged (see e.g., Wallerstein 1979), North and Thomas provided a careful examination of ruling societal elites located in contrasting historical conditions who made choices that gave rise to markedly different institutional arrangements regulating economic activity.

Field-Level Studies

Dezalay and Garth (1996) provide a detailed historical account of the creation of an institutional framework at the international level for resolving disputes between businesses in different countries: transnational commercial arbitration rules and practice. Although their scope is international, they focused on the creation of a specific organizational field. Their history depicts the construction of an "international legal field"—the gradual and conflictual development of an arena with defined boundaries, central players, and accepted ground rules for dispute resolution.

The focus of their history is the transformation that began to occur in the 1970s as an elite "club" of "grand old men" centered in Paris confronted increased demand for arbitration services fostered by burgeoning international trade and globalization. This demand brought into the arena a new generation of "technocrats" housed in U.S. corporate law firms. The delicate transition was negotiated by the International Chamber of Commerce, which succeeded in transferring the legitimacy of the former elite to an expanding set of arbitrators in a classic instance of increased bureaucratization and rationalization of the field. Personal charisma was gradually replaced by routinized, impersonal, specialized expertise. Maintaining legitimacy was essential for the continued success of arbitration if it was "to provide a basis to govern matters that involve powerful economic and political entities" (Dezalay and Garth 1996: 33).

Dezalay and Garth (1996: 41) provide a finely nuanced account of "the contests through which the field and the markets of arbitration are constituted." Although all participants are depicted as attempting to pursue their respective interests, the tale told is not one of rational design, but of improvisation, conflict, and compromise.

DiMaggio's (1991) study of the efforts by professionals to create the cultural conditions that would support the development and maintenance of art museums during the late 19th century in America is also cast at the organizational field level, but limited to a single society. In his historical account, DiMaggio gave primary attention to cultural-cognitive aspects of the professional project: the creation of distinctions between high and low forms of art, and the creation and selection among cultural models for constituting art museums as distinctive types of organizations. Struggles are depicted among contending professional factions debating the merits of a "curator" versus an "educational" model of museum, and between the interests of new types of professionals—curators, art historians, and acquisition experts—and those of museum managers. Philanthropic foundations, specifically the Carnegie Corporation, are shown to play a pivotal role as they work to advance the interests of the new museum professionals. This study underlines DiMaggio's contention that agency and interests are more apparent during the creation of a new institutional fields in contrast to the routine operation of an existing field.[2]

Another informative study of contending models for organizing at the field level is provided by Rao's (1998) account of the emergence of consumer protection organizations in the United States during the early part of the 20th century. The Consumers' Union (CU) embodied the model of watchdog as radical critic, overseeing both consumer interests and worker rights. By contrast, Consumer Research (CR) advanced the model of watchdog as impartial evaluator, limiting their purview to consumer goods. Pressure from conservative media and political bodies forced CU to abandon its more radical agenda and, like CR, operate as a "rational" scientific agency employing impartial testing methods to evaluate consumer products. Rao emphasizes that the institutionalization of such consumer interest agencies could not take place until a settlement had been reached between these competing institution-building projects.

Population-Level Studies

At the population level, institutional construction concerns primarily the creation of new organizational forms. In his now classic discussion of organizations and social structure, Stinchcombe (1965) identified organizational forms as an important topic of study and pointed out that organizational foundlings of the same type tend to be concentrated in particular historical periods. Moreover, because new organizations must rely on existing ideas, technologies, and social routines, organizations take on a similar character—are imprinted by their institutional environment—so as to reflect the historical conditions of their origin. Finally, although these differences reflect these somewhat arbitrary conditions of their birth, they tend to persist over time. Organizational forms exhibit substantial inertia. Stinchcombe assembled data on differences in the labor force composition of varying industries to illustrate this effect, demonstrating that industries founded in different periods tended to exhibit differing labor force characteristics and that these differences were maintained over long time periods.

These insights have provided an important touchstone for both population ecologists and institutional theorists. Ecologists are necessarily concerned with identifying meaningful organizational forms. After all, it is difficult to enumerate organizational populations if their identification is problematic. Theorists like McKelvey (1982) proposed the creation of a broad general taxonomy, but most ecological scholars utilize a more pragmatic approach that focuses on identifying similarities in key properties, such as stated goals, hierarchical forms, and core technologies (see Hannan and Freeman 1989).

Institutionalists Greenwood and Hinings (1993: 1055) stress the cognitive dimension in their attempt to identify distinctive organizational forms or *archetypes*, which they define as "a set of structures and systems that consistently embodies a single interpretive scheme." Although they emphasized the importance of environmental niches associated with distinctive patterns of resource usage, ecologists also increasingly recognize that organization forms and the boundaries between them are institutionally defined and constructed. While the differences involved may have their origins in technologies, the characteristics of clients served, or the resources consumed, particular arrangements come to be seen as the "natural" way to carry out certain types of activities. Institutionalizing processes ensue,

> transforming arbitrary differences into differences with real social consequences. In this sense, nominal classifications become real classifications. They become real in their consequences when they serve as bases for successful collective action, when powerful actors use them in defining rights and access to resources, and when members of the general population use them in organizing their social worlds. Thus, the clarity of a set of boundaries is not a permanent property of a set of classifications. Rather, the realism of distinction among forms depends on the degree of institutionalization that has occurred. (Hannan and Freeman 1989: 57)

In the following chapter, we consider the way in which ecologists measure degree of institutionalization.

Mohr and Guerra-Pearson (forthcoming) illustrate the application of such arguments in their study of the emergence of differentiated populations of welfare organizations in New York City during 1888–1907 (see also Mohr 1994). They suggested that differentiation in these populations occurred along three axes: the sorts of statuses recognized and the merit they were accorded, the kinds of social needs or problems identified, and the kinds of solution repertoires recognized. Client differentiation was driven by power struggles surrounding these three socially constructed dimensions.

> Organizational forms are significant because they provide the containers into which these three dimensions of institutional life are poured and they provide the empirical foundations around which conflicts over how these three primitive institutional elements will be combined are negotiated and struggled over. (Mohr and Guerra-Pearson forthcoming)

The researchers examined data from city directories at the turn of the century and, with the use of multidimensional scaling techniques, were able to map changes over time in the coherence of organizational boundaries as selected forms came to be seen as preferred ways of organizing specified services.

As another example of a study of institutional construction at the population level, Suchman (1995a, forthcoming) combined both historical and analytic approaches in his study of the creation of organizational forms for semiconductor firms in California's Silicon Valley. Creating a new organization requires not only resources, but also ideas or models on how to organize. Conventional histories celebrate the role of Stanford University engineers in providing the designs and early material resources for start-up companies (see e.g., Saxenian 1994). While acknowledging this contribution, Suchman and colleagues laid the groundwork for a "genetics of organization" that examines the flows of both operational resources and "constitutive information."

> Just as mating patterns shape organic populations by structuring the flow of constitutive genetic blueprints, institutional patterns— definitions, typologies, accounts of relevance, theories of causation, and so on—shape organizational populations by structuring the flow of constitutive cognitive models. Cognitive models carry the scripts for organizational competences, and in structuring the transmission of such models, cognitive institutions function as organizational reproduction mechanisms." (Suchman, Steward, and Westfall 2001: 358–359)

They proceed to outline an organizational genetics, concerned with the development and preservation of distinctive species or forms, to supplement organizational ecology, which focuses on competition

among existing species or types of organizations. In established organizational fields, most new organizations are "reproducer rather than
innovative" forms because they largely copy routines and competences
from existing organizations (Aldrich and Ruef 2006: 67). They follow
what Suchman and colleagues (2001: 359) termed a "filiation" mode of
reproduction: Here "new organizations draw competences directly
from specific existing organizations that embody those competences
themselves." But when fields are in their early stages of development,
organizations cannot simply copy successful recipes. Under such
circumstances, Suchman suggests, a process of "compilation" may be
employed, whereby "information intermediaries" such as consultants
or lawyers observe existing, relatively heterogeneous practices and
attempt to distill a core set of organizing principles. In their historical
account, Suchman and Cahill (1996) described how lawyers and venture capitalists in Silicon Valley functioned as "dealmakers," linking
clients with various transactional partners and as "counselors," formulating and disseminating standardized solutions to recurrent problems.

Shifting to a quantitative approach, Suchman (1995a; Suchman,
Steward, and Westfall 2001) analyzed data on 108 venture-capital
financing contracts from two Silicon Valley venture-capital funds. Such
contracts bring together the venture capitalists, lawyers, and entrepreneurs in the crucial founding event, constituting the structure of relations among these parties as they jointly form the start-up company.
The contracts were coded along numerous dimensions, and these
scores were then used to calculate measures of contractual standardization as an indicator of increasing institutionalization. Suchman's
analysis reveals that standardization was strongly correlated to both
date of filing and location of the law firm that drafted the contract. In
general, standardization of contracts was greater the later in the time
period they were filed and the closer the location of the law firm draft-
ing the contract was to the core of Silicon Valley.

Organization-Level Studies

Oliver Williamson (1994) embraces (boundedly) rational choice
assumptions and, as discussed in chapter 2, developed an explana-
tory framework within which economic agents are expected to devise
or select those governance forms that minimize transaction costs in
managing their enterprise. He left to economic historians and sociologists the tasks of accounting for the characteristics of "institutional
environments"—the "background conditions," including property
rights, norms, customs and similar frameworks—in order to focus on

the choice of "mechanisms of governance," which he views as the central focus of the economics of organizations. Designers of organizational governance arrangements must take into account these wider institutional conditions when fashioning their structures. Williamson recognized that, over time, their choices feed back to affect environmental conditions, including institutional environments, but his interest lies in accounting for the design of specific organizations.

Walker and Weber (1984) tested Williamson's arguments that transactions involving higher uncertainty and greater asset-specificity (specialized skills or machinery) would be more likely to be produced inhouse, rather than purchased by a firm. That is, organizational designers will elect to have such tasks governed by the firm's hierarchy rather than by the market. Their study of 60 "make or buy" decisions within a division of a large automobile company found results generally consistent with these predictions, although, unexpectedly, the researchers found that comparative production costs had a larger impact on these decisions than did transaction costs.[3]

Studies by Armour and Teece (1978) and Teece (1981) attempted to empirically evaluate Williamson's arguments regarding the relation between a firm's governance structure and its economic performance. Following Chandler's (1962) early insights and historical research, Williamson (1975) argued that firms adopting a multidivisional (M-form) structure would be more capable of separating strategic from operational decision making, allocating capital among divisions, and monitoring divisional performance. Armour and Teece studied a sample of diversified firms in the petroleum industry and found that those firms adopting the M-form structure performed better financially. Teece (1981) extended the test to evaluate the performance of pairs of firms matched by size and product line in 20 industries. The performance of the firm first adopting the M-form (the lead firm) was compared with that of the matched firm for two time periods. Again, the results confirmed the hypotheses.

Williamson, in concert with other practitioners of the new institutional economics, argues, in effect, that managers attempt to design the boundaries and governance structures of their firms so as to economize on transaction costs. This emphasis, as David (1992: 2–3) observed, assumes that these institutional arrangements represent "presently efficient solutions to resource allocation problems" and that "institutional arrangements are perfectly malleable." Such assumptions are at odds with those held by most sociologists and economic historians, who stress the effect of past events on present institutions and the likelihood of these structures to resist change. Williamson also employs functional explanations in accounting for changes in organizational governance structures (see Granovetter 1985). Such explanations attempt to account for the existence and maintenance of a given social structure by noting what functions it performs to assist adaptation. To be valid, such explanations need to specify the causal feedback loop by which the forces maintaining the structure are selected and reinforced, although most analysts are content to argue "as if" rather than to demonstrate such connections (see Elster 1983; Stinchcombe 1968).

Like Williamson, Terry Moe (1990a) focuses on the level of the individual organization. He has been particularly inventive in applying rational-choice perspectives to the design of public agencies. Adopting the perspective of institutional economists, Moe viewed organizations primarily as governance systems, emphasizing regulatory elements. Moe (1990a: 221) pointed out that governmental structures differ from those in the private sector in that, unlike the world of voluntary exchange, "people can be forced to [give up resources involuntarily] by whoever controls public authority." The legitimate use of coercive power distinguishes public from private authorities. The problem confronted by political actors in democratic systems is that, although they can use their power to design institutional arrangements that serve their interests, the possibility exists that opposing parties will come to power and employ the same instruments to serve their own ends. To deal with this problem of the uncertainty of political control, Moe argued, public authorities often restrict the discretion of agencies and envelop them in detailed rules and procedures.

> Obviously, this is not a formula for creating effective organizations. In the interests of political protection, agencies are knowingly burdened with cumbersome, complicated, technically inappropriate structures that undermine their capacity to perform their jobs well. Nor, obviously, is this a formula for effective hierarchical control by democratic superiors. Insulationist devices are called for precisely because those who create public bureaucracy *do not want* a truly effective structure of democratic control. (Moe 1990a: 228; italics original)

These pathologies are particularly likely to develop in political systems based on the separation of power, such as the United States, compared to parliamentary systems, such as the United Kingdom.

The "politics of structural design" become even more perverse in situations where the Congress and the White House are controlled by opposing parties. Moe (1989) provided a detailed historical account of the creation of the Consumer Product Safety Commission (CPSC), an agency created when Richard Nixon, a Republican, was President, but was compelled to work with a Democratic Congress. Consumer interests, allied with Congress, were successful in their struggle to create an independent agency, separate from cabinet departments that were viewed as overly conservative. Strict procedural rules were imposed to ensure that the agency would attend to consumer interests. However, business interests, with the support of the administration, made sure that ample provision was made for their input and review of all pending decisions, and that enforcement powers were not vested in the Commission, but in an independent agency, the Justice Department. The initial design of the agency reflected the contending interests of the parties, and subsequent modifications were governed by the shifting political power of consumer versus business interests.

Philip Selznick, like Moe, also examined the design of a public agency. However, in his well-known account of the evolution of the Tennessee Valley Authority (TVA), Selznick (1949) eschewed a rational-choice framework, as he depicted processes that undermine rational design. He provided a historical account of the development over time of a distinctive ideology and set of normative commitments on the part of TVA officials. As I noted in reviewing Selznick's views in chapter 2, his approach describes how the original structure and goals of this innovative government corporation were transformed over time by the commitments of its participants to the "means" of action. In Selznick's work, to institutionalize is "to infuse with value beyond the technical requirements of the task at hand" (Selznick 1957: 17) because intrinsic worth is accorded to a structure or process that originally possessed only instrumental value. Although Selznick emphasized normative beliefs and values in his analysis, he also attended to the importance of cognitive features of organizations. His discussion of the role played by the grassroots ideology in framing decisions and garnering support from important constituencies is central to his argument (see Selznick 1996).

Selznick's approach focuses on internal relations, especially informal structures rather than on formal structures, and on the immediate environment of the organization rather than on more general cultural rules or characteristics of the wider organizational field (see DiMaggio and Powell 1991). The carriers of institutionalized values are relational structures, in particular, informal structures and cooptative relations linking the organization with salient external actors, both individual and collective.[4]

Selznick's argument stresses the importance of power processes—the vesting of interests in informal structures and the cooptation of external groups that acquire internal power in return for their support. His analysis of the TVA examines the ways in which particular constituencies, such as the agricultural interests, on whom the organization was dependent, were able to modify agency programs in ways that compromised its conservation program. As discussed in chapter 2, Stinchcombe's (1968) amplification of Selznick's arguments stressed the ways in which power is used to perpetuate these interests and values over time.

Diane Vaughn (1996) wove together many of the same kinds of arguments to account for the continued use of a flawed design by Morton Thiokol engineers and the fateful decision by NASA officials to launch the Challenger missile. Her richly detailed historical account of the organizational routines—both technical and decision-making—leading up to the disaster depicted the development of a culture within which "signals of potential danger" were "repeatedly normalized by managers and engineers alike" (Vaughn 1996: xiii). Although production pressures played an important role, these pressures "became institutionalized and thus a taken-for-granted aspect of the worldview that *all* participants brought to NASA decision-making venues" (Vaughn 1996: xiv; italics original).

Selznick's interest in organizations that become defined by their commitments to distinctive values has been pursued by a new generation of researchers interested in "organizational identity." Defined as a commitment to values that are "central, enduring, and distinctive," organizational identity provides participants with a core set of normative elements around which to craft their narratives and sense-making activities (see Albert and Whetten 1985; Whetten and Godfrey 1999).

Interpersonal- and Intraorganization-Level Studies

Axelrod (1984) employed the "prisoner's dilemma" situation to examine the conditions under which individuals who pursue their own self-interest in the absence of a central authority will evolve norms of cooperation. The prisoner's dilemma involves a situation in which two players make one of two choices: cooperation (c) or noncooperation (n). The payoff matrix is such that if both players opt for c, then both receive an intermediate reward; if both select n, they receive a low reward; but if one player selects c when the other selects n, the former (sucker) receives no reward and the latter (exploiter) receives a high reward. Players are not allowed to exchange any type of information other than their choices, and the game is played over a number of trials.

The challenge for each player is to provide incentives and encourage the formation of norms to induce his or her partner to cooperate. However, the knowledge of each player is limited, and any normative structure that develops must be fashioned incrementally.

In a novel design, Axelrod (1984) invited other game theorists from many disciplines to compete in a computer tournament to select the best game strategy by submitting a program that embodies rules to select the cooperative or noncooperative choice on each move. Such a program provides a complete process description of the sequence of decisions during the course of the encounter. Of the 14 strategies submitted, the most successful was the "TIT FOR TAT" decision rule: a strategy that starts with a cooperative choice and thereafter selects whatever the other player did on the previous move. This simple strategy provided the best payoff to the player adopting it under a wide range of simulated conditions. Axelrod (1984: 54) summarized its virtues:

> What accounts for TIT FOR TAT's robust success is its combination of being nice, retaliatory, forgiving, and clear. Its niceness [never initiating noncooperation] prevents it from getting into unnecessary trouble. Its retaliation discourages the other side from persisting whenever defection is tried. Its forgiveness helps restore mutual cooperation. And its clarity makes it intelligible to the other player, thereby eliciting long-term cooperation.

Although it may be argued that the prisoner's dilemma is "just a game," it encapsulates an important dilemma built into many real-world situations, from the school yard to international diplomacy. It is to cope with such situations that security regimes and similar types of institutions develop (see Krasner 1983; Mares and Powell 1990). A particularly important element of the conditions supporting the rise of stable cooperative norms is that "the future must have a sufficiently large shadow" (Axelrod 1984: 174). The anticipation of future interaction provides an important stimulus to evoke norms of reciprocity. Indeed, such norms are argued to undergird the stability of much ongoing economic and social behavior, making it less necessary for parties to resort to such expensive alternative regulatory structures as the legal system and police force (see Macaulay 1963).

Elsbach (2002: 37) defines intraorganizational institutions as "taken-for-granted beliefs that arise within and across organizational groups and delimit acceptable and normative behavior for members of those groups." This definition encompasses a wide range of organizational research beginning during the 1930s and variously labeled studies of work group behavior and subgroup identities, human relations, organizational culture, organizational identity, and sense-making processes (see e.g., Dutton and Dukerrich 1991; Frost et al. 1985; Roethlisberger and Dickson 1939; Roy 1952; Weick 1995). Earlier studies tended to emphasize the normative facets of institution-building, whereas latter approaches have given more attention to shared schemas and identities—cultural-cognitive elements.

Comparative Comments

The studies briefly summarized here differ in a number of important respects. They are arranged by level of analysis, but it is important to emphasize that level is defined by the nature of the dependent variable: the level of the unit whose structure or behavior is to be explained. In many of the studies reviewed, multilevel processes are shown to be involved with, for example, societal structures affected by transnational phenomena or, alternatively, field-level processes being influenced by the actions of organizations embedded within the field. We believe that a hallmark of the more sophisticated institutional approaches is their openness to such multilevel causal processes.

The studies reviewed also vary in terms of the assumptions made about rationality of actors and salience of institutional elements. Among the various studies reviewed, Moe and Williamson assume a higher level of rational choice exercised by actors in designing institutional arrangements. In these studies, actors are assumed to be pursuing their individual interests armed with substantial knowledge of alternatives and their relation to consequences. Hence, the critical questions are when and why it is in an actor's self-interest to construct and maintain institutional structures that will govern not only others', but one's own, behavior. Other theorists embrace a less restrictive conception of rationality, assuming that while individuals attempt to pursue their interests, they do so with imperfect knowledge and intelligence. Errors in judgment occur and unintended consequences result. Rather than conceiving of institutions as "sets of predesigned rules," these theorists are more apt to see them as "unplanned and unintended regularities (social conventions) that emerge 'organically' " (Schotter 1986: 118). Among the studies reviewed, North and Thomas and Axelrod best exemplify these assumptions.

Although analysts in all of the studies presume that participants have interests and examine the processes by which contending interests are resolved, researchers such as Dezalay and Garth, DiMaggio, Mohr, Selznick, and Suchman view such interests not simply as preexisting, but as being constructed in the course of the interaction and negotiation processes.

With respect to institutional elements, North and Thomas, Moe, and Williamson place primary emphasis on regulatory structures. Axelrod, Dezalay and Garth, Selznick, and Vaughn attend largely to normative elements, although the latter three studies also considered cultural-cognitive elements. DiMaggio, Mohr and Guerra-Pearson, and Suchman highlight the role of cultural-cognitive processes of institutional creation.

❖ CONCLUDING COMMENT

From an early focus on how existing institutions affect organizations, institutional theorists have recently expanded their purview to include attention to the ways in which institutions are constructed. Accounts of construction processes vary according to how much intent and conscious design is emphasized, as opposed to less intentional, more evolutionary processes.

Institutional agents include both individual and collective actors, and they differ in whether they employ primarily regulative, normative, or cultural-cognitive tools in their construction efforts. The nation-state and the professions play high-profile roles in institutional constructions, whereas a variety of other types of actors, including other elites as well as social movement organizations and marginal and rank-and-file players, have a hand in the building of institutions.

Investigators have examined these processes at work across multiple levels. Institution-building at the transnational level represents a relatively new focus of interest and is one of the most active construction arenas as we enter the 21st century.

❖ NOTES

1. For a related discussion, see Strang and Sine (2002).

2. A possible limitation of this study is that it does not attend to potential sources of influence in field construction stemming from outside the United States. It is generally recognized that Americans at this time looked to Europe for their models of high culture.

3. More recent research suggests that this specific prediction may no longer hold in certain industries, including automobile manufacturing. To protect and develop specific assets, partnering relations with suppliers are now more likely to be used than vertically integrated structures (Helper, MacDuffie, and Sabel 2000).

4. In his monograph on the TVA, Selznick emphasized the crescive, unplanned, and unintended nature of institutional processes. Valued commitments were generated over time, unplanned structure having unintended consequences. However, in his later, more prescriptive writing on leadership, Selznick (1957) argued for a more intentional model: Effective leaders are those who can define and defend social values and obtain the support of others in preserving them.

6

Institutionalization

Z ucker (1977: 728) observed that "institutionalization is both a process and a property variable." It refers both to a process occurring over time as well as to a set of social arrangements "that has attained a certain state or property . . . ; social patterns that, when chronically reproduced, owe their survival to relatively self-activating social processes" (Jepperson 1991: 145). We concentrate in this chapter on institutionalization as process.

We begin by reviewing three versions of institutionalization as process—each relying on assumptions and arguments associated with one of the three pillars. These perspectives embrace not simply differing conceptions as to the elements or ingredients involved, but of the processes underlying their construction, maintenance, and change.

❖ THREE CONCEPTIONS OF INSTITUTIONALIZATION: UNDERLYING MECHANISMS

How and why does institutionalization occur? An important part of the answer to these questions is to examine the mechanisms involved in creating and sustaining institutions. *Mechanisms* focus attention on how effects are produced. Elster (1989: 3) regards mechanisms as the "nuts and bolts" of social processes, which Hernes (1998: 74) appropriately amends to "the cogs and wheels . . . the wheelwork or agency by which an effect is produced." A less colorful, but more useful, definition is provided by McAdam, Tarrow, and Tilly (2001: 24): "Mechanisms are a delimited class of events that alter relations among specified sets of elements in identical or closely similar ways over a variety of situations." Increasing attention to mechanisms is particularly salutary for institutional theorists who too often have neglected to address questions of the "who" and "how" with regard to institutional effects. We consider three alternative mechanisms underlying the process of institutionalization of social systems.

Institutionalization Based on Increasing Returns

A compelling version of institutionalization has been put forward by institutional economists to account for the development and persistence of institutional systems based on the process of positive feedback. The specific argument was first proposed by David (1985, 2000) and Arthur (1994) to explain unusual features detected in some types of technological trajectories.[1] They observed that, under specified conditions, technologies develop in such a manner that it is difficult, if not impossible, to reverse course or to consider the use of alternative approaches even if these would provide "superior" solutions. Such a path-dependent process is argued to occur because of "positive feedback": Further developments in the same direction are rewarded, whereas the costs of switching to an alternative increase over time. The necessary conditions supporting positive feedback as described by Arthur (1994) are: (a) the presence of high setup costs—once an approach is available, the development of alternatives involves additional, often substantial, costs; (b) learning effects—individuals who invest time and effort in learning a particular approach are reluctant to consider alternatives; (c) coordination effects—the multiple advantages that accrue to a user because others have adopted the same option; and (d) adaptive expectations—as late-comers perceive that a particular approach is widely accepted, they are more inclined to adopt it themselves. Consequential features of this process include indeterminacy (a number of solutions [multiple equilibria] are possible), inefficiencies (inferior technologies may be adopted), lock-in (the difficulty in withdrawing the selected solution), and the primacy of early events (small differences and chance events can create unlikely trajectories difficult to alter).

North (1990) suggests that, with modification, this framework is applicable to the analysis of institutional change. He argues that all of the factors identified by Arthur apply to institutions—perhaps even more so than to technologies. The learning and coordination effects, coupled with the associated growth of formal and informal rules, all reinforce the buy-in of multiple players. As a result of this combination of processes, North (1990: 95) asserts that "the interdependent web of an institutional matrix produces massive increasing returns."

In addition to the effect of increasing returns, institutional processes (more than technologies) are shaped by the existence of imperfect markets. If markets are competitive, North asserts, then imperfect institutions are detected and eliminated. However, if markets are flawed—if feedback is fragmentary, if subjective evaluations dominate objective information, and if transaction costs are high—then imperfect institutions are likely to persist. The combination of path dependence and suboptimal markets is employed by North (1990: 92) to account for (a) the substantial differences we observe in the "evolution of societies, polities, or economies over time"; and (b) the persistence of systems that, at least by standards stressing the value of economic growth, exhibit persistently poor performance.

The central thrust of the increasing returns argument for institutionalization is to highlight the role of incentives as a motivating force in social life.

Institutionalization Based on Increasing Commitments

Rather than emphasizing the role of incentives (costs and benefits), scholars embracing the normative pillar focus on the mechanism of commitments. Possible loci of commitment include norms and values, structures and procedures, and individuals and collective actors. The theorist who has most explicitly pursued this view of institutionalization is Philip Selznick (1948, 1949, 1957).

As described in chapter 2, Selznick (1957: 16–17; italics original) argues that, "in its most significant meaning, 'to institutionalize' is to *infuse with value* beyond the technical requirements of the task at hand." In a more general statement, Selznick (1992: 232) asserts

institutionalization is the emergence of orderly, stable, social integrating patterns out of stable, loosely organized, or narrowly technical activities. The underlying reality—the basic source of stability and integration—is the creation of social entanglements or commitments. Most of what we do in everyday life is mercifully free and reversible. But when actions touch important interests and salient values or when they are embedded in networks of interdependence, options are more limited. Institutionalization constrains conduct in two main ways: by bringing it within a normative order, and by making it hostage to its own history.

Selznick argues that organizations are transformed into institutions through a two-step process. First, the creation of a formal structure provides an "institutional" solution to problems of economy and coordination. Explicit goals and rules, coordination mechanisms, and communication channels—these provide the modes of governance referenced by institutional economists such as Williamson. But for Selznick (1992: 235), this first step is only a beginning.

> Beyond lies what we may call "thick" institutionalization. . . . Thick institutionalization takes place in many different ways. Familiar examples are: by sanctifying or otherwise hardening rules and procedures; by establishing strongly differentiated organizational units, which then develop vested interests and become centers of power; by creating administrative rituals, symbols, and ideologies; by intensifying "purposiveness," that is, commitment to unifying objectives; and by embedding the organization in a social environment.

Thick institutionalization is a cumulative process taking place over time. Knudsen (1995a: 144–145) notes the strong resemblance of Selznick's version of institutionalization to Nelson and Winter's evolutionary views described in chapter 2. In both conceptions, the firm is modeled as

> a "hereditary mechanism" that accumulates more and more complex behavioral patterns over a period of time. The organization structure of a firm can therefore no longer be regarded as determined by its transaction costs, but rather by its accumulated competences or capabilities.

The mechanism of commitment also plays a large role in discussions of relational contracts and network forms of organizing. Relational contracts are agreements between two parties in which as much or more attention is paid to preserving the relationship as to honoring the contract. Womack and colleagues (1991) provide a useful description of the types of relational contracts that developed between Toyota and its multiple suppliers in the 1970s and 1980s. In contrast to U.S. automobile companies, at least at that time, Toyota worked with a much smaller set of suppliers with whom it entered into long-term, flexible agreements, sharing proprietary information, providing equipment and training, and exchanging employees. The assembly plant-supplier relations were marked by reciprocity, trust, and mutual concern for the other's welfare—in short, commitments.

Similarly, in contrast to conventional markets or hierarchies, network forms of organizations rely more heavily on mutuality. In Powell's (1990: 303–304) description

> In network forms of resource allocation, individual units exist not by themselves, but in relation to other units. These relationships take considerable effort to establish and sustain, thus they constrain both partners' ability to adapt to changing circumstances. As networks evolve, it becomes more economically sensible to exercise voice rather than exit. Benefits and burdens come to be shared. . . . As Macneil (1985) has suggested, the "entangling strings" of reputation, friendship, interdependence, and altruism become integral parts of the relationship.

If the increasing returns argument privileges the role of incentives, then the commitment argument highlights the role of identity: Who am I (or who are we), and what is the appropriate way for me (us) to behave in this situation?

Institutionalization as Increasing Objectification

Anchored in the work of Berger and Luckmann (1967), scholars embracing the cultural-cognitive pillar emphasize the role of increasing objectification of shared beliefs in institutionalization. As described in chapter 2, Berger and Luckmann identify *objectification*—the processes by which the meanings produced in social interaction "come to confront [the actor] as a facticity outside of himself"—as one of the three phases of institutionalization. Berger and Luckmann stress the importance of transmission of shared beliefs to third parties—individuals who played no role in constructing them—as they are informed not "This is the way we do this," but rather "This is how these things are done." In the process of transmission to others—to a new generation—the objectivity of the institutional world "thickens and hardens" (59). In the following, we discuss how, as recipes or templates diffuse, in the

Figure 6.1   Component Processes of Institutionalization

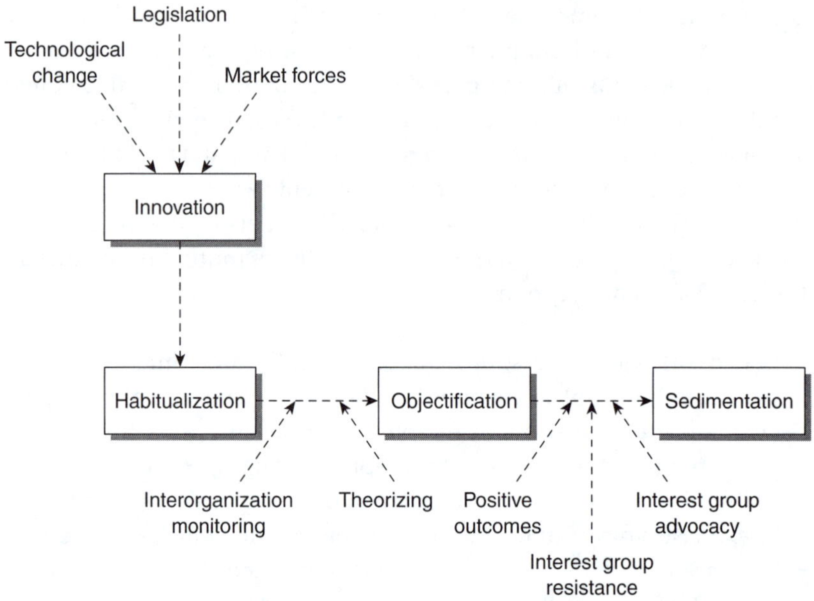

SOURCE: From "Component processes of institutionalization," (p. 182) by Pamela S. Tolbert and Lynn Zucker. In Stewart Clegg, Cynthia Hardy, and Walter R. Nord (eds.), Handbook of Organization Studies, Sage Publications. Used with permission.

form of "best practice" or advanced modes for organizing, their degree of institutionalization increases.

In an expanded view of the processes associated with objectification, Tolbert and Zucker (1996) propose a multistage model of institutional processes that occur within as well as between organizations (see fig. 6.1).[2] In response to changes in political, technological, or market conditions, actors in organizations innovate, advancing new ideas, solutions, and practices. They also scan the environment to determine what similar organizations are doing. Many of the proposed solutions invented or adopted prove to be unsatisfactory and are dropped. However, some innovations will prove more viable and come to the attention of others. They become more broadly accepted or habituated and, in interactions within and between organizations, become the object of formal "theorization"—a formulation of why and how the innovation is effective and an identification of the class of problems or organizations for whom it is suitable (Strang and Meyer 1993). These preinstitutionalization processes, if they proceed successfully, set the stage for objectification.

Objectification involves the development of some degree of social consensus among organizational decision-makers concerning the value of a structure, and the increasing adoption by organizations on the basis of that consensus. . . . The impetus for diffusion shifts from simple imitation to a more normative base . . . [the innovation is viewed as possessing] both general cognitive and normative legitimacy. (Tolbert and Zucker 1996: 182–183)

In a final stage of institutionalization, termed "sedimentation," the innovation is perpetuated across several generations and spreads to virtually all of the relevant population of potential adopters. (Tolbert and Zucker 1996: 184)[3]

Objectified beliefs often become embedded in routines, forms and documents (e.g., the types of classifications employed), and artifacts— our tools, hardware, and machinery. We organize our material world in accordance with our mental categories, and the two become self-reinforcing.

Although the increasing returns argument focuses on the role of incentives and the increasing commitment approach emphasizes identity, the increasing objectification view favors ideas. Cultural-cognitive theorists stress that ideas—beliefs, schema, and assumptions—play a powerful role in institutional processes. Campbell (2004: 93) indicates that ideas play this role in multiple ways. Among the most powerful are the taken-for-granted assumptions that reside in the background of debates. Such ideas "remain largely accepted and unquestioned, almost as principles of faith"; they are unnoticed unless and until others, holding contrasting assumptions, enter the scene pursuing unusual goals or employing unfamiliar or unacceptable means. Personnel or companies working in foreign cultures are likely to encounter surprising and inexplicable behavior stemming from differences in background beliefs (Hofstede 1991; Orr and Scott 2007). At a more conscious level, ideas provide the cognitive frames that are employed to justify one or another type of action, as well as the substantive programs that point the way to possible new approaches and ways of behaving. This is the realm of contested decision making and controversy over policy choices.

Thus, arrayed in line with the three pillars, we encounter three rather different accounts of the mechanisms leading to institutionalization. Although different aspects of institutions are privileged and different mechanisms are evoked, these arguments are not necessarily in conflict. Robust institutionalization is often the product of multiple mechanisms that interact and reinforce each other.

❖ MAINTAINING AND DIFFUSING INSTITUTIONS

Maintaining Stability

The concept of institution connotes stability and persistence. Are these conditions problematic? Once an institutional structure is in place, is there anything else to be said? A good many students of organizations assume that institutionalization is an absorbing state and, once completed, requires no further effort at maintenance. Simon (1945/1997: 106), for example, describes a number of reasons for the persistence of behavioral patterns once established. He emphasizes, in particular, cognitive patterns: "the activity itself creates stimuli that direct attention toward its continuance and completion." Such individual-level, attention-directing processes also act to decrease the individual's sensitivity to external stimuli. Organizational ecologists also assume that stability or, in their terms, *inertia* is a normal state for organizations. Inertia is the product of such organization-level processes as sunk costs, vested interests, and habitualized behavior shored up by the external constraints imposed by contractual obligations to exchange partners and regulatory regimes (Hannan and Freeman 1984, 1989). Change is assumed to be both difficult and dangerous for organizations.

Other theorists, however, argue that persistence cannot be taken for granted. Zucker (1988b: 26), for example, suggests that entropy—"a tendency toward disorganization in the social system"—is the more normal condition. Things—structures, rules, and routines—tend to break down. She argues, as a corollary, that deinstitutionalization is prevalent and has many roots. (These ideas are considered in chap. 8.) Persistence is seen to be tenuous and problematic. Theorists such as Giddens (1984) take an intermediate position. He emphasizes the extent to which the persistence of rules, norms, and beliefs require actors to actively monitor ongoing social activities and continuously attend to maintaining the linkages with the wider sociocultural environment. Structure persists only to the extent that actors are able to continuously produce and reproduce it.

In his most recent work, economic historian Avner Greif (2006: 14) embraces and elaborates this intermediate position, combining agency and structural views, by proposing an equilibrium perspective. Greif argues, as I have proposed, that institutions are supported by varying elements, including rules, beliefs, and norms. "These institutional elements are exogeneous to each individual whose behavior they influence." But they are also "endogenous institutions," which are self-reinforcing.

> Each individual, responding to the institutional elements implied by others' behavior and expected behavior behaves in a manner that contributes to enabling, guiding, and motivating others to behave in the manner that led to the institutional elements that generated the individual's behavior to begin with. Behavior is self-enforcing in that each individual, taking the structure as given, finds it best to follow the institutionalized behavior that, in turn, reproduces the institution in the sense that the implied behavior confirms the associated beliefs and regenerates the associated norms. (Greif 2006: 15–16)

In my reading, most institutional scholars accord little attention to the issue of institutional persistence, and those who do disagree over what mechanisms underlie stability. In particular, the underlying conception of institution—whether cultural-cognitive, normative, or regulative—affects views of maintenance mechanisms. Cultural-cognitive theorists tend to emphasize the important role played by unconscious, taken-for-granted assumptions defining social reality. Jepperson (1991: 145), for example, insists that the hallmark of an institution is its capacity for automatic maintenance and self-restoration. Institutional mechanisms are those requiring no conscious mobilization of will or effort. Similarly, Zucker (1977: 726) argues: "Internalization, self-reward, or other intervening processes need not be present to ensure cultural persistence because social knowledge once institutionalized exists as a fact, as part of objective reality, and can be transmitted directly on that basis."

To evaluate this claim, Zucker conducted an experimental study to assess the extent to which the degree of institutionalization was observed to affect the extent of uniformity, maintenance, and resistance to change exhibited by subjects. Her study utilized the classic Sherif (1935) stimuli, asking subjects to evaluate the amount of apparent movement by a stationary light in a darkened room. Extent of institutionalization was manipulated by instructions given to the subjects. To create lower levels of institutionalization, the subject was told only that the other person (a confederate) was "another person"; to create intermediate levels, the subject was told that she and her coworker (the confederate) were both "members of an organization," but their positions were unspecified; and to create higher levels of institutionalization, the subject was told that she and her coworker were both participants in an organization, and the coworker (confederate) was given the title of "Light Operator." Zucker (1977: 728–729) reasoned:

> Settings can vary in the degree to which acts in them are institutionalized. By being embedded in broader contexts where acts are viewed as institutionalized, acts in specific situations come to be viewed as institutionalized. Indicating that a situation is structured like situations in an organization makes the actors assume that the actions required of them by others actors in that situation will be . . . more regularized and that the interaction will be more definitely patterned than if the situation were not embedded in an organizational context. Any act performed by the occupant of an office is seen as highly objectified and exterior. When an actor occupies an office, acts are seen as nonpersonal and as continuing over time, across different actors.

Note the extent to which Zucker's experiment is built on a cultural-cognitive conception of institutionalization. The only factor manipulated to account for the behaviors of subjects was their cognitive framing of the situation, including their own identity within it. No sanctions or other types of regulative controls or normative pressures were involved in producing the observed effects.

Zucker found that extent of institutionalization exhibited the expected effects: Subjects working in more institutionalized (organization-like) conditions were more likely to transmit the standards they had learned in an initial series of trials (with the confederate supplying the standard) to a new naive subject, maintain their standards over time (subjects were asked to return one week later to perform the same type of activity), and resist attempts to change their judgments (having adopted the confederate's standard in the initial period, subjects were exposed to a second confederate who attempted to alter the standard). Zucker shows that in ongoing social systems, transmission of beliefs and practices to new actors is a vital process underlying persistence. Further, more highly institutionalized practices, being more "objectified," are more easily transmitted than less institutionalized behavior (Tolbert and Zucker 1996).

Theorists taking a normative view emphasize the stabilizing influence of shared norms that are both internalized and imposed by others. For example, in his examination of "the reproduction of inertia" in a multinational corporation, Kilduff (1993) stresses the role of social networks, whose members draw "on shared normative frameworks, [and] continually monitor interpersonal behavior," and of accounts that provide "an interpretive and normative base" to support ongoing behavior. The ease of maintenance and transmission of institutional practices is affected by the extent to which new recruits share similar beliefs and interpretive frameworks of current personnel. The more different the new members are, the more effort must be expended to transmit existing beliefs and practices. In her study of law firms, Tolbert (1988) found that firms employing recruits from more heterogeneous training backgrounds were more likely to utilize special training programs, mentoring systems, more frequent evaluations, and other socialization mechanisms, than firms employing recruits primarily from the same law school.

Other theorists focus on the central role of the environment not only in fostering the acceptance of innovations (see below), but in supporting and sustaining changes once they have occurred. In a study of public school districts in California, Rowan (1982: 261) demonstrates that districts were more likely to adopt and retain innovations—new programs and personnel—when they were supported by "key members of the institutional environments of local systems"—specifically, by state and federal legislatures, state educational agencies, state-level professional associations, and teacher-training institutions. If support was lacking from one or more of these external constituencies, districts were less likely to adopt and more likely to drop the innovation when viewed over a 40-year period.

Regulatory theorists are more likely to stress conscious control efforts, involving interests, agency and power, and the deployment of sanctions. Actors employ power not just to create institutions, but also to preserve and maintain them over time (see DiMaggio 1988; Stinchcombe 1968). Neoinstitutional economists, including both transaction cost and agency theorists, emphasize how important it is to devise appropriate governance structures and develop incentives and controls suited to the situation (see Pratt and Zeckhauser 1985). However, if regulation is institutionalized, the rewarding and sanctioning take place within a framework of rules. Power is stabilized and legitimized—that is, "institutionalized"—by the development of rules.[4]

Some studies attend to the full range of forces supporting persistence: cultural-cognitive, normative, and regulative. In Miller's (1994) examination of a Pietist mission organization that has survived for almost two centuries, all of the institutional elements appear to be at work. The Basel Mission was founded in the early 19th century to educate missionaries and establish evangelical outposts in various parts of the world. Miller examined the records of this organization, focusing on the period from 1815 to 1915, to ascertain the basis for its longevity. He argues that participants were recruited from a relatively homogenous social base; given intensive socialization so that participants came to share similar beliefs and values; placed in a strong authority structure combining aspects of charismatic, traditional, and bureaucratic control elements together with formalized procedures of "mutual surveillance"; and encouraged to develop a sense of "specialness and separation" that insulated them from being corrupted by the secular world.

In their study of the evolution over a 35-year-period of a new industry devoted to the cochlear implant—a device to restore hearing to the deaf—Van de Ven and Garud (1994) analyze a series of events coded as creating variation (novel technical events), selection (rule-making events), and retention (rule-following events). The latter events, retention, are indicators of institutional persistence because they refer to an event that "was programmed or governed by existing institutional rules and routines" (Van de Ven and Garud 1994: 429).[5] Viewed over the period of study, their data show how novel technical events dominated during the developmental period from 1956 to 1983, rule-making and rule-following events grew in an oscillatory fashion during the middle period from 1983 to 1986, and then, by 1989, "no more institutional rule-making events occurred while rule-following events continued to occur" (430). They also describe how institutional rules operated to suppress innovation and to "constrain the flexibility of private firms to adapt to changing circumstances" as existing technologies were "locked in" to specific technological paths.

Institutional Diffusion

The diffusion of an institutional form across space or time has a triple significance in institutional analysis. First, extent of diffusion of a set of rules or structural forms is often taken as an indicator of the growing strength of an institutional structure. In this sense, studies of institutional diffusion may be regarded as studies of increasing institutionalization. Second, because the diffusing elements are being adopted by and incorporated into organizations, studies of diffusion are also properly treated as studies of institutional effects. In such studies, early or later adoption is often argued to follow different principles because of the changing strength of the institutions and also because of the varying characteristics of the adopting organizations. Studies of factors affecting the adoption behavior of individual organizations are discussed in chapter 7. Third, the spread of a new form or practice is also an instance of institutional change—but change of a particular kind. It is *convergent change:* change that reinforces and diffuses existing patterns (see Greenwood and Hinings 1996). Most institutional theory and research emphasizes these convergent processes. Only recently has attention turned to disruptive and divergent change, a topic I consider in chapter 7.

Several distinctions are helpful in understanding the various ways in which institutions are diffused. DiMaggio and Powell's (1983) useful typology focuses attention on three contrasting mechanisms—coercive, normative, and mimetic—that identify varying forces or motives for adopting new structures and behaviors. As noted in chapter 3, these mechanisms map well onto the three types of institutional pillars I identify. Other analysts, such as Brown (1981), distinguish between demand- and supply-side explanations of diffusion. Demand-side approaches focus attention on the characteristics or conditions of new adopters, whereas supply-side approaches focus on the nature and efforts of agents attempting to spread the innovation. For many types of diffusion processes, it is more useful to examine the attributes or behavior of the diffusion agent or the "propagator" than those of the target or recipient units.

Early research tended to view diffusion as a rather mechanical process: the movement of technologies, models, and ideas from one place to another. Attention to the intermediary role of carriers, with the recognition that the mode of transmission affects the message transmitted, has helped to correct this problem (see chap. 4 and the following section). As noted in our earlier discussion, information is modified, edited, and translated in transmission by the carrier (Czarniawska and Joerges 1996; Sahlin-Andersson 1996). Even more important, there is increasing recognition that the end-user also alters the innovation, sometimes in small and other times in major ways. Institutional effects are not one-sided and determinant, but multifaceted and related to a nonergodic world (precise predictions assume constant states, whereas social contexts are constantly changing) (North 2005). As Latour (1986: 267) concludes:

> The spread in time and space of anything—claims, orders, artifacts, goods—is in the hands of people; each of these people may act in many different ways, letting the token drop, or modifying it, or deflecting it, or betraying it, or adding to it, or appropriating it.

These ideas are employed to frame a brief review of selected diffusion studies.

Regulative Processes

To be effective, the use of coercion requires relatively clear demands, effective surveillance, and significant sanctions. Beyond this, it also matters whether the mechanisms employed are primarily those of power, involving imposition of authority—where the coercive agent is viewed as a legitimate agent of control—or rely on the use of inducements (Scott 1987). We would expect institutional effects—the depth or shallowness of institutionalization—to vary by these mechanisms, higher penetration being associated with authority. Numerous institutional forms are diffused by some combination of these mechanisms in the world of public and private organizations. Djelic (1998) describes variation among Germany, France, and Italy in their response after World War II to the U.S. efforts to export the American model of corporate enterprise. Mechanisms involved included coercion, inducement (the Marshall Plan), and mimicry.

Nation-states with statist or corporatist traditions are more likely to successfully employ coercive, regulative power in introducing innovations and reforms than pluralist or individualist systems (Hall and Soskice 2001a, 2001b; Jepperson and Meyer 1991). Private organizations routinely utilize their legitimate authority as well as carrots and sticks to introduce new forms and practices. Coercive mechanisms emphasize supply-side processes, directing attention to the characteristics of the diffusion agent, and to relational carriers, noting the alignment of interests between principal and agent, and the adequacy of information, inspection, and control systems.

Three empirical studies are described to illustrate the study of diffusion supported by regulatory authority. In their well-known study of the diffusion of civil service reforms, Tolbert and Zucker (1983) examine the diffusion of municipal civil service reform in the United States at the turn of the century, from 1885 to 1935. They contrast two types of diffusion process: the situation in which particular states adopted the reform and mandated that cities under their jurisdiction embrace it, and the situation in which a state allowed individual cities to choose whether to adopt the reform. States mandating the reform employed legal procedures and official sanctions to enforce compliance; the institutional arrangement was that of a hierarchically structured authority system. By contrast, cities in states lacking mandates were responding to a social movement—a decentralized model of reform relying on normative and cultural-cognitive influences (beliefs that it is the right or modern thing to do and an awareness that other cities were adopting the reform). Cities in states mandating the reform were much more likely to adopt civil service provisions than those in states lacking such mandates. They did so much earlier and more completely: Mandated reforms were adopted by 60% of the municipalities within a 10-year period (all did so within 37 years), whereas it took 50 years for nonmandated reforms to approach the 60% level (Tolbert and Zucker 1983: 28–29).

In her study of profound social change in Japan in the late 19th century, during the Meiji period, Westney (1987) provides a historical account of the conscious selection by Japanese officials of various Western models regarded as successful for organizing particular organizational fields, such as police systems and postal services. These models, or organizational archetypes, were then imposed on the relevant sectors, employed as a basis for restructuring existing organizational arrangements. The diffusion of these models exhibited differing patterns, affected by the variable authority of the propagating officials, the presence of compatible preexisting cognitive models supplied by indigenous organizations (e.g., the army for the police), and the availability of a supportive organizational infrastructure in the immediate environment. Westney emphasizes that, although the original intent of the reformers had been to simply imitate and import successful practices from other societies, much inventiveness was required to fit these models into their new circumstances.

Cole (1989) examined differences among firms in Japan, Sweden, and the United States in the adoption and retention of innovative small-group activities, such as quality circles. His analysis emphasizes the role played by varying national infrastructures—governmental agencies, trade associations, and union organizations—in legitimating, informing, and supporting the innovations. Japan more than Sweden and Sweden more than the United States possessed such supportive structures, with the result that the innovations spread more widely and were more stable in the former than the latter societies. Although these three countries varied in the relative strength of regulatory statist authority, Cole's analysis also points to important differences in the extent to which trade associations and unions were mobilized to provide normative support for these innovations.

Normative Processes

Analysts focusing on normative processes stress the importance of network ties and commitments—relational structures as carriers. Many of the studies emphasizing normative processes focus on professional or collegial networks, interlocking directorates (individuals who serve on multiple director boards), or the support provided by informal ties.

Recent neoinstitutionalist scholars argue that regulatory activities thought to embody coercive pressures often depend more on normative and cognitive elements. Examining the effects of governmental influence in the United States on employers, Dobbin and Sutton (1998: 443) call attention to the "strength of a weak state" because the state's inability to craft clear unambiguous legislation on employment gives rise to processes by which managers "recast policy-induced structures in the mold of efficiency." The state's role in eliciting change is overshadowed and augmented by managers' interests in collectively crafting a normative justification that creates a market rationale for their conformity. In a related discussion, Edelman, Uggen, and Erlanger (1999: 407) suggest that it is not accurate to view legal actions by the state, such as the U.S. regulation of employment practices, as operating independently and from "on high." Rather, when law is contested, "organizations actively participate in the meaning of compliance" in ways that "renders law endogenous: the content and meaning of law is determined within the social field that it was designed to regulate." The meaning of laws "mandating" equal opportunity or affirmative action were negotiated and socially constructed by the actions and reactions of personnel managers, legislators, and the judiciary. The diffusion of new forms and procedures was more responsive to the spread of norms carried by professional networks (e.g., a firm's membership in personnel associations) than to changes in regulatory policies (e.g., the weakening of regulatory enforcement during the Reagan years had little effect on diffusion).

Often there is competition among those who promulgate normative models. For example, as discussed in chapter 5, DiMaggio (1991) described the contests occurring among professional camps holding competing visions for developing art museums during the early 20th century in the United States. Following Bourdieu, DiMaggio and Powell (1991: 70) view professionalization as "the collective struggle of members of an occupation to define the conditions and methods of their work." Research by Lounsbury, Ventresca, and Hirsch (2003), described in chapter 8, provides an apt example.

Normative standards may be explicitly established by self-appointed arbiters employing more or less representative bodies and deliberative procedures. Professional and trade associations present clear modern instances of such groups and processes. For example, after considerable struggle and compromise extending over many years, various medical associations joined forces with a managerial association, the American Hospital Association, to form the Joint Commission on Accreditation of Healthcare Organizations. Whereas licensure is a governmental, regulatory process, accreditation is a "nongovernmental, professional-sponsored process"—a normative process aimed at promulgating high standards for the industry (Somers 1969: 101). Although accreditation is not legally mandated, in professionally dominated arenas such as health care, organizations lacking accreditation are suspect and may not be eligible for reimbursement from certain funding sources. Empirical studies show that organizations such as hospitals, for example, accredited by appropriate professional bodies were considerably more likely to survive than those lacking such normative support (see Ruef and Scott 1998).

Greenwood, Suddaby, and Hinings (2002) describe negotiations and debates within the professional association of Canadian accountants as they worked to theorize and institute new models of governance for accounting firms. In other cases, the norms governing organizations may arise more incrementally and informally. Westphal and Zajac (1994) examine the emergence in business circles, during the period from 1970 to 1990, of an informal norm that the compensation of chief executive officers (CEOs) should be linked to the financial performance of their companies. Although based on theoretical arguments by economists and supported by some empirical data showing effects of such incentive plans on short-term stock prices, the argument took on moral weight as more and more boards of Fortune 500 companies adopted them. Corporate boards not taking such actions were regarded as negligent in their protection of stockholders' interests. The practice spread rapidly among companies, and those adopting the new model were rewarded by the stock market.

Most empirical work focuses on factors affecting the diffusion of a successful normative model, with much less attention given to proposed models that fail to catch on. Representative empirical studies of institutional diffusion of organizational forms and practices, perhaps the most widely studied aspect of institutional processes, are discussed in chapter 8.

Cultural-Cognitive Processes

Following Berger and Luckmann, Strang and Meyer (1993) stress the centrality of cultural-cognitive elements in institutional diffusion processes. They argue that diffusion is greatly affected by various theorization processes. For diffusion to occur, the actors involved need to regard themselves as similar in some important respect (the creation of categories such as the generic "organization" or particular subtypes such as "hospitals" facilitates this process). Theorization also provides causal accounts, explanations for why some kinds of actors need to add specific components or practices. As discussed earlier in this chapter, theorization contributes to "objectification" (Tolbert and Zucker 1996).

Organizational ecologists have embraced the cultural-cognitive conception of institutions by recognizing that the density of organizations exhibiting a given organizational form—the simple number of organizations of a given type—can be interpreted as a measure of the legitimacy of that form: the extent to which it is institutionalized. For some years, ecologists documented the importance of "density dependence," observing that the number of organizations of a given type was positively correlated with the founding of additional organizations of the same type. Research on numerous, diverse populations of organizations revealed that as a new form emerged, numbers increased slowly at first, then more rapidly, finally tailing off or declining (for a review of these studies, see Baum 1996; Hannan and Freeman 1989). Carroll and Hannan (1989: 525–526) were the first to provide a theoretical interpretation of this empirical finding, arguing that organizational density serves as an indicator of the cognitive status of the form: its cognitive legitimacy. They propose that

> an organizational form is legitimate to the extent that relevant actors regard it as the "natural" way to organize for some purpose. From this perspective, rarity of a form poses serious problems of legitimacy. When few instances of a form exist, it can hardly be the "natural" way to achieve some collective end. On the other hand, once a form becomes prevalent, further proliferation is unlikely to have much effect on its taken-for-grantedness. Legitimacy thus grows monotonically with density but at a decreasing rate.

However, as the numbers continue to increase in a given environment, legitimation processes give way to competitive processes—the dampening of new foundings and the consolidation of existing forms—so that the density curve levels out or declines over time.

This interpretation of density as connoting legitimacy has proved to be controversial. Zucker (1989) argues that Carroll and Hannan provide no direct measure of legitimacy, simply assuming the connection between prevalence and legitimacy (see also Baum and Powell 1995). Baum and Oliver (1992) suggest that prevalence may be only a proxy for other, related effects such as embeddedness. Their study of day-care centers in Toronto found that when measures of the latter, such as the number of relations between centers and governmental institutions, are included, then density effects disappeared. Carrol and Hannan (1989; Hannan et al. 1995) responded by noting the widespread use of indirect indicators in the sciences, the support for the association between prevalence and legitimacy provided by historical accounts related to the early experience of the populations studied, and the advantage offered by its generality—its applicability to any type of population.

Many other institutional scholars have studied the diffusion of ideologies or belief systems, forms or archetypes (conceptions as to how to organize), and processes or procedures. Nothing is as portable as ideas. They travel primarily by symbolic carriers, although they also are conveyed by relations and artifacts. They may circulate via specific social networks, but they also ride on more generalized media.

Mauro Guillén (1994) carried out detailed historical analyses comparing the diffusion of managerial ideologies in the first half of the 20th century in the United States, Germany, Great Britain, and Spain. He differentiated between management theory, transmitted among intellectuals and indexed by the flow of books, articles, and professional discourse, and management practice, the use of techniques by practitioners as indicated by surveys and case studies. Scientific management, one of the early major managerial ideologies, was discovered to be more highly diffused among practitioners than intellectuals and to have penetrated the United States and Germany much earlier than Great Britain and Spain. Guillén argued that differences among the four societies in international pressure, labor unrest, state involvement, and professional groups, among other factors, help to account for the differences in diffusion patterns observed.

Shocked out of their complacency by the fierce competition provided by Japanese automobile and electronics manufacturers in the mid-1970s, American firms began to explore and experiment with a range of practices that came to be labeled "total quality management" (TQM) (see Cole and Scott 2000). As described by Cole (1999), American businessmen were not quick to respond, unsure of the nature of the challenge they faced or what to do about it. A period of sense-making ensued as communities of actors crafted and sifted interpretations (see Weick 1995, 2000). Although expert gurus offered insights, consulting companies proffered advice, professional associations (such as the American Society for Quality) offered normative justification, and award programs (e.g., the Baldrige National Quality Award) offered prestige and financial incentives, little consensus developed regarding the core ingredients of TQM. The movement was not sufficiently theorized or supported by adequate normative and regulative structures to diffuse widely or to have deep effects in this country (see Cole's [1989] comparative research, described earlier in this chapter). Some practices, such as quality circles, were widely discussed, but tended to receive more lip service than use. Companies felt the need to change, but the directions and recipes offered did not provide clear guidelines. Perhaps the most important change associated with TQM was in the cognitive framing of quality, shifting attention from the concerns of internal engineers to external customers and from a "detect-and-repair" to a "prevent-and-improve" mentality. Although the quality fad seems to have run its course, it provided the basis for some useful organizational learning (see Cole 1999). All attempts at institutional diffusion do not succeed.

❖ CARRIERS AND INSTITUTIONAL MECHANISMS[6]

Four types of carriers were identified in chapter 4: symbolic systems, relational systems, routines, and artifacts. As I have emphasized, type of carrier affects the message being carried and in multiple ways.

Symbolic Systems

Attention to symbolic systems as carriers of institutional rules and beliefs emphasizes the important role played by such mechanisms as interpretation, theorization, framing, and bricolage—"mechanisms that operate through alterations of individual and collective perception" (McAdam, Tarrow, and Tilly 2001: 26). For ideas to move from place to place and time to time through the use of symbols, they must be encoded into some type of script that is then decoded by recipients who are necessarily embedded in different situations and possessed of differing agendas. As discussed in chapter 5, Strang and Meyer (1993: 103) employ the concept "theorization" to refer to this coding process. Theorization applies both to actors, because diffusion occurs more readily when "the actors involved are perceived as similar (by themselves, and others, and within social institutions more generally" (103), and to the diffusing practices themselves, as practices are abstracted, codified, and converted into models.

> Under these conditions, we suppose that what flows is rarely an exact copy of some practice existing elsewhere. When theorists are the carriers of the practice or theorization itself is the diffusion mechanism, it is the theoretical model that is likely to flow. Such

models are neither complete nor unbiased depictions of existing practices. Instead, theoretical models systematically capture some of the features of existing practices and not others, or even fundamentally revise the practices altogether. (Strang and Meyer 1993: 495)

A general problem encountered in focusing exclusively on isolated symbolic materials is that to do so disembeds them from their social context. As Brown and Duguid (2000: 31) note: "This makes [the information] blind to other forces at work in society." Thus, for example, although the appearance of newspapers makes it appear to be a simple record of what happened on a given day,

news is not some naturally occurring object that journalists pick up and stick on a paper. It is made and shaped by journalists in the context of the medium and the audience. . . .

The newspaper, then is rather like the library—not simply a collection of news, but a selection and a reflection. And the selection process doesn't just "gather news," but weaves and shapes, developing stories in accordance with available space and priorities. (Brown and Duguid 2000: 185–186)

Brown and Duguid point out that the older usage of the word *media* was employed to refer not only to the information, but also the associated technology and social institutions. Yet in today's digital world, any reference to media does not typically conjure up the background role of social institutions. Inattention to social context is not just a problem on the input side, where symbolic information is created, but also on output side, where it is translated and applied. In her study of the implementation of Western models in Meiji, Japan, discussed above, Westney (1987: 25) points out that departures from models occurred in part because the models needed to be adapted to "a different societal scale" and also because social organizations and institutional frameworks were missing in Japan that were present providing essential support in the West.

Students of social movements and institutions have recently stressed the important role played by the "framing" of information or issues. Adapting Goffman's (1974) original concept, Snow and colleagues (Snow and Benford 1992; Snow et al. 1986) emphasize the ways in which meaning is mediated by the use of varying cognitive frames. Campbell (2005: 48–49) usefully defines *frames* as "metaphors, symbols, and cognitive cues that cast issues in a particular light and suggest possible ways to respond to these issues." Frames are employed by disseminators to distill and sharpen messages and by recipients to capture and interpret them so that a critical component of successful transmission involves processes of frame alignment (Snow et al. 1986).

Bricolage involves the creative combination of symbolic and structural elements garnered from varying sources and traditions (Douglas 1986; Levi-Strauss 1966). Actors may arrive with ideas and templates derived from their previous experience, but when applying them to new situations often join them with local structures and ideas to form new hybrid combinations. Stark (1996: 1014) provides a graphic description of this process as East European capitalists struggled to craft new types of enterprise after the collapse of the socialist framework. He found that rather than completely discarding all aspects of the former enterprises, Hungarian businesspeople mixed and matched selected elements from the socialist and capitalist repertoires of structures and routines, constructing hybrid public-private organizations. Unclear as to which models to follow, they employed "organizational hedging that crosses and combines disparate evaluative principles." Crafting new combinations of symbolic and structural elements, Hungarian agents were engaged in "rebuilding organizations and institutions not *on the ruins* but *with the ruins* of communism as they redeploy available resources in response to their immediate practical dilemmas" (Stark 1996: 995; italics original).[7]

Relational Systems

Connections or linkages characterize all manner of things, from words and sentences in paragraphs, to pages on the World Wide Web, to the food chain. Here we emphasize social connections among individuals, groups, and organizations and the ways in which these channels carry institutional materials. Strang and Meyer (1993: 489) distinguish between relational and symbolic carriers of institutions. They point out that designs emphasizing relational carriers are based on social realist models, which assume that social actors are relatively independent entities who must be connected by specific networks or communication links if diffusion is to occur. By contrast, if symbolic carriers are privileged, "diffusion processes often look more like complex exercises in the social construction of identity than like the mechanistic spread of information."

In recent years, researchers interested in the diffusion of institutional ideas and forms have made extensive use of network measures and methods in examining these flows. Measures, including distance, centrality, clustering, density, structural equivalence, and centralization, have been employed to examine their effects on the rate of flow or type of information disseminated.[8]

For example, researchers have pointed out that similar or closely related ideas are likely to flow between friends and close associates. "Particularly when organized by homophily, strong ties lead actors to take the perspective of the other and to exert powerful pressures for conformity" (Strang and Soule 1998: 272). By contrast, following research by Granovetter (1973) and others, contacts with individuals or organizations differing from oneself—"weak" ties—are associated with the transmission of new or different ideas so that, as noted in chapter 5, institutional agents introducing innovations are likely to be situated in networks that cross conventional boundaries.

A multitude of studies on interlocking directorates in corporations—organizations that share board members—suggests that such connections are most likely to function as "weak" ties, providing organizations with information regarding the ways in which other organizations are dealing with one or another problem. Differing kinds of information travel through different networks. For example, a study by Davis and Greve (1997) compared the diffusion patterns of two recent governance innovations, "golden parachutes" and "poison pills," adopted by many U.S. corporations in response to the takeover waves of the 1980s.[9] Parachutes, perceived to principally advantage incumbent executives of takeover targets, were found to diffuse among Fortune 500 firms slowly during the 1980–1989 period. Their adoption was primarily related to geographic proximity: "firms adopted to the extent that other firms in the same metropolitan area had done so" (29). By contrast, pills, perceived as protecting the integrity of the firm against hostile takeover attempts, diffused rapidly after its introduction in 1985, its spread being strongly related to the pattern of board interlocks among firms. Thus, the spread of parachutes was associated with firm ties to local (regional) companies, whereas the spread of pills was associated with links to national elite networks. More important, Davis and Greve (1997: 33) propose that the two innovations were associated with different carriers and exhibited different diffusion patterns because they involved different institutional elements. Pills acquired "substantial normative legitimation in the eyes of the directors adopting them" and diffused via formally constituted national networks, whereas the spread of parachutes was based more on their cognitive legitimacy—the information available locally to managers that others occupying the same role had secured such protections.

There often exist gaps or structural holes in networks—locations between groups or organizations that are not occupied. Such conditions provide important opportunities for actors who can seize the chance to link together two or more previously unconnected social sites (Burt 1992). As McAdam, Tarrow, and Tilly (2001: 26) point out, brokerage is an important relational mechanism for relating groups and individuals in stable sites; alternatively, mobilization can be employed during periods of unrest to bring together previously disconnected parties.

A largely neglected topic playing a central role in relational carriers is the existence and increasing importance to a wide variety of *intermediary roles*—roles defined almost entirely by the activities they perform in carrying information among central players in organizational fields. Ranging from consultants to librarians to technicians, the existence of these and other information intermediaries is vital to the functioning of any complex field (see Sahlin-Andersson and Engwall 2002). For example, McDonough, Ventresca, and Outcalt (2000: 378) examined the role played by high school counselors, private counselors, and college admissions officers in mediating the selection and flow of students in the field of higher education. By focusing on contrasting interests and roles and on conflicts over values and meanings, they attempt to speed "the shift away from more disembodied social processes to situated social practices, [which] directs our attention to *how* activities take shape, the mechanisms by which forms emerge, acquire stability, and experience challenges to that stability."

Routines

Much contemporary institutional theory privileges symbols and beliefs over behavior. Indeed, scholars such as John Meyer assume that institutionalization frequently involves changes in rules and formal structures that have little effect on—are decoupled from—participant actions (Drori, Meyer, and Hwang 2006; Meyer and Rowan 1977). However, early students of organizations, often engineers such as Taylor (1911), paid close attention to workers' actions, believing these to be the core processes of organizations. As noted in chapter 4, this emphasis was revived and renewed by March and Simon (1958), in their attention to performance programs, and by Nelson and Winter (1982), who view routines as comparable to genes in preserving the distinctive competence of the organization.

Structuration theorists attempt to reconnect structure and behavior, ideas and actions by theorizing their mutuality and interdependence. Feldman and Pentland (2003: 101–102) applied these arguments to routines, suggesting that routines incorporate an ideal or schematic ("ostensive") aspect and a "performance" aspect—"the specific actions taken by specific people at specific times when they are engaged in an organizational routine." Thus, routines involve both a generalized idea and a particular enactment. In this manner, they propose to reintroduce ideas, but also agency back into the concept of routines. To carry out a routine is not simply to "reenact" the past, but to engage with and adapt to the context in ways that require "either idiosyncratic or ongoing changes and reflecting on the meaning of actions for future realities" (Feldman and Pentland 2003: 95).

As discussed in chapter 4, routines are indispensable in carrying information residing in the tacit knowledge of actors. Such information travels by direct contact among actors occupying similar roles and engaged in closely related activities. We have already described the importance of on-the-job training for many types of work. The concept of "communities of practice" (Brown and Duguid 1991) helps to extend such learning opportunities beyond the confines of a single organization. A good part of the power and attraction of network forms of organization are the opportunities they afford organizations and their participants to acquire the "sticky" knowledge embedded in the routines of other organizations—offset with the concern that there may be a "leakage" of their own proprietary knowledge to alliance partners or subsidiaries (see Oxley 1999).

Artifacts

As noted in chapter 4, although artifacts—tools, equipment, and technology—appear as hard and unyielding, like routines they lend themselves to a structuration perspective. As Orlikowski (1992) detailed, artifacts in use are adapted and modified by their users. Barley (1986) notes that technologies are not determinant, but rather their introduction provides an "occasion" for structuration. Previously discussed mechanisms such as interpretation, bricolage, and translation can be applied to artifacts as well as other types of carriers.

Artifacts, like resources, contain important material aspects, but their meaning and use can vary over time and space. As Sewell (1992: 19) argues, they "embody cultural schemas" whose meanings, like those of "texts or ritual performances . . . is never entirely unambiguous."

❖ CONCLUDING COMMENT

Because institutions are comprised of multiple elements, they spread through differing mechanisms. Regulatory institutions advance largely because they provide increasing returns to those who manage them. Normative institutions flourish on the basis of increasing shared commitments among the parties involved. Cultural-cognitive institutions depend, for their power and influence, on widening the circle of those who accept their claims as valid and self-evident.

How institutions persist, once created, is an understudied phenomenon. Our current understanding of social structures is that their persistence is not to be taken for granted. It requires continuing effort—both to "talk the talk" and to "walk the walk"—if structures are not to erode and dissolve. The ecological explanation for persistence, "inertia," seems on reflection to be too passive and unproblematic to be an accurate aid to guide studies of this topic.

By contrast, the diffusion of institutional forms over time and space has attracted considerable research attention across diverse scientific communities. Diffusion is of interest to the more theoretically oriented as a palpable indicator of increasing institutional strength; to those of a more practical bent and in a culture emphasizing modernity, such changes are viewed as a sign of progress and receptivity to innovation. Most studies of diffusion embrace a demand-side perspective, focusing attention on the characteristics of adopting organizations. However, a supply-side approach, focusing on the nature of the dissemination agents, appears as useful, if not more useful, in examining instances of contemporary institutional diffusion.

Diffusion, of necessity, highlights the role of institutional carriers who, depending on the type of message and the type of messenger utilizing mechanisms varying from theorization, framing, bricolage, brokerage, and mobilization, affect the meaning of the messages transmitted. Institutions are modified in transmission.

❖ NOTES

1. "Unusual" features referred, in particular, to the persistence of technical systems that, by objective tests, were demonstrably inferior to available alternatives. The canonical example is the continuing dominance of the QWERTY keyboard of the typewriter (and the word processor) (David 1985).

2. Note that their model resembles that developed by Suchman (1995a), as discussed in chapter 5 (see fig. 5.1).

3. A related, empirical study of the adoption by Canadian law firms of a new organizational template employs the concept of "sedimentation" somewhat differently to refer to situations in which an existing template is not replaced by the new, but rather layered on the old, providing a different, hybrid structure (Cooper et al. 1996).

4. Some have suggested that the new version of the "golden rule" is he or she who holds the gold makes the rules (Pfeffer 1992: 83). Still rules can operate to constrain the arbitrary exercise of power (see Dornbusch and Scott 1975).

5. This is not meant to imply that institutional processes are only relevant to the retention phase. They also play a significant role in the variation phase (e.g., affecting the cognitive frames determining which models are devised) as well as the selection phase (where concerns for legitimacy often determine which models survive).

6. This sections draws on materials first published in Scott (2003a).

7. For a helpful discussion of these related mechanisms, see Campbell (2004: chap. 3).

8. For a summary of definitions and measures employed in network studies, see Scott and Davis (2007: chap. 11) and Smith-Doerr and Powell (2005).

9. "Golden parachutes" provide severance benefits to top executives unemployed after a successful takeover. "Poison pills" give shareholders the right to buy shares at a two-for-one rate in the event of a hostile takeover attempt (Davis and Greve 1997: 10).

7

Institutional Processes
and Organizations

Most research on institutional processes by organizational scholars has focused on their effects on individual organizations. In this chapter, I review representative arguments and associated evidence. Earlier studies emphasized the effects of institutional context on all organizations within the relevant environment. The institutional environment was viewed as unitary and imposing structures or practices on individual organizations that were obliged to conform either because it was taken for granted that this was the proper way to organize, because to do so would result in normative approbation, or because it was required by legal or other rule-like frameworks. Later studies began to examine differences among organizations, recognizing that whether, when, and how organizations responded depended on their individual characteristics or connections. Recent theorists and researchers have stressed the varied nature of organizational responses to institutional demands. In some situations, individual organizations respond strategically, either by decoupling their structures from their operations or by seeking to defend themselves in some manner from the pressures experienced. In others, the demands are negotiated as organizations collectively attempt to shape institutional requirements and redefine environments. I review examples of studies that address these issues.

❖ ORGANIZATIONS AND INSTITUTIONS: THREE VIEWS

Three views are encountered in current writings about the relation between organizations and institutions. The first, most clearly developed by Douglas North (1990: 4–5) and embraced by many institutional economists, is based on a game analogy: Institutions provide the rules of the game, whereas organizations act as the players. Organizations may well assist in constructing the rules, attempting to devise rules favorable to themselves, and they often attempt to change the rules by political and other means. However, a consideration of rules and rule-setting and enforcement processes is to be clearly distinguished from concern with the playing teams and their structures and strategies. In his own work, North has attended primarily to the processes involved in constructing institutional rule systems.

Occupying a somewhat intermediate position, theorists such as Oliver Williamson (1975, 1985) view organizations, and their structures and procedures, as institutions: systems designed to exercise governance over production systems and minimize transaction costs. As noted, Williamson (1994) emphasizes the regulative aspects of institutions. However, rather than focusing attention on the "background conditions" involving property rights, contract law, and the like, he attends to the impact of these rules on the organization of economic activities at the level of individual economic enterprises. Designers of organizations construct institutional forms–governance structures—to more effectively manage economic transactions. In a parallel manner, but emphasizing normative forces as described in chapter 6, Selznick (1957) examines the ways in which individual organizations devise distinctive character structures over time, developing commitments that channel and constrain future behavior in the service of their basic values. For scholars such as Williamson and Selznick, organizations are relatively unique institutions that are either designed by or evolve out of the choices made by organizational agents.

Sociologists including Meyer, Zucker, and Dobbin act to elide the distinction between organizations and their institutional environments by stressing the strong connection between processes occurring at societal (and even transnational) levels and the structure and operation of individual organizations. Focusing on the cultural-cognitive aspects of institutions, organizational sociologists emphasize the extent to which the modern organization is an institutionalized form—in Zucker's (1983: 1) phrase, "the preeminent institutional form in modern society." Unlike economists, who view organizational systems as reflecting natural economic laws (primarily based initially on the British and subsequently on the American experience), these sociologists insist that "rationalized organizational practices are essentially cultural, and are very much at the core of modern culture precisely because modern culture is organized around instrumental rationality" (Dobbin, 1994a: 118). Not only is our overall conception of an instrumental organization based on a cultural model, but many of the components comprising any given organization are not locally designed to produce efficiency in a specific context, but taken "off the shelf" of available patterns. As Meyer and Rowan (1977: 345) point out:

> The growth of rationalized institutional structures in society makes formal organizations more common and more elaborate. Such institutions are myths which make formal organizations both easier to create and more necessary. After all, the building blocks for organizations come to be littered around the societal landscape; it takes only a little entrepreneurial energy to assemble them into a structure.

Again we see the wide range of assumptions and arguments guiding contemporary institutional studies.

❖ LEGITIMACY AND ISOMORPHISM

The general concept of legitimacy is defined and discussed in chapter 3. Weber was among the first social theorists to call attention to the central importance of legitimacy in social life. In his theoretical and historical work, he gave particular attention to those forms of action that were guided by a belief in the existence of a legitimate order, a set of "determinable maxims" providing models viewed by the actor as "in some way obligatory or exemplary for him" (Weber [1924] 1968: 31). In his analysis of administrative systems, both public and private, Weber examined the changing sources of legitimation as traditional values or a belief in the charismatic nature of the leader increasingly gave way to a reliance on rational/legal underpinnings. Organizations were regarded as legitimate to the extent that they were in conformity to rational (e.g., scientific) prescriptions and legal or law-like frameworks.

Parsons (1960a) applied the concept of legitimacy to the assessment of organizational goals. As specialized subsystems of larger societal structures, organizations are under normative pressure to ensure that their goals are congruent with wider societal values, as described in chapter 2. The focus of the organization's value system "must be the legitimation of this goal in terms of the functional significance of its attainment for the superordinate system" (Parsons 1960a: 21). This conception of legitimacy, emphasizing the consistency of organizational goals with societal functions, was later embraced by Pfeffer and colleagues (Dowling and Pfeffer 1975; Pfeffer and Salancik 1978).

Meyer and Rowan (1977) shifted the focus from organizational goals to the structural and procedural aspects of organizations. The structural vocabulary of modern organizations—their emphasis on formality, offices, specialized functions, rules, records, and routines— was seen to be guided by and reflect prescriptions conveyed by wider rationalized institutional environments. These structures signal rationality irrespective of their effects on outcomes. The master proposition they advanced was that "Independent of their productive efficiency, organizations which exist in highly elaborated institutional environments and succeed in becoming isomorphic with these environments gain the legitimacy and resources needed to survive" (Meyer and Rowan 1977: 352).

The principle of isomorphism was first applied to organizations by human ecologist Amos Hawley (1968), who argued that "Units subjected to the same environmental conditions . . . acquire a similar form of organizations" (see also Hawley 1950). However, ecologists proposed that isomorphism resulted from competitive processes because organizations were pressured to assume the form best adapted to survival in a particular environment (see Hannan and Freeman 1989), whereas neoinstitutionalists emphasized the importance of "social fitness": the acquisition of a form regarded as legitimate in a given institutional environment. DiMaggio and Powell (1983: 147) reinforced this emphasis on institutional isomorphism, focusing attention on coercive, normative, and mimetic mechanisms that "make organizations more similar without necessarily making them more efficient." More so than Meyer and Rowan, DiMaggio and Powell recognized that the models developed and the mechanisms inducing isomorphism among structural features operate most strongly within delimited organizational fields, rather than at more diffuse, societal levels (see chap. 8).

These arguments help to account for two notable features of all contemporary organizations. First, there exists a remarkable similarity in the structural features of organizational forms operating within the same organizational field. One university tends to resemble closely another university, and one hospital is much like other hospitals. The recognition that organizations must not only be viable in terms of whatever competitive processes are at work, but must also exhibit structural features that make them both recognizable and in conformity with normative and regulative requirements, goes a long way to explaining observed similarities among organizations in the same arena. Second, students of organizations at least since Barnard (1938) have long observed the presence of formal and informal structures, the former reflecting officially sanctioned offices and ways of conducting business, the latter actual patterns of behavior and work routines. An uneasy tension exists between these structures. What was not clear until the work of the neoinstitutionalists is why such tensions exist, but, more fundamentally, if they are disconnected from the work being performed, why do the formal structures exist at all? By positing an environment consisting not only of production pressures and technical demands, but also of regulative, normative, and cultural-cognitive elements, the relatively independent sources of informal versus formal structures are revealed.

Hence, there are good theoretical reasons for attending to isomorphism among organizational models and formal structures, and in the following sections I review additional research examining isomorphic pressures. However, to treat the existence of structural isomorphism as the litmus test for detecting institutional processes oversimplifies the complexity and subtlety of social systems. Varying, competing institutions and multiple institutional elements are often at work. Although they constitute new forms, they also interact with a variety of previously existing forms with varying characteristics and in differing locations. Conformity is one response to isomorphic pressures, but not the only one, because institutional processes are themselves conflicted or because they combine with other forces to shape structure and action.

Varying Elements and Mechanisms

The meaning of legitimacy and the mechanisms associated with its transmission vary somewhat with the three institutional elements, as previewed in chapter 3. General effects of institutional processes on organizational structures are readily apparent, but often overlooked. They become most visible when a longer time period is considered. A clear instance of the effects of regulatory forces—combined with cultural-cognitive constitutive processes—on for-profit organizations is represented by the structuring influence of incorporation statutes. These social arrangements, allowing for the pooling of capital from many sources along with limitations on liability for those who managed these assets, were created early in the 18th century in England, but the misadventures of the South Sea Company set back the acceptance of these forms until the mid-1800s (Micklethwait and Wooldridge 2003: chap. 2). In its early development, the corporate form was restricted to enterprises pursuing broadly public purposes, such as turnpikes and canals, but gradually it was appropriated for use by private firms, as detailed by social historians Seavoy (1982) and Roy (1997). Individually crafted charters granted by state legislatures were replaced by statutes providing a legal template for incorporation available to a wide range of organizations. These legal (and cultural) changes were associated with the rapid expansion of business enterprise in England and the United States during the second half of the 19th century, fueled in good part in America by competition among the several states to pass legislation favorable to businesses wishing to incorporate.

The effect on organizational structure of normative influences is illustrated by the distinctive features of the American community hospital. During the late 19th and early 20th centuries, American physicians consolidated their social and cultural authority, upgraded their training systems, and exercised increasingly strong jurisdictional controls over the medical domain (Starr 1982). Although they became increasingly dependent on hospitals, which provided the technical equipment, laboratory facilities, and nursing services required for effective acute care, physicians were able to remain independent of administrative controls, organizing themselves into an autonomous medical staff to oversee clinical activities. This "dual" control structure—one administrative, the other professional-collegial—provided the organizing principle for community hospitals throughout the 20th century (White 1982). Only during the most recent decades have managerial interests begun to exert more direct controls over rank-and-file physicians in hospitals (see Scott et al. 2000).

The power of shared cultural models as a basis for organizing is highlighted in Knorr-Cetina's (1999: 242–243) study of high-energy physics and molecular biology laboratories. She argues that, more so than most types of organizations, the structural blueprint for these knowledge societies is object- rather than person-centered. The work takes place in the context of shared scientific knowledge—"distributed cognition, which then also functions as a management mechanism: through this discourse, work becomes coordinated and self-organization is made possible." Moreover, legitimation of these organizations is based on the congruence between the theories and practices of these laboratories and the wider scientific community of which they are a part. Many of the distinctive features of professional organizations are possible because of the unobtrusive controls exercised by shared symbolic systems linking actors to the objects of their work based in understandings grounded in their invisible colleges.

We can supplement these more historical and process-oriented accounts with studies employing quantitative evidence. These studies provide evidence of the increasing variety and sophistication of indicators employed. With regard to studies emphasizing the cultural-cognitive pillar, as noted, some scholars infer legitimacy from the prevalence of an organizational form (Carroll and Hannan 1989), and others interpret the increasing diffusion of a form as an indication of increasing legitimacy (Tolbert and Zucker 1983). These indirect and somewhat controversial measures tap into the cultural-cognitive and, to some extent, the normative dimensions of legitimacy. However, more direct measures of cultural cognitive support have utilized a variety of archival materials to measure changes in meaning systems and legitimating ideologies. For example, in studies described in chapter 8, investigators have measured changes in legitimating "social logics" as assessed by changes in professional discourse or the media coverage (e.g., Rao, Monin, and Durand 2003; Scott et al. 2000). In an imaginative approach, Zuckerman (1999) assessed the "illegitimacy discount" imposed by stock analysts on those firms whose markets did not match conventional industry-based classifications.

Employing a more individual-level approach to legitimacy processes, Elsbach (1994: 58) conducted studies combining impression management and institutional theories to examine how organizational agents "use verbal accounts or explanations to avoid blame or gain credit for controversial events that affect organizational legitimacy." Managers of companies in the cattle industry in California were asked to respond to a number of controversial events occurring within the industry, and their responses were evaluated by informants representing influential groups (e.g., media, public officials). These qualitative studies provided the inputs for an experiment in which varying combinations of situations (vignettes) and company responses were reported to experimental subjects who then rated the legitimacy accorded to the organization. Acknowledgments of problems in contrast to denials, and references to widely institutionalized procedures, in contrast to technical measures, led to higher legitimacy scores.

Analysts emphasizing the normative pillar have stressed measures that assess certification and accreditation procedures utilized by professional associations (e.g., Casile and Davis-Blake 2002; Mezias 1995; Ruef and Scott 1998), opinions expressed by the public media (e.g., Hybels and Ryan 1996), and the endorsement of established community organizations such as schools and religious organizations (e.g., Baum and

Oliver 1992). Ventresca and Mohr (2002: 811) point out that the latter shift analysts' attention away from measures that "emphasize organizations as independent objects toward the measurement of relations among objects and the inherent connectivity of social organization."

Scholars favoring the regulative view of institution utilize measures that stress the extent to which organizations are under the jurisdiction of a given authority (e.g., Hannan and Freeman 1987; Tolbert and Zucker 1983), whether enforcement is vigorous or lax (Dobbin and Sutton 1998), and whether a specific organization has been approved by a licensing body or, conversely, has been subject to sanctions by an enforcement authority (e.g., Deephouse 1996; Singh, Tucker, and House 1986).

These and related studies demonstrate that it is possible to develop measures of legitimating processes in modern society, such that these institutional forces need not simply be asserted or assumed, but are subject to being assessed with empirical evidence.

Varying Sources and Salience

Who—which agencies or publics—have the "right" to confer legitimacy on organizations of a given type may not be a simple question in environments characterized by complexity or conflict. It is a truism of modern organization studies that organizations are highly differentiated, loosely coupled systems, in part, because they must relate to many different environments. Universities, for example, relate not only to educational accreditation agencies and professional disciplinary associations, but also to federal agencies overseeing research grants and contracts and student loans, to the National Collegiate Athletic Association for sports activities, to local planning and regulatory bodies for building and roads, among many other oversight bodies (see Stern 1979; Wiley and Zald 1968).

In his study of commercial banks operating in the Minneapolis–St. Paul metropolitan area, Deephouse (1996) examines the effects of two different sources of legitimation: state regulatory agencies that made onsite assessments of the safety and soundness of a bank's assets and metropolitan newspapers who reported information to the public about banking activities. Both sources were found to be positively associated with isomorphism in the asset strategies pursued by banks. Banks that experienced fewer enforcement actions from regulatory agencies and banks that received a higher proportion of positive reports in the public media were more likely to exhibit conformity to the industry average in their strategies for distributing assets across various categories of borrowers, such as commercial, real estate, and individual loans. This finding held up after the differences in their age, size, and performance (return on assets) were taken into account. Both of the legitimation sources were significantly associated with strategic isomorphism, although there was only a modest association of .34 between measures of regulatory assessment and public endorsement. This result suggests that legitimation sources vary in the attributes to which they attend in conferring legitimacy.

The salience of such legitimation agents can vary among organizational subunits or programs, and also over time. In our study of hospitals in the San Francisco Bay area, for example, Ruef and I (Ruef and Scott 1998) found that accreditation by an assortment of medical bodies, such as the American College of Surgeons, was independent of (and, in some cases, negatively associated with) accreditation by various managerial bodies, such as the American Hospital Association. Although the endorsement of both types of accreditation agencies was positively associated with hospital survival throughout the period 1945–1995, the strength of this relation was found to vary over time. During the period before 1980, when professional medical associations exercised greater influence in the field, medical association accreditations were more strongly associated with hospital survival than were managerial endorsements, whereas after 1980, managerial accreditations were a stronger predictor of survival than medical endorsements. We argue that market and managerial logics have become more prevalent in the health care field since 1980, challenging and, to some degree, supplanting the logics of the medical establishment. It appears that the influence of various regulatory and normative bodies varies depending on the institutional logics dominant within the wider institutional environments.

In summary, individual organizations exhibiting culturally approved forms and activities (including strategies), receiving support from normative authorities, and having approval from legal bodies are more likely to survive than organizations lacking these evaluations. Legitimacy exerts an influence on organizational viability independent of its performance or other attributes or connections.

In the following section, I review arguments and related research concerning the effects of the institutional context on organizational structures. In much of this work, the underlying rationale implied is that the effects are due to legitimacy processes. However, other causal processes may also be at work.

❖ INSTITUTIONAL CONTEXT AND
    ORGANIZATIONAL STRUCTURE

Imprinting

Stinchcombe (1965) was the first theorist to recognize the strong influences of social (including institutional) conditions present at the time of its founding on the structural forms of organization, but his focus was on organizational forms or populations, not on individual organizations (see chap. 5). However, his concept of imprinting has also been applied to the level of individual organizations accompanied by the same assumption: Imprinting processes are important because they tend to become institutionalized and persist over time. Kimberly (1975) evaluated the imprinting argument by studying a collection of 123 rehabilitation organizations (sheltered workshops) established in the New York region during the period from 1866 to 1966. During the latter part of this period, beliefs and norms supporting these workshops shifted from a commercial emphasis on the production of goods and services to a therapeutic one, emphasizing the psychological rehabilitation of the clients. Although only 18% of the workshops founded before 1946 were rehabilitation-oriented, 64% of those founded after that date exhibited this orientation. Moreover, the later in the period studied that a workshop was founded, the more likely it was that a rehabilitation orientation would be embraced. This study did not systematically assess changes in the normative and cultural-cognitive models and norms governing these organizations, yet it is clear that the more recently founded organizations differed substantially from earlier forms in their institutional logics and internal characteristics.

Boeker (1989) studied factors affecting the institutionalization of power differences present at the time of founding in a sample of 53 semiconductor companies. Boeker contrasts the impact of entrepreneurial and environmental effects present at the time of the firm's founding on current firm strategy. He found that the previous functional background of the entrepreneur influenced the selection of the firm's strategy, but also that this decision was independently influenced by the industry's stage of development at the time the firm was founded. Firm strategies were significantly impacted by industry stage in three of the four stages examined. For example, firms founded during the earliest era were more likely to embrace and continue to pursue first-mover strategies, whereas firms founded during the most recent period studied were more likely to develop and to pursue a niche strategy.

Cultural models of organizing precede the creation of organizations. Most organizational fields present not a single, but a (limited) number of organizational models or archetypes. Research by Baron, Hannan, and Burton (1999) assessed the types of models or blueprints governing employment practices present in the mind of the founding CEOs in a sample of startup firms engaged in computer hardware, software, and semiconductors in Silicon Valley. Examining the characteristics of these firms after their first few years of operation revealed that companies whose CEOs held a more bureaucratic conception of employment practices were more likely to exhibit higher managerial intensity (proportion of managers to full-time employees) than companies whose CEOs held a more egalitarian "commitment" models.

Environmental Complexity

Gradually, both theorists and researchers have come to realize that, although organizations confront and are shaped by institutions, these institutional systems are not necessarily unified or coherent. A variety of scholars have explored the effects on organizations of environmental complexity and inconsistency (see Brunsson 1989; Heimer 1999; Meyer and Scott 1983b; Zucker 1988a).

Several researchers have examined the effect of institutional complexity on organization structure. For example, Meyer and I proposed that organizations confronting more complex, fragmented environments—such as multiple authorities and/or funding sources—would develop more complex and elaborated internal administrative structures, holding constant the complexity of their work processes (Scott and Meyer 1983). Powell (1988: 126) found evidence consistent with this prediction in his study comparing a scholarly book-publishing house and a public TV station. He concluded that "organizations, such as [the public television station] WNET, that are located in environments in which conflicting demands are made upon them will be especially likely to generate complex organizational structures with disproportionately large administrative components and boundary-spanning units." Meyer, Scott, and Strang (1987) employed data on the administrative structure of districts and elementary and secondary schools to demonstrate that schools and districts depending more on federal funding, which involves many independent programs and budgetary categories, had disproportionately large administrative structures compared to schools relying primarily on state funding, which tended to be more integrated.

D'Aunno, Sutton, and Price (1991) examined effects on community mental health organizations exposed to two conflicting models for staffing and service provision in drug abuse programs. The conventional mental health approach prescribed a psychosocial model of treatment administered by mental health professionals, whereas the competing model, more common in the drug abuse treatment sector, endorsed the Alcoholics Anonymous (AA) model, relying on ex-addicts and client-centered approaches. Because some mental health centers, termed *hybrids*, elected to treat drug abuse cases, they were confronted with the two conflicting institutionalized models of treatment. These organizations reflected the conflicts in their environments by attempting to incorporate some features consistent with both the mental health and drug abuse institutional practices. These organizations "responded by combining hiring practices" from the two sectors: "hybrid units also adopted conflicting goals for client treatment and somewhat inconsistent treatment practices" (D'Aunno, Sutton, and Price 1991: 655–656). Conflicts in the institutional environment were mapped into the structure and practices of these organizations.

Interactive Processes

Although all organizations within a given institutional field or sector are subject to the effects of institutional processes within the context, all do not experience them in the same way or respond in the same manner. Just as social psychologists call attention to "individual differences"—differences among individuals in their definition of and response to the same situation—students of organization have increasingly attended to differences among organizations in their response to the "same" environment. I review here studies examining how adoption responses vary because of differences among organizations in the amount of pressure they experience, in their characteristics, or in their location within the field. In a later section of this chapter, I consider a broader array of responses by organizations to their institutional environments.

The general question addressed is: Why are some structures or practices adopted by some organizations, but not others in similar situations? This question is of interest not only to institutionalists, but also to students of the diffusion of innovation (see Abrahamson 1991; Rogers 1995; Strang and Soule 1998) and organizational learning (see Haunschild and Miner 1997; Ingram, 2002; Levitt and March 1988). The latter ask in this connection how organizations learn both from their own experience as well as from the experience of others. Institutional arguments, emphasizing the effects of rules, norms, or constitutive beliefs, shade off into stratification and instrumental arguments, for example, that organizations imitate others whom they perceive to be successful or prestigious (see e.g., Burns and Wholey 1993; Haunschild and Miner 1997; Haveman 1993). Many motives conduce toward conformity: fads, fashion, status enhancement and vicarious learning. All mimetic behavior does not involve (exclusively) institutional processes.

Variable Institutional Pressures

All organizations in the "same" field are not equally subject to the institutional processes at work there. Organizations vary in the extent to which they are under the jurisdictional authority of oversight agencies. Regulative requirements regarding employee protections such as health and safety rules often apply only to organizations of a given size. Equal opportunity laws apply more clearly to public sector organizations and to organizations receiving federal grants and contracts than to other employers (see Dobbin et al. 1988; Edelman 1992). As another example, Mezias (1990) examined the adopting of new procedures for reporting income tax credits by the 200 largest nonfinancial firms in the United States from 1962 to 1984. He discovered a number of organization-level factors that influenced adoption, including whether the firm was under the jurisdiction of the Interstate Commerce Commission. Casile and Davis-Blake (2002) found that business schools located in public universities were more responsive to changes in accreditation standards than those affiliated with private colleges.

Variation in institutional pressures also comes from differences over space and time in the strength of cognitive beliefs or normative controls. As described in chapter 5, both ecologists and institutional scholars view the increasing prevalence of a form or practice as an indicator of increasing legitimation. This temporal variation has given rise to an interesting line of research that contrasts the characteristics of early versus late adopters. Two studies were particularly influential in shaping the arguments.

The first was the study of the diffusion of civil service reforms among municipalities at the turn of the century conducted by Tolbert and Zucker (1983), portions of which were discussed in chapter 6. Turning their attention to those states in which civil service was not mandated, Tolbert and Zucker show that its adoption by cities during the initial period varied according to their characteristics: Larger cities, those with higher proportions of immigrants and a higher proportion of white-collar to blue-collar inhabitants, were more likely to adopt the reform. The authors argue that these cities were rationally pursuing their interests: Some local governments confronted more severe governance problems, encouraging them to adopt changes that would buffer them from "undesirable elements." Although such city characteristics were strongly predictive of adoption during the earliest period (1885–1904), in each subsequent period, the associations became weaker, so that by 1935, these variables no longer had any predictive power. The authors interpret these weakening correlations as evidence of the development of widespread and powerful cultural beliefs and norms supporting civil service reform, such that all cities were under increasing pressure to adopt the reform regardless of their local needs or circumstances.[1]

The second study, by Fligstein (1985), was briefly discussed earlier, but merits more detailed examination. Fligstein tested a number of alternative arguments for why large firms adopted the multidivisional (M-form) structure. His data were collected to reflect five periods, each a decade between 1929–1939 and 1969–1979, and included information on the 100 largest U.S. industrial corporations for each period.[2] During the earlier periods, firms that were older, pursuing product-related strategies in their growth patterns, and headed by managers from sales or finance departments were more likely to adopt the M-form than firms lacking these characteristics. During the 1939–1949 time period, these same factors continued to operate, but another variable also became relevant. If firms were in industries in which other, similar firms had adopted the M-form, they were more likely to adopt this structure. All of the factors, with the exception of age, continue to be significantly correlated with M-form adoption during the last two decades included in the study.

Fligstein's study provides empirical support for two different versions of institutional arguments. The findings linking structural forms to strategies supports Williamson's (1975) arguments that organizational managers attempt to devise governance structures that will economize on transactions costs—the alignment of structure with strategy. The findings relating M-form adoption to the number of other similar firms employing the structure are consistent with DiMaggio and Powell's (1983) views of mimetic—and perhaps normative—processes operating in uncertain environments.

These findings have been replicated in a number of later studies, some of which are described below. They suggest the following general pattern. In the early stages of an institutionalization process, adoption of the practice by organizations represents a choice on their part that can reflect their varying specific needs or interests. As the institutionalization process proceeds, normative and cultural pressures mount to the point where adoption becomes less of a choice and more of a requirement. Differences among individual organizations are of less consequence when confronted by stronger institutional impera- tives. Although in one sense the logic of action has shifted from one of instrumentality to appropriateness, in another sense, the situation con- fronting each organization has changed so that it is increasingly in the interest of all to adopt the practice. Not to do so is to be regarded as deviant, inattentive, or behind the times, resulting in a loss of legiti- macy and, perhaps, attendant material resources.

The question of what types of benefits are associated with early and late adoption is further explored in a study of over 2,700 U.S. hospitals encouraged to adopt total quality management (TQM) pro- cedures in response to increased normative pressures from the Joint Commission on Accreditation of Healthcare Organizations. Westphal, Gulati, and Shortell (1997) found that hospitals slower to adopt these practices conformed more highly to the pattern of practices imple- mented by other hospitals to which they were connected or to a par- ticular, standardized approach, compared to early adopters. That is, hospitals adopting early were more likely to customize their TQM practices to their specific situation; those adopting later exhibited a more ritualistic pattern, mechanically following standard TQM mod- els or imitating the practices of other hospitals with which they were connected in alliances or systems. The adoption of TQM improved hospital legitimacy (overall ratings by the Joint Commission) for both early and late adopters, but only early adopters of TQM also improved their productivity and efficiency, as measured by a number of objective and subjective indicators. We see again that, although early and late adoption showed different effects, all hospi- tals adopting TQM improved their legitimacy and some improved their performance.

Organizational Factors Associated With Adoption

A generation of recent studies has attempted to identify what orga- nizational features are associated with early adoption. Of course, these features vary greatly depending on the nature of the innovation. Most of the studies reviewed examine the adoption of some type of administra- tive innovation (e.g., new managerial structures or employee systems). A number of general characteristics appear to be associated with adoptive behavior. Without attempting to be comprehensive, I identify three classes of variables that have received attention from recent scholars.

Attributes. Organizations vary in many ways, but only a few of these differences have been found to be regularly associated with early adoption. Numerous studies have found that organization size is important, larger organizations being more prone to early adoption. Size effects have varying interpretations, each of which is conducive to earlier response. Larger organizations tend to be more resource-rich; larger organizations are more differentiated and, hence, more sensitive to environmental changes; and larger organizations are more visible to external publics, including governance bodies (see Dobbin et al. 1988; Edelman 1992; Greening and Gray 1994). Organizations that operate within or are more closely aligned with the public sector are more likely to be responsive to institutional pressures, particularly legal and regulatory requirements, but also normative pressures (see Dobbin et al. 1988; Edelman 1992; Casile and Davis-Blake 2002). Organizations possessing differentiated personnel offices are more likely to be receptive to innovations, particularly those pertaining to employment matters (e.g., the adoption of hiring, training, and due-process procedures; see Baron, Dobbin, and Jennings 1986; Baron, Jennings, and Dobbin 1988; Dobbin et al. 1988; Edelman 1992; Kalleberg et al. 1996). Unionization has been shown to affect selected types of adoption, in particular, grievance procedures and internal labor market practices (Pfeffer and Cohen 1984; Sutton et al. 1994; Kalleberg et al. 1996). In private sector organizations, the characteristics of CEOs have been found to affect adoptive behavior. CEO background—for example, whether their experience comes from production, marketing, or finance (Fligstein 1985, 1990)—and CEO power vis-à-vis the corporate board (Westphal and Zajac 1994)—is associated with the adoption of new structural forms and with CEO compensation protections and incentive systems. Firms experiencing turnover in their top management teams are more likely to adopt new accounting procedures (Mezias 1990). Finally, organizational performance has been found to influence the adoption of CEO income protection and incentive plans (Westphal and Zajac 1994).

Linkages. Networks of organizations exhibit structure. Linkages among organizations vary by frequency and nature of exchanges, multiplicity and absence of connections, and central and peripheral location. Participants within organizations are linked together at high levels (e.g., interlocking boards of directors, friendship, and school ties among executives) and low levels (e.g., occupational affiliations and communities of practice that cross organizational boundaries).

For example, Haunschild (1993) demonstrates that corporations sharing directors were more likely to make acquisitions during the 1980s, and Palmer, Jennings, and Zhou (1993) reported that interlocking directors predicted the adoption by corporations of an M-form structure during the 1960s. Rao and Sivakumar (1999) report that firms with similar ties were more likely to create an investor relations office when they learned about it from other board members.

The distinction between being connected and being similar to another social unit is an important one to network theorists. The former, referred to as *cohesion*, pertains to the presence of exchange relations or communication links between two or more parties. The latter, termed *structural equivalence*, refers to social units that "occupy the same position in the social structure"; they "are proximate to the extent that they have the same pattern of relations with occupants of other positions" (Burt 1987: 1291). In situations where information is widely available (e.g., via the mass media), social contagion—the diffusion of some practice or structure—may be more influenced by the behavior of those we regard as similar to ourselves than by those with whom we are in contact (recall the similar arguments made by Strang and Meyer [1993], discussed in chap. 6).

The relative importance of cohesion versus structural equivalence is evaluated in a study by Galaskiewicz and Burt (1991), who examined factors affecting diffusion of norms and standards among Contributions Officers in corporate firms pertaining to the evaluation of nonprofit organizations seeking donations. The study examines how common norms develop within an organizational field, affecting how individual officials come to view their social environment, adopt standards, and arrive at similar evaluations. Results were based on evaluations made by 61 contributions officers of 326 local nonprofit organizations eligible to receive donations from corporations. Judgments by officers (as to whether they recognized the nonprofits and, if so, regarded them as worthy prospects) were correlated with the evaluations of other officers who were either (a) in contact, or (b) in equivalent structural positions. "The results show weak evidence of contagion by cohesion and strong evidence of contagion by structural equivalence" (Galaskiewicz and Burt 1991: 94). Differences in judgment were also influenced by differences in the personal characteristics of officers, such as gender and prominence, but these did not eliminate the structural effects.

Reference Groups. These and related studies raise this general question: If organizations imitate the behavior of other organizations, how do they determine which organizations to emulate? Clearly, organizations must choose among their many network connections, and they must decide what criteria to employ to assess similarity. A number of recent scholars explore these questions utilizing network approaches. Notably, much of this research focuses on the adoption by market-based organizations of various competitive strategies, including acquisition behavior, entry into new markets, and choice of an investment banker or construction of a comparison set (e.g., for justifying CEO compensation). Illustrative findings are that organizations are prone to imitate the behavior of organizations that are geographically proximate (Davis and Greve 1997; Greve 1998), perceived to be similar to themselves (e.g., operating in the same industry; Haunschild and Beckman 1998; Palmer, Jennings, and Zhou 1993; Porac, Wade, and Pollock 1999); closely connected by ties, including resource, information, and board interlocks (Galaskiewicz and Bielefeld 1998; Haunschild 1993; Kraatz 1998; Uzzi 1996); have high status or prestige (Burns and Wholey 1993); and are more (visibly) successful (Haunschild and Miner 1997; Haveman 1993; Kraatz 1998). In contrast, firms may select less successful others as a comparison set to justify or place their own actions in a favorable light (Porac, Wade, and Pollock 1999).

The arguments associated with reference group variables range from strictly institutional to vicarious learning to political maneuvering. More important, however, these studies begin to show the ways in which institutional processes interact with interest-based motivations to guide organizational choices and behaviors (see also Baum and Dutton 1996; Dacin, Ventresca, and Beal 1999).

Institutional and Organizational Processes

The public policy literature contains numerous studies providing examples of the ways in which organizations both engage in regulatory activities and respond to attempts to control their behavior. Some of these accounts take a top-down perspective (e.g., Wilson 1980), focusing on the structure and tactics of the enforcement agency, whereas others take a bottom-up view, examining how the policies are interpreted and carried out at local sites (e.g., Lipsky 1980). Organizations operate at every level in these accounts: as policymakers, units of the implementation machinery, and targets of policy reform. Although these studies have received scant attention from mainstream organizational scholars, they contain important insights concerning how organizations participate in and respond to regulatory efforts (see e.g., Hoffman and Ventresca 2002; Landy, Roberts, and Thomas 1990; McLaughlin 1975; Peterson, Rabe, and Wong 1986). Pierson (2004: chap. 1) provides a perceptive discussion of political organizations, public policy setting, and institutional processes.

A more general process-oriented perspective is provided by organizational scholars who focus attention on organizations as information systems: as symbol-processing, sense-making, and interpretation systems. Pfeffer and Salancik (1978) stress the importance of the information system developed by the organization: the specialized units and routines that determine the variety and types of information routinely collected by the organization. Information is more likely to be salient and used simply because it is available. The availability of information thus influences the "attention-structure" of decision makers. Because "time and capabilities for attention are limited," as March (1994: 10) notes, "theories of decision making are often better described as theories of attention or search than as theories of choice." Rather than assuming a straightforward, unified, demand-response model, a more ambiguous, complex, and nuanced portrait is painted of organizations staffed by multiple actors with conflicting agendas and interests confronting diverse and imperfect information. Demands or requirements trigger not automatic conformity, but multiple questions: Does this apply to us? Who says so? Is this something to which we should respond? What might we do about it? Who else may be in the same situation? What are they doing? They become occasions for interpretation and initiate sense-making processes (Barley 1986; Daft and Weick 1984; Whetten and Godfrey 1999). Weick (1995) provides a penetrating and provocative analysis of these processes—reminiscent of Suchman's (1995a) discussion of theorization—that occur within and across organizations.

Related efforts to foster the development of more interactive and subtle models of the ways in which organizations relate to institutional environments have been carried out by law and society scholars, who complain that institutionalists too often embrace a "legal formalism" stressing the external, objective, rational nature of law. Rather, as Suchman and Edelman (1997; see also Edelman and Suchman 1997) propose, laws and regulations are socially interpreted and find their force and meaning in interactions between regulators and regulatees. This approach is well illustrated in a series of studies examining the response of a diverse sample of U.S. organizations to equal opportunity/affirmative action laws passed in the early 1960s (see Dobbin et al.

1988, 1993; Edelman 1992; Edelman, Uggen, and Erlanger 1999; Sutton et al. 1994). All laws are subject to variable interpretation, but these statutes—in part reflecting underlying, unresolved political conflicts—were particularly ambiguous to the point where even cooperative organizational managers could not determine what it meant to be in compliance. The passage of the legislation set in motion an elaborate sense-making process in which personnel managers engaged in discourse with their counterparts—within their organizations, in their professional journals, at conventions—attempting to discern what measures would be found acceptable. Proposals were floated, prototype programs were developed, and, over time, these responses were evaluated by the federal courts (yet another collection of state-based, professional actors), which served as the final arbiters of adequate compliance. Personnel managers were much more willing to initiate procedural rather than substantive solutions (that focused on the consequences of employer actions) (Edelman 1992), although their proposals were often couched in language emphasizing their contributions to organizational efficiency (Dobbin and Sutton 1998). Hoffman (2001: 143) amplifies this argument, noting that organizational actors attempt to reframe environmental demands in terms that make sense from their specialized perspective:

> When buyers and suppliers impose environmental pressures on the firm, they become framed as an issue of operational efficiency through resource acquisition, processing, and sales. When imposed by banks, shareholders, and investors, they become framed as an issue of capital acquisition. When consumers begin to consider environmental concerns in their purchasing decisions, the issue becomes framed as an issue of market demand. When competitors begin to use the environment as a strategic issue or challenge how others use it, the issue becomes translated into one of competitive strategy.

When eventually selected kinds of programs were declared to meet the requirements of the law—governance processes having shifted to the judiciary—these models diffused rapidly through the field. The overall process that occurred was one in which legal changes could best be understood as an endogenous process engaging various actors and working through sense-making and problem-solving activities within the organizational field. This process was guided more by normative constructions among professional actors than by coercive mechanisms emanating from the state, and it was better understood as a structuration process changing rules and behaviors across the entire field, rather than as a simple process by which individual organizations were confronted by and conformed to centralized directives.

❖ STRATEGIC RESPONSES

Studies emphasizing institutional processes rather than effects, such as those described above, begin to suggest that organizations may not be quite so powerless or passive as depicted in earlier institutional accounts. Noting the oversocialized conception of organizations and the limited response repertoire proffered by early formulations—in effect, Conform, either now or later!—a number of scholars have joined voices in calling for more attention to power and agency, particularly on the part of individuals and organizations subject to institutional pressures (see DiMaggio 1988; Perrow 1986). Pfeffer (1981; Pfeffer and Salancik 1978) was among the first to emphasize that managers often manipulated symbols to "manage" their legitimacy in the larger environment.

In an important development of these arguments, Christine Oliver (1991) called for an expansion of the choice set available to organizations. Drawing on resource-dependence arguments, she outlined a broad range of potential responses, emphasizing throughout the possible use of more self-interested, strategic alternatives.[3] I begin by reviewing her arguments and typology. However, because they focus on responses by individual organizations, I conclude by pointing to the possibility of more collective strategic actions.

Individual Organizational Responses

Although it is useful to recognize that organizations can react to institutional pressures in a number of ways, it is also important to observe the extent to which institutional environments operate to influence and delimit what strategies organizations can employ. Just as institutions constitute organizations, they also define and set limits on their appropriate ways of acting, including actions taken in response to institutional pressures. Strategies that may be appropriate in one kind of industry or field may be prohibited in another. For example, public agencies are frequently encouraged to coordinate services, whereas private organizations are expected to refrain from becoming overly cozy (or collusive). Tactics that can be successfully pursued in one setting may be inconceivable in another. As we have noted in studies previously reviewed, structures, as well as strategies are institutionally shaped.

Oliver (1991: 152), however, concentrates primarily on types of strategies that organizations can pursue irrespective of such field-level constraints. She delineates five general strategies available to individual organizations confronting institutional pressures:

- *Acquiescence* or conformity is the response that has received the lion's share of attention from institutional theorists.

As we have seen, it may entail either imitation of other organizations selected as models or compliance to the perceived demands of cultural, normative, or regulative authorities. It may be motivated by anticipation of enhanced legitimacy, fear of negative sanctions, hope of additional resources, or some mixture of these motives.

- *Compromise* incorporates a family of responses that include balancing, placating, and negotiating institutional demands.

Compromise is particularly likely to occur in environments containing conflicting authorities. Earlier, we described D'Aunno, Sutton, and Price's (1991) research on the compromises devised by mental health agencies incorporating drug abuse programs. Although this seems a special case, as we noted in chapter 6, in liberal, pluralist societies like the United States, inconsistent and contested institutional frameworks are commonplace (Berman 1983; Friedland and Alford 1991). This implies that organizations will frequently find themselves in situations in which they have considerable room to maneuver, interpret, bargain, and compromise. For example, Abzug and Mezias (1993) detail the range of strategies pursued by organizations responding to court decisions regarding comparable worth claims under Title VII of the Civil Rights Act of 1972. The federalized structure of the court systems, permitting quasi-independent rulings by federal, state, and local courts, allowed a greater variety of appeals and also provided avenues for reform efforts to continue at one level if blocked at another.

Alexander (1996: 803) describes a combination of "compromise" strategies as being pursued by curators of fine arts museums in the United States, whose organizations increasingly rely on diverse funding streams—wealthy individuals, corporations, governments, and foundations—each of which holds different goals in providing support. Alexander finds that curators, whose prestige "rests on the scholarliness and quality of their work, including the exhibitions they mount," tend to alter the format of exhibitions to please their funders—for example, creating "blockbuster" and traveling exhibitions to please corporate and government sponsors—but to compromise less on the content of exhibitions. Other specific strategies employed included "resource shifting," "multivocality"—sponsoring exhibitions with many facets that appeal to a variety of stakeholders—and "creative enactment"—inventing linkages between particular types of art and the specific interests of a potential sponsor.

- The strategy of *avoidance*, as defined by Oliver, includes concealment efforts and attempts to buffer some parts of the organization from the necessity of conforming to the requirement.

One mode of avoidance has received considerable attention from the outset of neoinstitutional theory. In their seminal essay on institutional environments, Meyer and Rowan (1977) argued that organizations confronting demands frequently respond by "decoupling" their structural features from their technical activities. This is assuredly a possible response. Loose coupling among differentiated units is a characteristic feature of all organizations—indeed, of all open systems (see Glassman 1973; Orton and Weick 1990; Weick 1976). Organizations, in particular, are known to deal with external demands by developing specialized administrative units mapping onto these external sources (Buckley 1967; Thompson 1967/2003). Organizations under pressure to adopt particular structures or procedures may opt to respond in a ceremonial manner, making changes in their formal structures to signal conformity, but then buffering internal units, allowing them to operate independent of these pressures. Although this is certainly a possible response, Meyer and Rowan imply that this response is widespread. Indeed, some theorists treat decoupling as the hallmark of an institutional argument. I believe this interpretation to be incorrect.

To begin, these decoupled responses are often seen to be merely symbolic, the organizational equivalent of "smoke and mirrors" (see Perrow 1985). However, to an institutionalist, the adjective "merely" does not fit comfortably with the noun "symbolic." The use of symbols involving processes by which an organization connects to the wider world of meaning exerts great social power (see Brunsson 1989; Pfeffer 1981). Second, numerous studies suggest that, although organizations may create boundary and buffering units for symbolic reasons, these structures have a life of their own. Personnel employed in these units often play a dual role: They both transmit and translate environment demands to organizations, but also represent organizational concerns to institutional agents (see Hoffman 1997; Taylor 1984). In addition, the very existence of such units signals compliance. Edelman (1992: 1544) elaborates this argument in her discussion of organizational responses to equal employment opportunity/affirmative action requirements:

> Structural elaboration is merely the first step in the process of compliance. Once EEO/AA structures are in place, the personnel who work with or in those structures become prominent actors in the compliance process: they give meaning to law as they construct definitions of compliance within their organizations. . . . But while actors within organizations struggle to construct a definition of compliance, structural elaboration signals attention to law, thus helping to preserve legitimacy.

Finally, rather than assuming that decoupling automatically occurs, we should treat this as an empirical question: When and under what conditions do organizations adopt requisite structures but then fail to carry out the associated activities? Consistent with our pillars framework, which elements are involved can be expected to affect the response. Organizations are more likely to practice avoidance when confronted with external regulatory requirements than with normative or cognitive-cultural demands. Thus, research by Coburn (2004: 233), who studied the effect of curricular changes in elementary school reading programs, found that teachers were more likely to respond to "normative messages than to regulative messages by incorporating them into their classroom and doing so in ways that altered their preexisting practice." Organizations are also more likely to decouple structure from practice when there are high symbolic gains from adoption but equally high costs associated with implementation. Westphal and Zajac (1994) studied the behavior of 570 of the largest U.S. corporations over two decades when such firms were adopting long-term CEO compensation plans in an attempt to better align CEO incentives with stockholder interests. Although many companies adopted these plans, a substantial number failed to use them to restructure executive compensation within a subsequent 2-year period. Adoption of a plan was found to enhance organizational legitimacy with stockholders and stock purchasers. Westphal and Zajac (1994, 1998) found that plan adoptions, regardless of whether they were used, resulted in improved market prices, and they found adoption to be associated with greater CEO influence over the board. At the same time, use of these plans could negatively impact CEO compensation. Accordingly, the researchers found that nonimplementation was also associated with greater CEO influence. In addition, Westphal and

Zajac (1994) observed the familiar pattern involving late versus early adoption: Late adopters were less likely to implement the plan than early adopters, suggesting that decoupling is more likely to occur among reluctant adopters responding to strong normative pressures.

- The strategy of *defiance* is one in which organizations not only resist institutional pressures to conform, but do so in a highly public manner.

Defiance is likely to occur when the norms and interests of the focal organizations diverge substantially from those attempting to impose requirements on them. Covaleski and Dirsmith (1988) describe one organization's attempt to defy the state's efforts to impose a new budgetary system on them. The University of Wisconsin system attempted to devise and obtain public support for an alternative budgetary system that would more clearly reflect their own interests in research and educational programs and retaining top-flight faculty. In the end, state power prevailed, and the university was forced to accept the state's enrollment-based approach.

- Organizations may respond to institutional pressures by attempting to *manipulate*—"the purposeful and opportunistic attempt to co-opt, influence, or control" the environment (Oliver 1991: 157).

Numerous scholars, from Selznick (1949) to Pfeffer and Salancik (1978) to Alexander (1995), have examined the ways in which organizations attempt to defend themselves and improve their bargaining power by developing linkages to important sources of power. Of special interest to institutional theorists are the techniques used by organizations to directly manage views of their legitimacy. Elsbach and Sutton (1992: 702) report a process study of impression-management techniques employed by Earth First! and ACT UP, two militant reform organizations that employed "illegitimate actions to gain recognition and achieve goals." Their analysis suggests that such techniques were employed to gain media attention to the organization and its objectives. Once such attention was forthcoming, spokespersons for each organization stressed the more conventional aspects of the organization and attempted to distance their organization's program from the illegal activities of some of its members. They sometimes claimed innocence or justified their actions in the light of the greater injustices against which they were contending. Endorsements and support received from other constituencies were emphasized. In these and related ways, organizations attempt to manage their impressions and improve their credibility. However, as Ashforth and Gibbs (1990) point out, organizations that "protest too much" run the risk of undermining their legitimacy.

One final caution: In recognizing the possibility of strategic action by organizations confronting institutional pressures, it is also important that institutional theorists not lose sight of the distinctive properties of institutions, in particular those associated with the cultural-cognitive forms. As Goodrick and Salancik (1996: 3) point out:

> A problem with the direct incorporation of a strategic choice per-spective into institutional theory is that it discounts the social-fact quality of institutions. Rather than being social facts that make up the fabric of social life, they assume the special and arbitrary posi-tions of dominant social agents. . . . The notion that organizations act at times without choice or forethought is lost. . . . The institu-tional context [then becomes] . . . of no special importance for understanding organizational action. It is simply a constraint to be managed like any other constraint, a choice among many choices.

Goodrick and Salancik (1996) examined the behavior of various types of California hospitals in adopting Cesarean operations from 1965 to 1995, a time when the rates for this procedure increased greatly. Professional practice norms encourage the use of Cesarean sections for high- but not low-risk births. Comparing Cesarean rates among for-profit and nonprofit hospitals, the researchers observed differences among them only for births of intermediate risk. For-profit hospitals were more likely to carry out these relatively profitable procedures under these conditions than nonprofit forms. But this self-interested, strategic behavior only occurred for intermediate-risk patient condi-tions for which professional norms did not provide clear guidelines. Institutional rules set the limits within which strategic behavior occurs.

More generally, there is clear tension between a strategic approach and the view of many institutional theorists. As previewed in chapter 3, a strategic perspective views legitimacy as another type of resource—a cultural resource—to be extracted from the environment. As Suchman (1995b: 576) points out, given the "almost limitless malleability and symbols and rituals," in contrast to the hardness of material resources and outcomes, the former provides ready targets for manipulation by managers. Institutionalists, however, emphasize the limits of this view.

In a strong and constraining symbolic environment, managers' decisions are often constructed by the same belief systems that determine audience reactions. Consequently, rather than examining the strategic legitimation efforts of specific focal organizations, many institutionalists tend to emphasize the collective structuration (DiMaggio and Powell 1983) of entire fields or sectors of organizational life (Suchman 1995b: 576).

Collective Responses

More so than the actions of single organizations, concerted responses by multiple organizations have the potential to shape the nature of the demands and even to redefine the rules and logics operating within the field. We review several studies dealing with these collective responses to institutional environments, but reserve for chapter 8 a discussion of more general field-level changes.

Earlier in this chapter, we discussed a number of empirical studies depicting the ways in which organizations subject to some type of normative or regulative pressure respond in ways that reshape or redefine these institutional demands. Recall the behavior of personnel officers confronted by equal opportunity legislation. We suspect that such processes—in which rules or normative controls are proposed or legislated, interpretations and collective sense-making activities take place among participants in the field to which they are directed, and then the requirements are redefined and clarified—are more often the rule than the exception.

A study by Kaplan and Harrison (1993: 423) examines the reactions by organizations to changes in the legal environment that exposed board members to a greater risk of liability suits. Corporations pursued both proactive strategies, adapting so as to conform to environmental requirements, and reactive strategies, attempting to alter environmental demands. Both involved collective as well as individual efforts. The Business Roundtable, a voluntary governance association, "took the lead in coordinating the conformity strategy by making recommendations on board composition and committee structure" consistent with the concerns raised by such regulatory bodies as the Security and Exchanges Commission. Proactive collective strategies included lobbying efforts directed at states to broaden the indemnification protection for outside directors as well as the creation of insurance consortia to underwrite the costs of providing director and officer liability insurance to companies. The strategies pursued were judged to be highly successful: "New legislation and the insurance consortia enabled most corporations to substantially improve director liability protection. As a result, most board members are less at risk of personal liability now than they were a decade ago" (Kaplan and Harrison 1993: 426–427).

A somewhat more contentious process of negotiation and compromise is detailed by Hoffman (1997) in his historical account of reactions by the U.S. chemical and petroleum firms and industries during the period 1960–1995 to increasing regulatory pressures intended to reduce treats to the natural environment. Trade journals were examined to assess industry response to these challenges. During the 1960s, relatively little attention was devoted to environmental concerns; most accusations and concerns were dismissed as groundless. However, with the formation of the Environmental Protection Agency in 1970— in response to a number of highly visible environmental accidents— governmental scrutiny of both industries increased dramatically, as did the mobilization of environmental activists. The Chemical Manufacturers Association and the American Petroleum Institute initially pursued primarily confrontational strategies in an attempt to influence regulatory behavior—in particular, standard-setting—but by the late 1980s, a more cooperative framework had evolved as the industries and related corporations began to embrace a policy of corporate environmentalism. Public agencies and corporate actors accommodated to one another's interests, erecting new types of understandings, norms, and hybrid public/private governance arrangements.

But more conflict-laden collective reactions have occurred whose resolution has proved more difficult. Miles (1982) examined the interesting case of the response by the "Big Six" tobacco companies in the United States to the Surgeon General's report linking smoking and cancer. Each of these companies reacted individually, some developing their foreign markets and others diversifying their products. But they also engaged in collective action, creating the Tobacco Industry Research Committee to conduct their own scientific studies and cooperating to hire lobbyists and create Political Action Committees (PACs) to guide legislation and resist the passage of punitive laws. Collective efforts to shape the regulative and other governance structures to which they are subject continue up to the present day in response to heightened activities on the part of federal and state officials.

A different kind of negotiation process and redefinition of the organization field is described by Halliday and colleagues (Halliday, Powell, and Granfors 1993) in their study of U.S. state bar associations These associations were formed at the turn of the 20th century as market-based organizations competing for the support of lawyer members. However, during the early decades, failure rates were high. A different model of organizing was developed in the early 1920s, which relied on state support: Membership in the association was mandated as a condition for practicing in the state, and annual fees were imposed on all members. This new form, which required either legislative action or a ruling by the state supreme court, rapidly diffused through a number of states, although it did not supplant the market-based form in all states. Event-history analysis revealed that the state-based mode was more likely to be adopted in states in which the market-based form had attracted only a small proportion of lawyers (i.e., states favorably disposed to licensing professions) and in rural states. The state-based form was also promoted by a centralized, propagator association, the American Judicature Society, created to advance legal reform and diffuse the new structure. Collective action in this case resulted in the transformation of an organizational form, moving it out of the competitive marketplace and under the protective wing of the state.

❖ SOURCES OF DIVERGENCE

Collecting arguments from this and previous chapters, we see that, although institutional pressures under many conditions conduce toward isomorphic organization structure and practices, there are many ways in which "identical" institutional forces can result not in convergent, but divergent outcomes. Among the mechanisms and processes discussed, consider the following:

- Varying carriers whose characteristics or mode of transmission alters the message
- Varying translations of institutional rules
- Misunderstandings or errors in the application of rules
- Varying exposure or susceptibility to institutional rules
- Varying attributes or relational connections that affect knowledge of or response to institutional pressures
- Adaptations or innovations by users adopting institutional forms
- Competing models being combined into varying hybrid forms
- Strategic responses by individual organizations to institutional pressures
- Strategic responses by networks or associations of organizations

Given the variety and prevalence of these factors, it would appear that if more nuanced institutional arguments are used, investigators may discover that it is easier to account for divergence than convergence of response by organizations to common institutional pressures.

❖ CONCLUDING COMMENT

Although organization analysts early embraced an open systems conception of organizations, it has taken a long time for us to comprehend the extent to which organizations are creatures of their distinctive times and places, reflecting not only the technical knowledge, but also the cultural rules and social beliefs in their environments. As Schrödinger (1945: 75) observed in his treatise on open systems: "The device by which an organism [or organization] maintains itself stationary at a fairly high level of orderliness . . . really consists in continually sucking orderliness from its environment."

Much of the important work by institutional theorists over the past two decades has been in documenting the influence of social and symbolic forces on organizational structure and behavior. Empirical research has examined how institutional systems shape organizations, variably, as a function of their location in the environment, their size and visibility, and their nearness to the public sphere, structural position, and relational contacts.

Organizations are affected, and even penetrated, by their environments, but they are also capable of responding to these influence attempts creatively and strategically. By acting in concert with other organizations facing similar pressures, organizations can sometimes counter, curb, circumvent, or redefine these demands. Collective action does not preclude individual attempts to reinterpret, manipulate, challenge, or defy the authoritative claims made on them. Organizations are creatures of their institutional environments, but most modern organizations are constituted as active players, not passive pawns.

In this chapter, I have tried to reflect the gradual but significant shift in scholarly treatments of institution-organization relations. From a concern with one-way, determinant institutional "effects," most contemporary researchers are instead crafting research designs to examine the complex recursive processes by which institutional forces both shape and are shaped by organizational actions.

❖ NOTES

1. Tolbert and Zucker here use density or prevalence of adoption of reforms as an indicator of their increasing legitimacy, although later Zucker (1989) criticized Hannan and Carroll for employing a similar "indirect" indicator.

2. Note that this sample design is unusual in that each of the decades represents a different set of firms. In subsequent analyses, Fligstein (1990, 1991) examined the strategic behavior of both firms that had entered and left so that the characteristics of "stayers" and "leavers" could be compared.

3. This conception was instrumental in attracting the attention of management scholars to institutional ideas. After all, an approach that views organizations as shaped largely by environmental forces—whether ecological or institutional—may appeal to academic social scientists, but is unlikely to attract scholars who consult with present and prepare future business managers for leadership responsibilities.

8

Institutional Processes and Organization Fields

I believe that no concept is more vitally connected to the agenda of institutional processes and organizations than that of organization field. Previously defined in chapter 4 and referred to from time to time in subsequent chapters, the concept of *field*—both as a unit and a level of analysis—figures sufficiently large in institutional approaches to organizations to merit extended attention. Like so many concepts in institutional theory, the conception of organization field is a work in progress. Although its introduction into organization theory can be dated with precision, it builds on previous work and has been subject to criticism, amendment, and improvement up to the present moment. It is, at one and the same time, widely accepted and hotly contested.

❖ CONCEPTUALIZING ORGANIZATION FIELDS

The concept of field usefully incorporates important previous levels of analysis employed in organization studies, including individual organizations, organization sets, and organization populations. That is, it encompasses:

- a diverse array of organizations working within a given arena or domain;
- attention not only to the producer organizations, but to their exchange partners, customers, competitors, intermediary actors, regulators, and funding agents—their *organization set*; and
- recognition that organizations are particularly attentive to and influenced by the existence of organizations exhibiting the same general features and competing for the same resources—their *organization population.*

The concepts of *organization set*, *population*, and *field* have all served to make more visible and palpable what had formally been vaguely regarded as the "environment" of the organization. For many years, this relatively passive framing led investigators to envisage a random collection of resources and other organizations that might be of use (or a threat). Some investigators (e.g., Dill 1958; Emery and Trist 1965; Lawrence and Lorsch 1967) came to conceive of the environment as a disembodied set of dimensions—such as complexity, stability, and munificence—whose states could impact the organization (for a review, see Scott 1992). There was little sense that the organization's environment was organized, and there was little awareness that organizations operating within the "same" environment might inhabit quite distinctive locations, providing diverse threats and opportunities.

The concept of organization field celebrates and exploits the insight that "local social orders" constitute the building blocks of contemporary social systems. It urges the benefits of the "mesolevel of theorizing," which recognizes the centrality of these somewhat circumscribed and specialized realms in the construction and maintenance of social order (Fligstein 2001b: 107). The field concept is productively employed in examining delimited systems ranging from markets to policy domains to the less structured and more contested arenas within which social movements struggle. Thus, for example, to view a product or labor market as a field is to embed the competitive processes that are the primary focus of most economic analyses within a larger canvas that includes multiple types of players, each working to "create and maintain a stable world within [each participating organization] and produce social relations across firms [and other units] in order to allow them to survive" (Fligstein 2001a: 70).

The field concept also fulfills a vital role in connecting organization studies to wider, macrostructures—sectoral, societal, and transnational. Organizations are major actors in modern society, but to understand their broader significance, it is necessary to see their role as players in larger networks and systems. As DiMaggio (1986: 337) asserts, "the organization field has emerged as a critical unit bridging the organizational and the societal levels in the study of social and community change."

Precursor Conceptions

Numerous precursors paved the way for the concept of organizational field. Among the more important was psychologist Kurt Lewin's (1951: 57) use of field as a tool to assess an individual's "life space"— encompassing "the person and the psychological environment as it exists for him." Important features of Lewin's approach were his insistence on the mutual interdependence of the many elements and forces surrounding the individual and on the centrality of the individual's perception and interpretation processes: life space conceived as a cognitive map of one's social environment (see Mohr, forthcoming). Also influential was the work of sociologist Pierre Bourdieu (1971, 1984), who employed the concept of field to refer "to both the totality of actors and organizations involved in an arena of social or cultural production and the dynamic relationships among them" (DiMaggio, 1979: 1463). Bourdieu suggests that, "to think in terms of field is to *think relationally* (Bourdieu and Wacquant 1992: 96; italics original), and he employs the analogy of a game, with rules, players, stakes, competition, and contestation, to depict its central features. For Bourdieu, fields are not placid and settled social spaces, but arenas of conflict in which all players seek to advance their interests; some are able, for longer or shorter periods, to impose their conception of "the rules of the game" on others. Bourdieu's treatment of field provided the foundation for DiMaggio and Powell's conception.

Within the organizational area, yet another important forerunner was the ecological conception of interorganizational community. Ecologists such as Hawley (1950), Warren (1967), and Astley (1985) employed the concept to focus on a geographically bounded collection of organizations rendered interdependent because of functional ties or shared localities. In contrast to population ecologists, who emphasized competitive processes among similar organizations, community ecologists pointed out that communities of organizations could develop structures that were mutually beneficial. As elaborated by Astley and Van de Ven (1983: 250–251):

> Rather than view organizations as pitched in a competitive battle for survival through a direct confrontation with the natural, or exogenous environment, [community theorists] emphasize

collective survival, which is achieved by collaboration between organizations through the construction of a regulated and controlled social environment that mediates the effects of the natural environment.

From today's vantage point, a limitation of this useful work was its tendency to focus more on colocation than on functional interdependence, with the effect that important connections and exchanges among organizations outside the spatial boundaries of the community were ignored (Scott and Meyer 1983: 132–133).[1]

Founding Conception

Because it has been so influential, let me repeat here DiMaggio and Powell's (1983: 148) founding definition of the concept of *organization field*, first discussed in chapter 4:

> those organizations that, in the aggregate, constitute a recognized area of institutional life: key suppliers, resource and product consumers, regulatory agencies, and other organizations that produce similar services or products.

Their definition identifies a collection of similar "producer" organizations working within a delimited social arena, together with their exchange partners, consumers, and regulators. They emphasize that the conception is not restricted simply to competing firms or networks of interacting organizations, but refers to "the totality of relevant actors." As noted, related conceptions of "societal sectors" (Scott and Meyer 1983: 137–138) and "industry systems" (Hirsch 1985) developed at about the same time. Another formulation by Whitley (1987, 1992b) of "business systems" reflects many of the same features. However, all of these views tended to emphasize shared conceptions and information and compatible (in the extreme case, isomorphic) structures.

More recent approaches have suggested that fields can develop not only around settled markets, technologies, or policy domains, but also around central disputes and issues. Thus, Hoffman (1999: 352) argues:

> I suggest that a field is formed around the issues that become important to the interest and objectives of a specific collective of organizations. Issues define what the field is, making links that may not have previously been present. Organizations may make claims about being or not being part of the field, but their

membership is defined through social interaction patterns. . . .
Field membership may also be for a finite time period, coincid-
ing with an issue's emergence, growth, and decline.

Hoffman arrived at this formulation from his study, described in
the previous chapter, of the U.S. chemical and petroleum industries
confronting the issue of corporate environmentalism.

Key Components of Organizational Fields

Relational Systems

DiMaggio and Powell's (1983) original conception focused much
attention on the relational systems linking organizations into larger
networks. Drawing on network theory, they emphasized that the
relevant relations may reflect either "connectedness"—with direct and
indirect links between organizations—or "structural equivalence"—
similarity of position in a network structure (e.g., the structure of local
school districts in adjacent states; Laumann, Galaskiewicz, and
Marsden 1978). In addition to interaction patterns and information
flows, DiMaggio and Powell (1983: 148) also noted the importance of
"interorganizational structures of dominance and patterns of coalition."
Similar to DiMaggio and Powell, Meyer and I (Scott and Meyer
1983) stress relational or structural features at the field (or sector) level,
focusing attention, for example, on centralization and fragmentation of
decision making, extent of federalization, and types of sector controls.
In a similar fashion, in his discussion of business systems, Whitley
(1992b) examines the extent of specialization within firms, whether
market ties are characterized by arms length or more relational contracting, and a variety of authority and coordination mechanisms at the
system level. More so than other organizational scholars at the time,
in his examination of corporate systems at the societal level, Fligstein
(1991: 314), like Bourdieu, stresses the centrality of power and control
processes—"the ability of a given organization or set of organizations to
capture or direct the actions of the field."[2] For Fligstein (1990: chap. 1),
the relevant relations for large corporations are (a) those involving
other, similar organizations; and (b) those with the nation-state, which
is in a position to ratify settlements or modify the terms of competition.
More recently, scholars like Podolny (1993) and Owen-Smith (forthcoming) highlight the role of status processes as more or less prestigious
actors work to shape the directions of field development.
An important subset of relational systems is the governance
systems that operate at the field level (Scott 1994a). *Governance systems*

are those "arrangements which support the regularized control—whether by regimes created by mutual agreement, by legitimate hierarchical authority or by nonlegitimate coercive means—of the actions of one set of actors by another" (Scott, Mendel, and Pollack, forthcoming). Each organizational field is characterized by a somewhat distinctive governance system composed of some combination of public and private actors employing some combination of regulatory and normative controls over activities and actors within the field. Among the common actors exercising these functions are public regulatory bodies, trade associations, unions, professional associations, and judicial systems. For a sampling of empirical studies of field governance systems, see Brunsson and Jacobsson's (2000) study of standard setting by professional associations, Campbell and colleagues' study of the governance of economic sectors (Campbell, Hollingsworth, and Lindberg 1991; Campbell and Lindberg 1990), Djelic and Quack's (2003b) and Djelic and Sahlin-Andersson's (2006) collection of studies of transnational regulatory systems, Holm's (1995) study of Norwegian fishing regimes, and our study of the changing governance systems controlling health care delivery organizations in the United States (Scott et al. 2000).

Cultural-Cognitive Systems

Truth be told, attention to the cultural aspects of fields has lagged behind relational approaches. Although in their early formulation DiMaggio and Powell (1983: 148) included in their delineation of field factors "the development of a mutual awareness among participants in a set of organizations that they are involved in a common enterprise," this factor is not further elaborated. Substantial progress was stimulated, however, by the appearance of Friedland and Alford's (1991: 248) essay stressing the importance of institutional logics to the existence of an institutional order. They defined *institutional logic* as "a set of material practices and symbolic constructions which constitutes its organizing principles and which is available to organizations and individuals to elaborate." Multiple frameworks are available within developed societies, which are differentiated around numerous specialized arenas—political, political, economic, religious, kinship, and so on—and each of which is governed by a different logic. Organizations, working at mesolevels within these arenas, are hence confronted by and have available to them multiple, often contradictory, logics:

Some of the most important struggles between groups, organizations, and classes are over the appropriate relationships between institutions, and by which institutional logic different activities are to be regulated and to which categories of persons they apply. Is access to housing and health to be regulated by the market or by the state? Are families, churches, or states to control education? Should reproduction be regulated by state, family, or church? (Friedland and Alford 1991: 256)

Thus, institutional logics vary in their content—the nature of beliefs and assumptions—but also in their penetration or "vertical depth" (Krasner 1988). For example, Fligstein (2001a: 32) distinguishes between "general societal understandings about how to organize firms or markets . . . and specific understandings about how a particular market works." Institutional logics also vary in their breadth or extent of horizontal linkage (Krasner 1988). One of the most significant pre-dictors of institutional stability and influence is the extent to which it is compatible with or complementary to related institutional arrange-ments (Hall and Soskice 2001a: 17). Finally, institutional logics within a field vary in terms of their exclusiveness or, conversely, the extent to which they are contested (Scott 1994a: 211; see also Thornton and Occasio 1999). Whitley's (1992b: 127) concept of "business recipes"— varying modes of organizing economic activities—provides alternative language for discussing institutional logics. His empirical work exam-ines the extent of variation in these recipes or logics among European and Asian industries (Whitley 1992a, 1992c). A good example of orga-nizations confronted by contrasting logics is provided by Haveman and Rao's (1997) study of early thrifts being organized as mutual aid societies, whereas later forms adopted the capitalist enterprise model, as discussed in chapter 6.

A second concept that has proved helpful in examining cultural-cognitive systems is that of *cultural frame*. The perceptive social psy-chologist, Erving Goffman (1974: 21), first employed the concept to refer to "schemata of interpretation" that enable individuals "to locate, perceive, identify, and label" events occurring to them in ways that establish their meaning. The concept was employed after modification by David Snow and colleagues, who eschewed the noun for the verb, emphasizing "framing processes" to better inform social movement theory (Benford and Snow 2000; Snow et al. 1986). As they noted:

This denotes an active, processual phenomenon that implies agency and contention at the level of reality construction. It is active in the sense that something is being done, and processual in the sense of a dynamic, evolving process." (Benford and Snow 2000: 614)

The concept of framing proved useful to social movement theo-rists, who realized that much of the work of activist and reform groups involves a "reframing" of issues and problems in ways that illuminate injustice or identify possible ways forward (McAdam 1994; Zald 1996). In short order, however, the concept was embraced by organizational and institutional scholars.

In their study of the recycling industry, Lounsbury, Ventresca, and Hirsch (2003) describe the contest waged between two competing visions—"field-level frames"—for managing solid waste. The waste-to-energy (W-T-E) model, which involves capturing usable energy from the burning of trash, was favored in the 1970s. This approach gen-erated opposition from environmentalists, who promoted an alterna-tive frame that favored recycling—the collection and breaking down of materials such as paper and glass that can be remanufactured into con-sumer products. The recycling view remained marginal until it was repackaged from a volunteer model to a for-profit model favored by federal, state, and local legislation to resist the building of incinerators and favor recycling efforts. The researchers tracked changes in dis-course reflected in the meetings of the Solid Waste Association of North America and its trade magazine providing "a cognitive representation of how key industry issues were to be thought about and discussed" (2003). Although attention to cultural frames stresses "the interweav-ing structures of meaning and resources as well as their wider cultural and political context" (Lounsbury, Ventresca, and Hirsch 2003), it is obvious from this example that the concept of frame is closely associ-ated with that of institutional logic: Issues of how things are interpreted and represented connects fairly seamlessly to considerations how things are to be done.

Organizational Archetypes

Two other families of concepts are useful because they help to bridge the analytical gap between attention to cultural and structural components of institutions. In addition to the examination of wider sys-tems of relations and meanings that provide essential context for actors, we note that within any given field one finds a delimited number of models both for individual actors (roles) and collective actors (organiza-tions). The concept of *organizational archetype,* as discussed in chapter 5, provides a useful mode of characterizing the ways in which a given interpretive scheme or conceptual model is embodied within an organizational structure and its operating systems (Greenwood and Hinings 1993). Of course, the extent to which organizational activities correspond with the model is always a matter for empirical investigation, but archetypes provide templates around which rules, administrative systems, and accounts of activities can be structured. Following the lead of population ecologists as well as "configurational" arguments (Van de Ven and Drazin 1985), Greenwood and Hinings (1993) propose that field-level pressures will encourage organizations to utilize structures and systems that manifest a single underlying interpreting scheme, and that, once adopted, organizations tend to retain the same archetypes.[3]

Attention to the power of organizational archetypes underlines the importance of the constitutive properties of cultural-cognitive elements: their capacity in the guise of typifications, scripts, or conceptions of agency to provide the forms and "categories and understanding that enable us to engage in economic and social action" (Dacin, Ventresca, and Beal 1999: 329; see also DiMaggio 1994: 35).

Most fields include a variety of organizational forms (populations) that constitute the primary modes of producer organizations (e.g., various types of health care delivery organizations, as described below), along with those different, supporting organizations that supply essential resources, including funding, and exercise controls. In addition, it is important not to overlook the critical role played in most fields by a variety of intermediary organizations and occupations—for example, stock analysts in markets (see Zuckerman 1999) or such information brokers as librarians, computer scientists, and online database services (Ventresca and Mohr 2002).

Repertoires of Collective Action

Another useful concept linking culture and social structure was first introduced into the analysis of social movements by Charles Tilly. Tilly (1978: 143) was among the first to point out that even apparently disorganized and disruptive behaviors were likely to take on "well-defined forms already familiar to the participants," including collective actions such as strikes, rallies, and demonstrations. Moreover "given the innumerable ways in which people could, in principle, deploy their resources in pursuit of common ends . . . at any point in time, the repertoire of collective actions available to a population is surprisingly limited" (Tilly 1978: 151). If such an observation holds for social movements, which tend to operate under less structured or institutionalized conditions, think how much more applicable it is to the world of everyday organizations operating in settled fields. As Hoffman (1997: 148) observes:

the institutional environment, in large part, defines the range of the organizational reality. In setting strategy and structure, firms may choose action from a repertoire of possible options. But the range of that repertoire is bound by the rules, norms, and beliefs of the organizational field.

Clemens (1996, 1997) connects the idea of repertoires to that of organizational archetype. She suggests that any field contains a limited repertoire of organizational forms that contain a limited set of culturally defined tools (Swidler 1986) or repertoires of collective action. Clemens also suggests ways in which social movement organizations participate in inducing institutional change, work we review in a later section.

Concepts such as organizational archetype and repertoires of collective action help us to better understand the ways in which cultural-cognitive models act to both constrain and empower social action. By providing clear templates for organizing—whether designing structures, strategies, or procedures—institutional forms constrain actors from selecting (or even considering) alternative forms and modes, on the one hand, but provide essential support for actors carrying on the selected activities in the guise of comprehensibility, acceptability, and legitimacy, on the other.

❖ FIELD STRUCTURATION PROCESSES

Multiple Levels

As described in chapter 4, Giddens (1979, 1984) defines the concept of structuration quite broadly to refer to the recursive interdependence or social structures and activities. The verb form is intended to remind us that structures only exist to the extent that ongoing activities produce and reproduce them. In applying the concept to organizational fields, DiMaggio and Powell (1983: 148) employ the term *structuration* more narrowly to refer to the degree of interaction and the nature of the interorganizational structure that arises at the field level. As noted above, the indicators proposed to assess structuration include the extent to which organizations in a field interact and are confronted with a larger amount of information to process, the emergence of "interorganizational structures of domination and patterns of coalition," and the development of "mutual awareness among participants in a set of organizations that they are engaged in a common enterprise." To these indicators, others can be added, including extent of agreement on the institutional logics guiding activities within the field, increased isomorphism of structural forms within populations in the field (i.e., organizations embracing a limited repertoire of archetypes and employing a limited range of collective activities), increased structural equivalence of organizational sets within the field, and increased clarity of field boundaries (see Scott 1994a; Scott et al. 2000: chap. 10).

We stressed earlier the important locus of the organization field as an intermediate unit between, at microlevels, individual actors and organizations and, at macrolevels, systems of societal and transocietal actors. Figure 8.1 depicts a generalized multilevel model of institutional forms and flows. Trans-societal or societal institutions provide a wider institutional environment within which more specific institutional fields and forms exist and operate. These, in turn, provide contexts for particular organizations and other types of collective actors that themselves supply contexts for subgroups and individual actors. Various top-down processes—constitutive activities, diffusion, translation, socialization, imposition, authorization, inducement, and imprinting (see Scott 1987)—allow higher level (more encompassing) structures to shape, both constrain and empower, the structure and actions of lower level actors. Simultaneously, counterprocesses are at work by which lower level actors and structures shape—reproduce and change—the contexts within which they operate. These bottom-up processes include, variously: selective attention, interpretation and sense-making, identity construction, error, invention, conformity and reproduction of patterns, compromise, avoidance, defiance, and manipulation (see Oliver 1991). Research by Schneiberg and Soule (2005) on the changing forms of rate regulation of fire insurance by the several U.S. states during the beginning of the 20th century depict policies resulting from contested, multilevel processes as competing regimes developed in different regions of the country. Forces at work in crafting a "middle way," which subsequently became widely adopted, included within-state differences in the power of relevant associations, attention to policies adopted by neighboring states, and decisions at the national level by the U.S. Supreme Court.

Earlier neoinstitutional sociologists emphasized top-down processes, focusing on the ways in which models, menus, and rules constituted and constrained organization-level structures and processes. Neoinstitutional economists and rational-choice political scientists continue to focus on bottom-up processes as actors pursue their interests by designing institutional frameworks that solve collective action

Figure 8.1   Top-Down and Bottom-Up Processes in Institutional Creation
and Diffusion

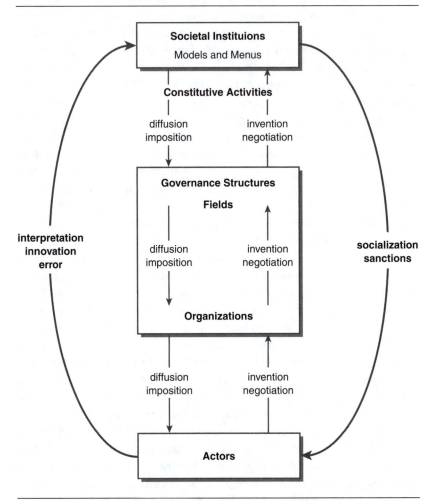

SOURCE: Adapted from Scott 1994c (Figure 3.1, p. 37).

problems or improve the efficiency of economic exchanges. Thelen
(1999: 380) proposes that, although the time may not have arrived
for a synthesis of economic and rational choice with more
historical and sociological views of institutions, we might "strive for
creative combinations that recognize and attempt to harness the
strengths of each approach." Recent work has begun to surface that
emphasizes the interweaving of top-down and bottom-up processes as
they combine to influence institutional phenomena (Barley and
Tolbert 1997). We previously discussed the studies by Edelman and

associates (Edelman 1992; Edelman, Uggen, and Erlanger 1999) and Dobbin and associates (Dobbin et al. 1993; Dobbin and Sutton 1998), who explored how top-down regulative processes initiated by federal agents trigger collective sense-making processes among personnel managers and who construct new structures and procedures that are reviewed and, eventually, authorized by the federal courts. Regulative (federal laws), normative (professional managerial codes), and cognitive (sense-making) processes are connected in complex and changing mixtures.

In formulating a recursive, iterative model of institutional change, Holm (1995) proposes that it is helpful in examining the processes connecting adjacent levels to distinguish between two, nested types of processes: practical versus political actions. The former are actions taken within a given framework of understandings, norms, and rules serving to reproduce the institutional structure or, at most, stimulate incremental changes. The latter, political processes are actions taken whose purpose is to change the rules or frameworks governing actions. For example, explicit rules govern the activities of professional sports teams, but, from time to time, team representatives and officials meet to review and make alterations in the rules based on accumulated experiences or specific problems encountered. Although in some cases, changes in rules are based on collective mobilization and conflict, in many organized systems, formal structures are in place to support routine reviews of and revisions in rule systems. The creation of such formalized decision-making and governance systems serves to institutionalize the process of institutional change.[4]

Widening Theoretical Frameworks

In addition to employing more multilevel and recursive models in institutional studies, institutional scholars have begun to widen their theoretical frames, taking advantage of ideas and approaches developed in related areas. I have already discussed, in chapter 6, the constructive connections being developed between students of the legal environment and institutionalists. Edelman and Suchman (1997) distinguish three dimensions of legal environments relevant to organizational studies. Legal systems offer a facilitative environment, supplying tools, procedures, and forums that actors can employ to pursue goals, resolve disputes, and control deviant and criminal behavior within and by organizations (see Sitkin and Bies 1994; Vaughn 1999). They provide a regulatory environment consisting of a set of "substantive edicts, invoking societal authority over various aspects of organizational life"

(Edelman and Suchman 1997: 483; see also Noll 1985). Most fatefully, they offer a constitutive environment that "constructs and empowers various classes of organizational actors and delineates the relationships among them" (Edelman and Suchman 1997: p. 483; see also Scott 1994c). Edelman and Suchman suggest that we need much more research on the ways in which constitutive legal processes function to construct interorganizational relations (e.g., tort law, bankruptcy law), construct distinctive forms of organization structure (e.g., corporate law), and contribute to an underlying cultural logic of legal rationality.

Another rapidly developing intersection, noted earlier in this chapter, is that between social movement theory and institutional change. For many years, social movement theory has productively borrowed from organizational theory as Mayer Zald, John McCarthy, Charles Tilly, and others showed us how collective movements, if they were to be sustained, required the mobilization of resources and leadership to create social movement organizations (Zald and Ash 1966). As numerous movement organizations pursued similar types of reforms, they identified social movement industries or fields within which such similar organizations competed, cooperated, and learned from each other (McCarthy and Zald 1977).

As social movements have become more organized and as the more nimble and flexible newer forms of organizations have become more movement-like, the flow of ideas between the two fields has increased apace (Davis et al. 2005).

Among their contributions to institutional theory, social movement scholars have called attention to the openings and opportunities provided to suppressed groups and interests by the contradictions or inconsistencies in political institutions or governance structure, the mobilizing processes that give rise to new kinds of organizations, and the reframing processes that involve the creative construction of new meanings and identities enabling new possibilities for collective action (McAdam, McCarthy, and Zald 1996: 2–3; McAdam and Scott 2005: 14–19).

All of these ideas are brought to bear by Elizabeth Clemens (1993, 1997) in her analysis of women's political groups at the turn of the last century in the United States. Lacking access to normal forms of political action (the right to vote), they "adapted existing nonpolitical models of organization for political purposes" (Clemens 1993: 758). The repertoire of collective action—the "set of organizational models that are culturally or experientially available" for women at this time and place—included unions, clubs, and associations. Employing these conventional models in unconventional ways mobilized around new purposes led to significant institutional change.

At the institutional level, women's groups were central to a broader reworking of the organizational framework of American politics: the decline of competitive political parties and electoral mass mobilization, followed by the emergence of a governing system centered on administration, regulation, lobbying, and legislative politics (Clemens 1993).

A neglected area of study has been the processes at work in the transitional period during which successful movement objectives are "handed off" to legislatures and public agencies for follow-through and implementation. In our study of advocacy groups for youth development in urban areas, we have observed the ways in which issues and objectives are reframed and revised as the action moves "from the streets to the suites" (McLaughlin et al. forthcoming). Institutional theory will benefit greatly by continuing to cultivate connections with law and society scholars and with social movements theorists, as well as with other rapidly developing research communities, such as network theorists (Nohria and Eccles 1992; Smith-Doerr and Powell 2005), students of society and accounting (Hopwood and Miller 1994), economic sociology (Smelser and Swedberg 1994, 2005), and international and comparative management (Ghoshal and Westney 1993; Guillén 2001b). All of these communities can bring theoretical insights and useful methodologies to our understanding of institutions and institutional change processes.

❖ STRUCTURATION, DESTRUCTURATION, AND RESTRUCTURATION

On the one hand, change poses a problem for institutional theorists, most of whom view institutions as the source of stability and order. If the nature of actors and their modes of acting are constituted and constrained by institutions, how can these actors change the institutions in which they are embedded? On the other hand, much theory and research on institutions focuses on change: the creation of new institutional forms and associated changes in organizational fields, and populations and individual organizations as these entities respond to pressures to adopt new structures or practices. Much of this attention to change, however, tends to privilege two moments: the formation of new elements and their diffusion across host forms, work reviewed in chapters 5 and 6. Emphasis has been on institutional construction and convergent change processes. This focus assumes that institutions are put in place and then exert their effects, but are not subject to further change. Only in the last two decades have theorists and researchers begun to examine arguments and situations involving institutional change that witnesses the deinstitutionalization of existing forms and their replacement by new arrangements, which, in time, undergo institutionalization. Using Gidden's language, institutionalists have focused attention on structuration processes, but have neglected processes leading to destructuration and restructuration.

This section begins by reviewing ideas and evidence concerning deinstitutionalization (destructuration) processes and then considers the ways in which institutions are reconstructed. Although these processes occur at any and all levels, the organizational field level provides, I believe, the most advantageous vantage point.

Deinstitutionalization Processes

As noted in chapter 5, persistence of institutional beliefs and practices cannot be presumed. Deinstitutionalization refers to the processes by which institutions weaken and disappear. As expected, some analysts emphasize primarily the regulative systems, noting enfeebled laws, diluted sanctions, and increasing noncompliance. Others stress eroding norms and evidence of the diminished force of obligatory expectations. Still others point to the erosion of cultural beliefs and the increasing questioning of what was once taken for granted. Regardless of which elements are emphasized—of course, these elements interact, and all or various combinations may be involved—analysts should attend to both beliefs and behaviors: to schemas and resources. Beliefs and behaviors are loosely coupled, as generations of sociologists have emphasized, but changes in our ideas and expectations put pressure on related activities and vice versa.

The possible causes of deinstitutionalization are multiple. As noted, Zucker (1988b) emphasizes the general phenomenon of entropy associated with "imperfect transmission" and modification of rules under the pressure of varying circumstances and the erosion of roles by the personal characteristics of occupants. Oliver (1992) describes three general types of pressures toward deinstitutionalization: functional, political, and social. *Functional* pressures are those that arise from perceived problems in performance levels associated with institutionalized practices. For example, U.S. public schools have clearly suffered loss of legitimacy in recent years due to lower scores on standardized educational tests compared to children in comparable societies (see National Commission on Excellence in Education 1983). Reduced legitimacy allows increased consideration of alternative policies—for example, No Child Left Behind—and approaches such as vouchers. There is an ecology of institutions, organizations, and actions. When institutional structures are found by some important constituency to be inadequate in the guidelines they provide, these structures are candidates for reform or replacement as problems accumulate.

Functional pressures can also arise from changing consumer preferences. Kraatz and Zajac (1996) studied the effect on private liberal arts colleges of changes in student educational goals beginning in the 1970s as students became less motivated by humanistic purposes and self-fulfillment goals and more concerned with making a living and succeeding financially. Data from over 600 U.S. colleges during the period 1971–1986 revealed that, despite strong normative and cultural-cognitive commitments to the value of liberal arts programs, virtually all the schools responded to student enrollment pressures by introducing vocationally oriented professional programs. As expected, those more dependent on student tuition were more likely to add such programs, whereas the most prestigious colleges were more resistant to these changes. Kraatz and Zajac interpret their findings as demonstrating the limits of institutional arguments: In the face of changes in consumer preferences, strongly institutionalized values and their associated structures gave way to market pressures. An alternative interpretation, which I prefer, is that their study depicts the undermining (delegitimation) of one institutional logic—the virtues of the liberal arts—and its gradual replacement by a second—embracing market-oriented institutional logics.

Political pressures result from shifts in interests or underlying power distributions that provided support for existing institutional arrangements. Changing voter preferences can lead to new political alignments and changing majorities in legislative groups can result in changes in regulatory legislation or enforcement practices. Thus, as discussed in chapter 7, when the U.S. Surgeon General finally summoned the courage and political resources to "blow the whistle" on tobacco companies, although the Big Six companies responded collectively to defend themselves, all companies attempted to adapt to the new environment in a variety of individual ways (Miles 1982). The Big Six companies survived, many by diversifying into other markets. Population ecologists remind us, however, that it is important not to focus exclusive attention on the largest companies in an industry. Research by Hannan and Freeman (1989: 23–33) reports that, during the period of interest, "of the 78 companies in the U.S. tobacco business in 1956, 49 had left the industry by 1986." About a quarter of these shifted into other business lines, but the rest failed to survive.

Business interests can lobby legislative bodies to change corporate governance frameworks, as discussed in chapter 5. As noted in our review of social movement contributions in the previous section, changes in the alignment of political groups can provide weakened support for existing institutional settlements and welcome opportunities for new players and divergent interests to enter the arena. The rise of environmental interests during the 1960s and the responsiveness of the political establishment to the increasing demands for clear air and water led to a major shift in the institutional environment within which the petrochemical industries operated, resulting in changes in the organizational structure and strategies of these companies and the institutional logics employed by their managers, as Hoffman (1997, 1999) details (see also chap. 7).

Social pressures are associated with differentiation of groups and increasing fragmentation of normative consensus, causing divergent or discordant beliefs and practices. In our health care study, we show how the long-term reduction in membership in the American Medical Association (AMA), associated with the rise of specialty associations, resulted in the weakening and fragmentation of physician normative consensus and, as a consequence, a disintegration of the unified voice of "American medicine" regarding health care matters (Scott et al. 2000). The presence of multiple competing and overlapping institutional frameworks undermines the stability of each. For example, we have "the numerous studies from Eastern Europe documenting parallel and contradictory logics in which ordinary citizens were already experiencing, for a decade prior to 1989, a social world in which various domains were not integrated coherently" (Stark 1996: 994).

We are beginning to see more empirical studies of deinstitutionalization. As might be expected, the indicators employed to assess the extent of deinstitutionalization range from weakening beliefs to abandonment of a set of practices. Geertz (1971: 17) describes a subtle and barely discernible pattern of deinstitutionalization underway in two Islam societies as fundamentalist belief systems gradually loosen their hold on believers:

> What is believed to be true has not changed for these people, or not changed very much. What has changed is the way in which it is believed. Where there once was faith, there now are reasons, and not very convincing ones; what once were deliverances are now hypotheses, and rather strained ones. There is not much outright skepticism around, or even much conscious hypocrisy, but there is a good deal of solemn self-deception.

Sine and Tolbert (2006: 7) describe an intermediate stage of deinstitutionalization based on changing practices. They examine a decline in the use of tenure systems in American institutions of higher education from 1965 to 1995. Although only a few colleges and universities abandoned the tenure system, "many higher education institutions have, in the last three decades, steadily increased the number and proportion of non-tenure-track faculty positions." The tenure institution, strongly supported by the normative structures of the teaching profession, persists, but its scope is narrowing so that the protections apply to ever smaller numbers of faculty members. Using data from 1989 to 1995, Sine and Tolbert show that, although there are costs, primarily labor costs, associated with compliance to the tenure system, other costs, primarily legitimacy costs, attend to reduced compliance.

Analyzing changes over time in the normative and cultural-cognitive conventions governing grand opera, Robinson (1985: 10) describes how the use of "two clocks"—the real-life tempo of the recitative as "things move along more or less as they do in real life," in contrast to the "slow time" devoted to an aria or ensemble number—which characterized 17th- and 18th-century productions gave way to the "continuous" musical style of the 19th century. Transitional composers paved the way by employing, but ridiculing, earlier styles. Thus, in his opera, *The Barber of Seville* (1816), Rossini self-consciously adhered to 18th-century conventions, but employed them to comic effect so that "one sees in Rossini an operatic convention at the very end of its artistic life: he makes fun of it; the next generation simply abandons it."

Outright abandonment of an institutionalized practice represents the extreme case of deinstitutionalization. Ahmadjian and Robinson (2001) examine the gradual abandonment, by Japanese companies, of their celebrated practice of permanent employment, viewed as a cornerstone of their distinctive employment system (Abegglen 1958; Cole 1979; Dore 1973; Ouchi 1981). For many years during the postWorld War II period, Japanese firms had an implicit contract with their mainline employees, who were given extensive in-company training, to provide them with employment until retirement. This commitment was viewed by many observers, including Cole and Ouchi, as a critical contributor to the remarkable productivity associated with the Japanese industry during this period. However, under the pressure of a severe economic downturn during the 1990s, Japanese firms began to abandon their normative commitment to employees. In their examination of over 1,500 companies arrayed across diverse industries, Ahmadjian and Robinson (2001: 644) found that, while downsizing strategies were first utilized by poorly performing companies and more slowly adopted by larger and more prestigious firms, as time passed, more and more companies abandoned the commitment to permanent employment.

Over time, "social and institutional concerns gave way to economic pressures as downsizing became increasingly widespread across the population, and firms found safety in numbers." However, as was the case with the study of the dilution of the liberal arts curriculum within colleges, although economic pressures played a role in destabilizing existing practices—whether regarding curriculum or personnel practices—the changes observed do not reflect the naked play of market forces or the adaptive efforts of independent, individual organizations, as Kraatz and Zajac (1996) would have us believe, but the emergence and diffusion of a new institutional logic concerning the right way to conduct the activities in question. As Burdros (1997: 230) makes clear in his study of U.S. corporate adoption of downsizing programs, these practices are supported by beliefs espoused by neoliberal arguments and advanced by investment managers who have proved persuasive to many businesses, although "available research indicates that these events generally have adverse human and organizational effects" (see also Campbell and Pedersen 2001). Deinstitutionalization is associated not only with the growing recognition that current institutional patterns are ineffective, but also with the development of a challenging alternative institutional logic.[5]

Four Studies of Field Structuration/Destructuation

Evolving Corporate Structure

We can better understand some of the forces and mechanisms at work in field-level change processes if we approach them as they were observed in a few selected studies of particular fields operating in specific times and places. We begin by revisiting Fligstein's (1990, 1991) study of changes in the structure of large U.S. corporations during the 20th century (see chap. 7). This research is particularly effective in pursuing three aspects of field structuration: the interplay of (a) private power and public authority, (b) ideas and interests, and (c) field logics and internal organization processes. We review each in turn.

Recall that Fligstein's study examined a (changing) sample of the 100 largest nonfinancial corporations from 1920 to 1980. These companies became increasingly diversified throughout this period, but the diversification strategies varied over time, in part, because of changing federal antitrust policies.

Whereas Alfred Chandler's (1977) detailed history of changes in corporate structure stressed the role of market forces and managerial decisions, as described in chapter 5, Fligstein reminds us of the power of the state both to ratify institutional settlements enforced by the dominant companies in an industry as well as to establish and change the general rules governing competitive practices and growth strategies for all firms. For Fligstein (2001a: 18), markets are not simply arenas of competition, but organizational fields whose members, in combination with state agencies, attempt to

> produce a social world stable enough that they can sell [their] goods and services at a price at which their organization will survive. Managing people and uncertain environments to produce stability is a sizable task. . . . The theory of fields implies that the search for stable interactions with competitors, suppliers, and workers is the main cause of social structures in markets.

Fields are vehicles for producing some stability and order for their members.

As for the interplay of ideas and interests, Fligstein (2001a: 15–20), more than most analysts, employs what he terms a *political-cultural* approach, melding the role of cultural-cognitive elements or interpretive frameworks with the play of power among actors struggling to achieve a "system of domination" that will serve their interests. Fields are arenas for the interplay of incumbents, who benefit from existing arrangements, and challengers, who seek to change the rules to advance their own interests. Governments, which can be conceived of as a "set of fields," interact with markets, another set of fields, imposing rules to help ensure stability. Fligstein (1991) asserts that the changing strategies reflected changing institutional logics regarding competitive practices and growth strategies. But what is the process by which field logics result in organizational change? One obvious mechanism is environmental selection: Firms not pursuing the favored strategy were more likely to drop out of a sample of the largest corporations over time, particularly during the later period Another mechanism explored by Fligstein is that changes in field logics trigger political processes within organizations so that corporations changed the criteria used to select their chief executive officer (CEO). Fligstein (1991: 323) categorizes CEOs in terms of their background under the assumption that "a manufacturing person will tend to see the organization's problems in production terms, a sales and marketing person will tend to view the nature, size and extent of the market as critical to organizational survival, and a financial person will see the basic profitability of firm activities as crucial." Empirically, he shows that the hiring of a CEO with a manufacturing background was associated with the subsequent adoption of a dominant strategy focusing on a single market, the hiring of a CEO from a sales background was associated with the adoption of a strategy of diversification into related markets, and the hiring of a CEO with a financial background was associated with the adoption of strategy of diversification into both related and unrelated markets. Greenwood and Hinings (1996) generalize these arguments by embracing Cyert and March's (1963) conception of organizations as coalitions of participants holding varying interests. Changes in field logics are likely to be viewed as advancing the interests of some types of organizational participants and undercutting those of others. In this manner, they propose to link the old institutionalism that focused more on power processes within organizations (think Selznick) with the new institutionalism that stresses field-level templates and logics.

Destructuration of a Health Care Field

My colleagues and I (Scott et al. 2000) decided to study health care delivery in the United States because this appeared to represent an instance of a relatively settled and stable institutional arena, which, within the past few decades, has become increasingly conflictual and unstable. For our primary empirical data, we focused on changes in health care delivery systems within a limited geographic area—the San Francisco Bay area—but in accounting for these developments, we took account of actors and forces at state and national levels. Data were collected over a 50-year period from 1945 to 1995.

To empirically capture changes in the field, we selected three components on which to gather data:

- *changes over time in the types and numbers of social actors—both individual (roles) and collective actors (organizations)*

For example, we measured changes in the number and types (specialties) of physicians, changes in the membership of leading professional associations, and changes in the major organizational forms (archetypes) comprising the delivery systems, including physician groups, hospitals, home health agencies, health maintenance organizations (HMOs), renal dialysis units, and integrated health care systems. We also assessed changing relational connections among these various forms (e.g., clinics and home health agencies contracting with hospitals or hospitals joining integrated healthcare systems; Scott et al. 2000: chap. 3).

I can think of no better single indicator for assessing changes in organizational fields than tracking changes in the number and types of organizations that operate within its boundaries. Organizations archetypes are critical aspects of the field's "structural vocabulary." During the period of our study, the number and size of medical clinics, home health agencies, HMOs, and specialized treatment units such as dialysis centers expanded greatly, whereas the overall number and size of hospitals remained relatively stable. Given that the population of the region more than tripled during this time, the lack of expansion in hospitals, the traditional delivery unit, indicates that they were being displaced by other types of organizations. Of equal significance are the new types of organizations that emerged. Newcomers such as home health agencies, staffed largely by nurses who deliver care in patients' homes, and HMOs, which ensure that physicians are financially at risk for failing to control costs incurred by the care they prescribe, represent radically different approaches to health care delivery. These forms embodied novel organizational archetypes that challenge earlier models.

Of course, it is possible for existing organizations to change their archetype, substituting one template or "interpretive scheme" for another, as Greenwood and Hinings (1993) and Fligstein (1990) demonstrated. However, both of these studies focused attention on a single population of organizations, municipal governments or large corporations. A distinctive advantage of field-level designs is that they widen the lens, allowing researchers to observe the rise of new forms that challenge and, sometimes replace, existing forms. Although it appears that we are interested primarily in structural and relational changes— merely counting organizations—we are in fact attending to the constitutive work of changing cultural-cognitive beliefs.

- *changes over time in the institutional logics that guide activities in the field*

Multiple indicators were employed to ascertain changes in logics, including changing patterns in the financing of health care,[6] changes in public policy at the state and federal levels, changes in consumer beliefs regarding health care, and changes in professional discourse as revealed by an examination of physician-oriented and health care administration journals (Scott et al. 2000: chap. 6). The use of such archival sources to reveal changes over time in the meaning structures employed to interpret and guide actions of field participants provides a promising avenue for assessing the codependence of cultural and structural elements (see Ventresca and Mohr 2002).

Composite indicators suggest that three contrasting institutional logics were dominant during different periods. To the mid-1960s, the dominant logic was an overriding concern with quality of care as determined by medical providers. In the mid-1960s, this logic was joined with a political logic emphasizing improved equity of access—the defining event being the passage of Medicare-Medicaid legislation in 1965. Somewhat later, in the early 1980s, yet another logic was introduced, which emphasized the importance of cost containment employing both market and managerial controls. None of the three logics—each of which was associated with differing types of actors—succeeded in replacing the other, but the contradictions and conflicts among them have greatly reduced the coherence and stability of field structure.

- *changes in governance structures that oversee field activities*

As defined earlier in this chapter, governance structures are combinations of public and private, formal and informal systems that exercise control within the field. During the period of our study, dramatic changes were observed in the kinds of actors exercising control and in the mechanisms employed. During the first half of the 20th century, the health care delivery field was firmly under the control of a hegemonic professional group—doctors of medicine. Having warded off a variety of rival claimants for jurisdiction over the field (see Starr 1982), subordinated a variety of ancillary groups (see Freidson 1970), and secured the backing of the several U.S. states exercising their licensure power, the medical establishment ruled by moral authority, exercising normative control.

As already described, by the mid-1960s, fragmentation of physician interests and the coming to power of the Democrats resulted in the passage of the Medicare/Medicaid Act, which overnight made the federal government the largest single purchaser of acute care and hospital services. Paying for a substantial proportion of the bills—which resulted in increasing demands—public authorities became more and more active in regulating health services. The number of health-related regulatory bodies operating at the county, state, and national levels grew from a handful in 1945 to well over 100 agencies (Scott et al. 2000). The normative power of the medical establishment, although weakened, remained in force, but was now joined by public regulative powers.

Beginning in the early 1980s, new approaches to cost containment were introduced based on neoliberal economic assumptions regarding the effectiveness of more business-like and market-based approaches. For-profit delivery systems were endorsed featuring stronger managerial controls, and incentives were employed to encourage patients to consume fewer services and providers to restrict treatments. New "health plans" emerged to define benefits, collect payments, and enlist panels of eligible providers. Thus, added to the mix of professional and public controls were private market and managerial governance mechanisms (Scott et al. 2000: 217–235).

Some time ago, Meyer and I (1983a: 201) argued that it is useful to view an organization's legitimacy as varying by the extent of coherence in the cultural environment underlying it—"*the adequacy of an organization as theory.* A completely legitimate organization would be one about which no question may be raised" (italics original). From this perspective, given the inconsistency of views regarding health care expressed by professional, public, and private oversight authorities, the legitimacy of health care systems markedly declined in this country during the last half of the 20th century. This is represented not only in the overelaborated and complex administrative units at the organizational level required to respond to the multiple and conflicting demands, but also in the overgrown jungle of financial and regulatory units and infrastructural apparatus—lawyers, accountants, health economists, actuaries, and insurance brokers—that contribute so much to the costs and confusion-making of the current state of this field.

Similar Pressures—Divergent Responses

Nicole Biggart and Mauro Guillén (1999) examine the response of the auto industries of four countries—South Korea, Taiwan, Spain, and Argentina—to mounting competitive pressures from the global environment (see also Guillén 2001b). For many decades, manufacturing fields serviced primarily domestic markets and did not have to take into account the productivity or performance of similar fields in other countries. However, in recent decades, as a result of numerous political, technological, and economic developments, formerly "local" industries were compelled to compete for survival with distant producers (Albrow 1997; Berger and Huntington 2002; Ó Riain 2000).

Biggart and Guillén (1999) employ an institutional approach to their study, emphasizing:

- the different kinds of actors available in each society (e.g., the nature of the state, families, large firms, small firms, business networks)
- the "pattern of social organization that binds actors to one another" (e.g., the relation of states to industrial firms, of large to small firms, of firms to business networks; 723)

- the organizing logics characteristic of the society. In their terms: "organizing logics are not merely constraints on the unfolding of otherwise unimpeded social action, but rather are repositories of distinctive capabilities that allow firms and other economic actors to pursue some activities in the global economy more successfully than others" (726)
- the industrial policies pursued by the state. Nation-states vary in the development policies they pursue, as well as in how actively they intervene in economic matters

Employing a distinction developed by Gereffi (1994), they note that societies characterized by more vertical linkages between strong states and firms or between large firms and subordinate units are more likely to excel at producer-driven activities linked to the global economy, whereas economies comprised of small firms connected by horizontal linkages are more nimble and, hence, can be more responsive to "buyer-driven" global demands. Thus, for example, South Korea, with its vertically integrated *chaebol* (business units) and strong state, has been relatively successful in auto assembly (producer-driven) operations, but much less successful in creating a competitive system of components manufacturers. By contrast, Taiwan, with its highly developed small firms economy, was unresponsive to state initiatives to promote auto assembly plants and instead has been able to compete globally in its manufacture of (buyer-driven) components. It is also possible for states to bypass their own business community and allow "foreign actors unrestricted access to the country" by encouraging foreign firms to make investments and establish direct ownership ties (Guillén 2001b: 17). This was the policy pursued by Spain. Biggart and Guillén (1999: 743) do not conclude that all strategies pursued are equally successful, but rather that the more successful strategies are those that build on a society's existing institutional logics. Such differences are not obstacles or constraints, but "the very engine of development. . . . Development is about finding a place in the global economy, not about convergence or the suppression of difference."

In short, we have a situation parallel to that described in chapter 7, where we considered the reaction of organizations with differing characteristics to similar institutional forces. Like organizations, organizational fields are likely to vary substantially in their history, structural features, and capacities so that, when confronted by similar challenges, they are likely to respond not in parallel, but in divergent, ways. This institutionally informed perspective varies considerably from that of a number of global observers, who emphasize the "flattening" of societal differences (Friedman 2005) or the rapid convergence of economic institutions and firm structures (McKenzie and Lee 1991) as the hallmark of globalization. Gray (2005) points out that, in this respect, such neoliberal arguments bear a close relation to earlier Marxist arguments because they assume that "it is technological advances that fuels economic development, and economic forces that shape society. Politics and culture are secondary phenomena."

The Revolt of the Chefs

As a final example of field-level restructuring, Rao, Monin, and Durand (2003) creatively combined social movement and institutional theory arguments to account for revolutionary changes occurring in the world of French *haut cuisine*. The study examines the introduction by a rebel breed of chefs of a new culinary rhetoric, replacing classic with nouvelle cuisine. The upstart chefs emerged during the period of general political turmoil associated with student protests against the Vietnam War during 1968, a cause that rapidly became connected to a range of other antiestablishment grievances. I like to think the organizing slogan for this revolution was: "Chefs of the world unite. You have nothing to lose but your sauces!"

Rao and colleagues suggest that the two cuisines—classic and nouvelle—represent differing institutional logics—rules of cooking, types of ingredients, and bases for naming dishes—as well as contrasting identities for chefs in relation to waiters. Their imaginative method of tracking the progress of the new logic was to examine changes over time in the menus of leading restaurants, coding a random sample of the signature dishes of chefs between 1970 and 1997.

In conducting their study, the authors draw on a distinction within social movement theory between "interest group" and "identity" politics (Rao, Monin, and Durand 2003: 796). Most studies of social movements focus on interest groups pursuing some instrumental movement (e.g., increased fairness or equality), whereas identity movements seek opportunities for authentic self-expression and opportunities to celebrate and display "who we are." Identity movements seek autonomy, not social justice (Armstrong 2002; Taylor and Whittier 1992). Employing historical materials as well as in-depth interviews, Rao and colleagues examined biographies of selected chefs who personally challenged existing rules—in some cases, rules embraced by their fathers—to convert to the new cuisine. However, for such ideas to diffuse into a movement, they needed to be "theorized" (see chap. 6). This process was greatly facilitated by the media and specialized culinary journalists, who developed the "10 commandments"—including "thou shall not overcook" and "thou shall use fresh quality products"—guiding the new cuisine and advancing rationales for its adoption. Systematic counts of the number of articles published between 1970 and 1997 extolling nouvelle cuisine in culinary magazines—cultural-cognitive legitimation—were found to correlate with adoption by chefs listed in annual directories of *Guide Michelin.*

Evidence concerning the normative legitimation of the movement came from two sources: the number of highly coveted stars from the *Guide Michelin* received by chefs who added a minimum of one nouvelle cuisine dish as part of his signature trio of dishes, and the number of nouvelle cuisine activists elected to the executive board of the professional society of French chefs. Both were positively associated with the abandonment of classical for nouvelle cuisine. In short, the new logic was eventually endorsed by the relevant governance systems.

A particularly valuable aspect of this study by Rao and associates is its recognition of the important role played by intermediary actors in field structuration. The contributions of journalists who helped focus, frame, and diffuse the new logic as well that of influential arbiters of consumer tastes—the editors of *Guide Michelin*—who gave their all-important stamp of approval to the insurgent band of chefs are systematically incorporated in the design of the study.[5]

❖ CONCLUDING COMMENT

The concept of organization field expands the framework of analytic attention to encompass relevant actors, institutional logics, and governance structures that empower and constrain the actions of participants in a delimited social sphere. It includes within its purview all of these parties who are meaningfully involved in some collective enterprise—whether producing a product or service, carrying out some specific policy, or attempting to resolve a common issue. The concept has not only encouraged attention to a higher (more encompassing) level of analysis, but it has also stimulated interest in organizational processes that take place over longer periods of time. To adequately comprehend the determinants, mechanisms, and effects of significant institutional change—or stability for that matter—demands attention to longer time periods.

Organization fields vary considerably among themselves and over time. The concept of field structuration provides a useful analytic framework, allowing investigators to assess differences among fields and to track changes over time in the extent of the field's cultural coherence and nature of its structural features.

Although it would appear that a field-level focus would detract attention from our attempt to understand the behavior of individual organizations, I believe that this is far from being true. Just as the attributes and actions of a character in a play are not fully comprehensible apart from knowledge of the wider drama being enacted—including the nature and interest of the other players, their relationships, and the logics that guide their actions—so we can better fathom an organization's behavior by seeing it in the context of the larger action and meaning system in which it participates.

❖ NOTES

1. Although this criticism holds generally for the community ecologists' conception of field, an important exception is Warren's later work on American communities, in which he laid great stress on the (vertical) connections between local organizations and more distant organizations and systems of ideas external to a given community (Warren 1972; Warren, Rose, and Bergunder 1974).

2. Fligstein (1990) developed a novel conception of field. Beginning with a more conventional view of a field as demarcated by product markets, because he studied large corporations in the process of differentiating into multiple markets, he argued that field boundaries for these organizations also shifted so that eventually the largest diversified corporations operated in a field comprised of other actors like themselves.

3. We consider in a later section processes leading to the replacement of one archetype with another.

4. Other notable studies of field-level structuration processes include Dezalay and Garth (1996), Lauman and Knoke (1987), Hoffman (1997), and Thornton (2004).

5. In addition to those noted above, see also Davis, Diekmann, and Tinsley's (1994) examination of the processes involved in the delegitimation of the conglomerate form in business enterprise, Greve's (1995) analysis of the abandonment by radio stations of one format for another, Zilber's (2002) study (at the organizational level) of changes over time in the meanings associated with organizational action, and Simons and Ingram's (1997) study of the gradual abandonment of ideological commitments regarding the use of labor by Israeli kibbutzim.

6. Financing issues are never just about material resources. In this case, Congress decided that the nation-state, rather than the individual, was responsible for financing medical care for the elderly and the indigent.

9

An Overview
and a Caution

I begin this brief coda by commenting on what I see as the distinctive flavor and texture of an institutional approach. Then I attempt to sum up some of the developments during the past 40 years that, in my opinion, are signs of progress—indicators of a maturing intellectual field. Finally, I briefly comment on a special type of metaphysical pathos that institutional theory is prone to that we would do well to guard against.

❖ DISTINCTIVE FEATURES

Institutional theory differs from alternative approaches to the study of organizations in a number of ways that are important to identify. The following appear to be important:

• *Institutionalists eschew a totalistic or monolithic view of organizational and societal structures and processes.*

The institutional perspective, more so than others, emphasizes the importance of the social context within which organizations operate.

Indeed, the "figure" (organization) is often defocalized to stress the centrality of the "ground" (environment). In many institutional accounts, "the figure is not simply embedded in, but also penetrated and constituted by, the ground" (Scott and Christensen 1995: 310). As suggested in chapter 8, institutional theorists suggest the value of attending to the larger drama, rather than to the individual player.

In addition, institutionalists are more likely than many other analysts to conditionalize their generalizations. Rather than seeking universal social laws, on the one hand, or reverting to "pure description and story-telling," on the other, they tend to work at an "intermediary level" that offers "sometimes true theories" of selected social phenomena (Coleman 1964: 516). As Swiss historian and economist Simonde de Sismondi (1837: iv) observed nearly two centuries ago:

> I am convinced that one falls into serious error in wishing always to generalize everything connected with the social sciences. It is on the contrary essential to study human conditions in detail. One must get hold now of a period, now of a country, now of a profession, in order to see clearly what a man is and how institutions act upon him.

As Fligstein (2001b) more recently pointed out, it is essential to assess the multiple "local orders" of which modern society is comprised, each representing its distinctive social meanings and social structures.

- *Institutionalists insist on the importance of nonlocal (as well as local) forces shaping organizations.*

An important addendum to the primacy given to context is the recognition that this concept—particularly in the modern world—can no longer safely be delimited by geographical boundaries. Many, if not the majority of, organizations are affected by and responsive to forces far removed from their local environment. This has long been the case, but is truer in today's world of intensified media and migrations (Appadurai 1996). As described in our discussion of institutional carriers in chapter 4, institutional elements are highly portable and can arrive in the briefcases of consultants, by the hiring of contract workers, on via the Internet or images of the cinema.

- *Institutionalists have rediscovered the important role played by ideas, specifically, and symbolic elements, generally, in the functioning of organizations.*

Reigning approaches to organization analysis in our time have for too long privileged the importance of material resources, technological drivers, and exchange/power processes in the shaping of organizations. From contingency theory to resource dependence and population ecology, analysts have examined in detail the power and resource constraints to the neglect of cultural forces and cognitive processes. Indeed, throughout much of the second half of the 20th century, organizations have been treated as if they were "culture-free" systems driven by instrumental objectives and governed by "natural" economic laws. Institutional theorists reclaim organizations as creators of man-made culture.

- *Institutionalists accord more attention to types of effects occurring over longer time periods.*

Too much of the work in social science concentrates on structures and processes of the here and now. As Paul Pierson (2004: 79) elaborates:

> Many important social processes take a long time—sometimes an extremely long time—to unfold. This is a problematic fact for contemporary social science [where] the time horizons of most analysts have become increasingly restricted. Both in what we seek to explain and in our search for explanations, we focus on the immediate—we look for causes and outcomes that are both temporally contiguous and rapidly unfolding. In the process, we miss a lot. There are important things that we do not see at all, and what we do see we often misunderstand.

Pioneering institutional work by Selznick and his students emphasized the value of seeing institutionalization as a process occurring over time (see Clark 1960, 1970; Selznick 1949; Zald and Denton 1963; see also chap. 2). These quasihistorical studies followed the development of a single organization over a relatively long period of time. Not long after, however, organizational ecologists began to conduct their longitudinal studies of organizational populations, beginning with the birth of the first organization of a given type and following the subsequent development of that population. Such studies emphasized the importance of taking a longer time perspective, ideally capturing the entire history of a given form (Carroll and Hannan 1989). Although this approach recognized the importance of studying organizations through time, these studies collected only minimal data about the organizations being tracked and, as Zucker (1989: 544) emphasized in her critique of this work, ecologists attended to time passing, but not to "historical time," assuming that one year is equivalent to another.

By contrast, during the past two decades, institutionalists have pioneered in the development of what Ventresca and Mohr (2002: 810) label the *new archival tradition*, which "tends to share key sensibilities in the historiographic approach, sharing its concerns for employing the nuanced, meaning-laden, action-oriented foundation of organizational processes." Key features of this work include its reliance on "formal analytic methodologies," "emphasis on the study of relations" rather than attributes, concern with "measuring the shared forms of meaning that underlie social organizational processes," and attention to "the configurational logics" that produce organized activity. The studies by my colleagues and I (Scott et al. 2000) and by Rao, Monin, and Durand (2002), reviewed in chapter 8, exemplify most of these characteristics.

- *Closely related to this concern with time, institutionalists also accord more attention to an examination of social mechanisms.*

As described in chapter 6, interest in mechanisms directs attention away from questions regarding *what* happened to questions of *how* things happen. Attending to processes of various kinds—fueled by environmental, relational, or cognitive mechanisms (McAdam, Tarrow, and Tilly 2001: 25–26)—is also a way of uncovering the sources of agency in structure and action.

- *Institutionalists embrace research designs that support attention to examining the interdependence of factors operating at multiple levels to affect the outcomes of interest.*

Institutionalists recognize that societies operate within and are affected by transnational processes and structures, organizational fields are affected by societal- as well as organizational-level phenomena, and organizations operate within fields that shape, constrain, and empower them, but are also influenced by the interests and activities of their own participants. To my mind, the most interesting institutional studies are those examining the interplay of such top-down and bottom-up processes as they shape organizations.

❖ THE MATURATION OF
INSTITUTIONAL THEORY AND RESEARCH[1]

More than 20 years ago, I wrote an article entitled "The Adolescence of Institutional Theory" (Scott 1987). In reexamining that article, I think it accurately portrayed, even more than I realized, the undeveloped state of theoretical development of the field at that time, while also recognizing its promise and potential. Taking stock now, I believe it is possible to point to indicators of substantial progress. During the past few decades, we have moved:

- *from looser to tighter conceptualizations of institutions and their distinctive features.*

As reviewed in chapter 1, early formulations about institutions and their effects were literally "all over the map." I believe that by focusing on a few key elements and examining the distinctive mechanisms associated with their operation, we have arrived at a more coherent conception of the phenomena of interest. Institutional forces are recognized to be complex and diverse in their makeup and mode of acting, but identifiable in their manifestation and measurable in their behavior and effects.

- *from determinant to interactive arguments*

Early formulations saw institutions as being monolithic and uniform in their features and determinant in their consequences. Researchers sought evidence of institutional "effects" on organizational forms and structures. More recent work recognizes that the institutional environments of many organization fields are fragmented and conflicted; because organizations have varying attributes and occupy different positions within the field, those institutional effects are far from uniform. In addition, organizations viewed early as passive victims of institutional pressures are increasingly recognized to exercise varying degrees of agency, responding in diverse ways, ranging from abject conformity to outright defiance.

- *from assertions to evidence*

Early institutionalists, and I was among them, often simply asserted the existence of institutional effects. Thus, in our early study of U.S. public schools, my colleagues and I (Meyer et al. 1988: 166) assembled data over a 40-year period to substantiate increased uniformity of structure. We demonstrated empirically that this evidence of increased structuration was not a consequence of heightened centralization of funding, concluding instead that the changes reflected "the expansion and imposition of standard models" of organizing. However, no data were adduced to validate this claim.

However, over time, as I have tried to demonstrate, institutional researchers have devised imaginative and appropriate ways of testing their arguments. Our study designs and measures are far from perfect, but signs of progress are apparent in contrasting recent with earlier studies.

- *from organization-centric to field-level approaches*

The earliest organizational studies focused almost exclusive attention on the inner workings of organizations and the behavior of their participants (see Scott and Davis 2007 for a review). When the importance of the environment first became apparent to scholars, during the 1960s, substantial work followed, which adopted an "organization-centric" perspective—viewing the environment from the vantage point of a single focal organization. The organization's exchanges and strategies became the focus on interest. With the development of organizational ecology and institutional approaches, however, the level of analysis shifted to higher levels, to organizational populations and fields. Attention shifted from the organization *in* an environment to the organization *of* the environment. I tried to describe in chapter 8, and I elaborate below, why I believe the organizational field level to be an especially appropriate venue for the application and testing of institutional arguments.

An interest in more macroapproaches has not supplanted, but supplemented, work at more microlevels. As I have noted, some of the more fruitful designs are those that attend to the interdependence and interaction of actors and forces at multiple levels—individual, organization, population, and field. Studies of top-down structuration processes, together with equal attention to bottom-up processes, have illuminated important facets of organizational life.

- *from institutional stability to institutional change*

Institutions, by definition, connote stability and change; therefore, it is not surprising that early scholars and researchers focused primarily on settled institutions to observe their effects on organizations. It was not long, however, before organizational researchers began to examine the social processes by which institutional frameworks come into being and by what means the more successful of them became more widely diffused and accepted. Studies attending to construction and convergent change processes were joined, during the 1990s, by new research examining processes of conflict and contention and of divergent change. This latter work was both inspired and infused by parallel studies by social movement scholars; over time, each of these two camps has stimulated and enriched the work of the other.

- *from institutions as irrational influences to institutions as frameworks for rational action*

A good many early formulations carried the implicit assumption that institutions undercut rational decisions and actions. Terms such as *myth, ceremonial,* and *superficial conformity* all smacked of subterfuge or skullduggery. Many organizational scholars dismissed institutionalists as dealing with superficial aspects of nonserious organizations. Although I believe this was a misreading of some of the early founding texts, it is an interpretation that has been hard to combat and eradicate.

For me, the concept of institution provides a way of examining the complex interdependence of nonrational and rational elements that together comprise any social situation. Values, beliefs, and interests,[2] along with information, habits, and feelings, are critical ingredients of social behavior. Which of us would claim that all our decisions represent "rational" choices? Of course, organizations were thought to be different from ordinary, less disciplined social actors like you and me. As discussed in chapter 4, the kinds of ideas that gave rise to organizational forms are those that can be formulated as "rule-like principles" that give rise to "means-ends chains"—the basis for rationalized systems. However, as noted, rationalization is a broad tent. These formulations vary enormously in their empirical foundation.

The subtitle of DiMaggio and Powell's (1983) seminal article was: "Institutional Isomorphism and Collective Rationality in Organizational Fields." Much attention has been lavished on the first idea: "institutional isomorphism" (see chap. 7), but far less on the second. Nevertheless, the second idea is the more powerful, and it is the reason that I am so enamored of the possibilities offered by the field level of analysis. As I have tried to argue, it is at the field level where organizations in interaction construct their "collective rationality." It is at this level that one can most readily comprehend the construction of socially constructed frameworks of beliefs, rules, and norms—where we can observe contentious processes involving the participation of various types of actors with varying levels of understanding and influence, and always under the watchful eye and, sometimes, the active intervention of the state. If one looks across the myriad fields that comprise a modern society—banking, manufacturing, mental health, education—one finds multiple worlds of collectively rationalized action, each different from the other.

Even within the same field, if one looks across societies, it is to observe the same activities being carried out in diverse, rational ways. This truth is graphically documented in Frank Dobbin's (1994b) comparative study of the building of the railroad industry in the United States, England, and France during the 19th century. Dobbin details the divergent models of organizing, funding, and state involvement that emerged due to what he terms the diverse "political cultures"— I would call them societal and field institutional frameworks—at work in these countries. The institutions within each country constructed an arena of rational action within which individual and collective actors pursued their interests in diverse competitive and cooperative ways as guided by their cognitive frames and cultural assumptions. We observe collective rationality at work.

Surpassing even my own enthusiasm for the possibilities afforded by organization field-level studies, Fligstein (2001b: 29) puts forward the proposition that "The theory of fields is a generic theory of social organization in modernity." That sounds as if it might be an important area in which to work.

Progress in a given realm of social inquiry takes many forms, including theoretical elaboration and clarification, broadened scope of application of the ideas, improvement in empirical indications, and strengthened methodological tools. Another type of progress is signified by a growing set of connections intellectually linking the area of study with related fields—in the case of institutional scholarship—with work in organizational ecology, law and society, social movements, and cultural sociology. Although there is not cause for complacency, there is much to celebrate in the recent history of our field.

Some observers skeptically wonder whether recent developments in institutional theory may have overly extended the scope of the enterprise. Is there a significant danger that institutional theory will become too broad, too encompassing? Have we staked out too wide a theoretical and empirical domain? Perhaps, but I doubt it. It is true that the range of concepts we employ is large (but the fact is that institutions are complex social systems) and that the levels of analysis to which they are applicable seems boundless. But no one study attempts to comprehend all meanings and levels in a single design. We have devised a rich tool kit of concepts and methods from which scholars may choose as they approach selected problems of interest. Rather than being apprehensive about the direction of our work, I am continually impressed and emboldened by the imagination of my colleagues and the sophistication of their research designs and analytic methods. The fecundity of recent contributions to the field lay to rest any doubts raised in my mind by the skeptics.

However, there is another concern about institutional approaches to social structures that merits attention.

❖ A CAUTIONARY COMMENT

If one examines the grand march of ideas across the centuries, it is possible to make a case for the regular repetition, and alternating dominance, of either more liberal or more conservative accounts of the human condition. Thus, for example, European intellectual circles during the 18th and 19th centuries experienced the heady period of the Enlightenment, with its celebration of Reason and Nature and Progress as the defining virtues—as espoused by such notables as Voltaire, Hume, Locke, Rousseau, and Mill. This exhilarating and optimistic moment gradually gave way (particularly after the failures of the 1848 revolutions) to a sober consideration of the limits of rational design and the impotence of mere individuals confronted with suprapersonal forces. Scholars such as Burke, Dilthey, Schleiermacher, and, most centrally, Hegel, emphasized the overpowering force of "History": the constellation of structures and the flow of historical processes as having a life of their own (Berlin 1956, 2006; Collingwood 1948; Dupri 2004; Robinson 1985). Such arguments became incorporated into the work of the early institutionalists—including Marx, Durkheim, Weber, and Schmoller (see chap. 1)—who stressed the play of larger "historical" forces in the affairs of man.

Fast-forwarding to 20th-century organization theory, a period of relatively optimistic work on organization design and strategy by such scholars as Taylor, Galbraith, Lawrence and Lorsch, and Thompson, along with the more strategic, political perspective of resource-dependence theorists, such as Pfeffer and Salancik and Porter, gave way, during the late 1970s, to much more pessimistic views, crafted by ecologists and institutional theorists, of an organization's ability to control its own destiny. These accounts variously emphasize the importance of imprinting and inertial forces or, alternatively, constitutive and embedding processes that foster increasing returns, commitments, and objectification processes that reinforce current paths of development. These arguments inevitably introduce a sense of constraint and caution to those who would attempt to intervene in or alter trajectories of change.

In short, institutional interpretations seem tailor-made to support conservative forces and voices in the social realm. As Albert Hirschman (1991), the perceptive observer of contemporary economic and political matters, has pointed out in his treatise on *The Rhetoric of Reaction,* conservative critics are poised to employ a "futility thesis" that asserts that any attempt at reform is doomed to failure because of the "intractable" nature of society's social fabric. Let me be clear. This is not a text about social reform. I am not advocating that it is our responsibility to take arms against inequities and injustice in our social structures (although some of us may choose to do so). However, we should see to it that our scholarship does not give aid and comfort to those who would seek to stifle such efforts.

To redress the imbalance, it is important that we recognize and publicize the more complex view of institutions as a double-edged sword. By stressing the role of institutions as curbing and constraining choice and action, we ignore the ways in which institutions also empower actors and enable actions. Those interested in redressing inequalities or pursuing other types of reforms can find inspiration and support from surveying and making judicious use of the variety of schemas, resources, and mechanisms that are to be found in any complex institutional field. Institutional forces can liberate as well as constrain. They can both enable and disarm the efforts of those seeking change. We must call attention to these possibilities in our scholarship.

❖ NOTES

1. This section draws from arguments elaborated in Scott (forthcoming-a).

2. Hirschman (1996) points out that "interests" are a modern conception, a refined and sanitized version of "passions."

References

Abbott, Andrew. 1992. An old institutionalist reads the new institutionalism. *Contemporary Sociology* 21:754–756.

Abegglen, James C. 1958. *The Japanese Factory*. Glencoe, IL: Free Press.

Abell, Peter. 1995. The new institutionalism and rational choice theory. In *The Institutional Construction of Organizations: International and Longitudinal Studies*, edited by W. Richard Scott and Søren Christensen (pp. 3–14). London: Sage.

Abernethy, David B. 2000. *The Dynamics of Global Dominance: European Overseas Empires, 1415–1980*. New Haven, CT: Yale University Press.

Abrahamson, Eric. 1991. Managerial fads and fashions: The diffusion and rejection of innovations. *Academy of Management Review* 16:586–612.

Abzug, Rikki, and Stephen J. Mezias. 1993. The fragmented state and due process protections in organizations: The case of comparable worth. *Organization Science* 4:433–453.

Ahmadjian, Christina L., and Patricia Robinson. 2001. Safety in numbers: Downsizing and the deinstitutionalization of permanent employment in Japan. *Administrative Science Quarterly* 46:622–654.

Albert, Stuart, and David A. Whetten. 1985. Organizational identity. In *Research in Organizational Behavior*, vol. 14, edited by L. L. Cummings and Barry M. Staw (pp. 263–295). Greenwich, CT: JAI.

Albrow, Martin 1997. *The Global Age*. Stanford, CA: Stanford University Press.

Alchian, Armen A., and Harold Demsetz. 1972. Production, information costs, and economic organization. *American Economic Review* 62:777–795.

Aldrich, Howard E. 2005. Entrepreneurship. In *The Handbook of Economic Sociology*, 2nd ed., edited by Neil J. Smelser and Richard Swedberg (pp. 451–477). Princeton, NJ and New York: Princeton University Press and Russell Sage.

Aldrich, Howard E., and Martin Ruef. 2006. *Organizations Evolving*, 2nd ed. Thousand Oaks, CA: Sage.

Alexander, Ernest R. 1995. *How Organizations Act Together: Interorganizational Coordination in Theory and Practice*. Luxembourg: Gordon and Breach.

Alexander, Jeffrey C. 1983. *Theoretical Logic in Sociology*: Vols. 1–4. Berkeley: University of California Press.

Alexander, Victoria D. 1996. Pictures at an exhibition: Conflicting pressures in museums and the display of art. *American Journal of Sociology* 101:797–839.

Anderson, Benedict 1983. *Imagined Communities: Reflection on the Origin and Spread of Nationalism.* London: Verso.

Ansell, Chris. 2005. *Pragmatism and Organization.* Unpublished paper, Department of Political Science, University of California, Berkeley.

Appadurai, Arjun. 1996. *Modernity at Large.* Minneapolis: University of Minnesota Press.

Armour, H. O., and David Teece. 1978. Organizational structure and economic performance. *Bell Journal of Economics* 9:106–122.

Armstrong, Elizabeth A. 2002. Crisis, collective creativity, and the generation of new organizational forms: The transformation of lesbian/gay organizations in San Francisco. *Social Structure and Organizations Revisited* 19:361–395.

Aronowitz, Stanley. 1992. *The Politics of Identity: Class, Culture and Social Movements.* New York: Routledge, Chapman and Hall.

Arthur, W. Brian. 1994. *Increasing Returns and Path Dependence in the Economy.* Ann Arbor: University of Michigan Press.

Ashforth, Blake E., and Barrie W. Gibbs. 1990. The double-edge of organizational legitimation. *Organization Science* 1:177–194.

Astley, W. Graham. 1985. The two ecologies: Population and community perspectives on organizational evolution. *Administrative Science Quarterly* 30:224–241.

Astley, W. Graham, and Andrew H. Van de Ven. 1983. Central perspectives and debates in organization theory. *Administrative Science Quarterly* 28:245–273.

Axelrod, Robert. 1984. *The Evolution of Cooperation.* New York: Basic Books.

Barley, Stephen R. 1986. Technology as an occasion for structuring: Evidence from observations of CT scanners and the social order of radiology departments. *Administrative Science Quarterly* 31:78–108.

Barley, Stephen R., and Pamela S. Tolbert. 1997. Institutionalization and structuration: Studying the links between action and institution. *Organization Studies* 18:93–117.

Barnard, Chester I. 1938. *The Functions of the Executive.* Cambridge, MA: Harvard University Press.

Barnett, William, and Glenn R. Carroll. 1993. How institutional constraints affected the organization of early U.S. telephony. *Journal of Law, Economics, and Organization* 9:98–126.

Baron, James N., Michael T. Hannan, and M. Diane Burton. 1999. Building the iron cage: Determinants of managerial intensity in the early years of organizations. *American Sociological Review* 64:527–547.

Baron, James N., Frank R. Dobbin, and P. Deveraux Jennings. 1986. War and peace: The evolution of modern personnel administration in U.S. industry. *American Journal of Sociology* 92:350–383.

Baron, James N., P. Deveraux Jennings, and Frank R. Dobbin. 1988. Mission control? The development of personnel systems in U.S. industry. *American Sociological Review* 53:497–514.

Baum, Joel A. C. 1996. Organizational ecology. In *Handbook of Organization Studies*, edited by Stewart R. Clegg, Cynthia Hardy, and Walter R. Nord (pp. 77–114). London: Sage.

Baum, Joel A. C., and Jane E. Dutton. eds. 1996. The embeddedness of strategy. In *Advances in Strategic Management*, vol. 13, edited by Paul Shrivastava, Anne S. Huff, and Jane E. Dutton. Greenwich, CT: JAI Press.

Baum, Joel A. C., and Christine Oliver. 1992. Institutional embeddedness and the dynamics of organizational populations. *American Sociological Review* 57:540–559.

Baum, Joel A. C., and Walter W. Powell. 1995. Cultivating an institutional ecology of organizations: Comment on Hannan, Carroll, Dundon, and Torres. *American Sociological Review* 60:529–538.

Becker, Howard S. 1982. *Art Worlds*. Berkeley: University of California Press.

Becker, Howard S., Blanche Geer, Everett C. Hughes, and Anselm Strauss. 1961. *Boys in White: Student Culture in Medical School*. Chicago: University of Chicago Press.

Bellah, Robert N., Richard Madsen, William M. Sullivan, Ann Swidler, and Steven M. Tipton. 1985. *Habits of the Heart: Individualism and Commitment in American Life*. Berkeley: University of California Press.

Bendix, Reinhard. 1956/2001. *Work and Authority in Industry: Managerial Ideologies in the Course of Industrialization*. New York: John Wiley, 1956; New Brunswick, NJ: Transaction Publishers, 2001.

Bendix, Reinhard. 1960. *Max Weber: An Intellectual Portrait*. Garden City, NY: Doubleday.

Benford, Robert D., and David A. Snow. 2000. Framing processes and social movements: An overview and assessment. *Annual Review of Sociology* 26:611–639.

Berger, Peter L. 1992. Reflections on the twenty-fifth anniversary of The Social Construction of Reality. Perspectives: The Theory Section Newsletter. *American Sociological Association* 15(2):1–2, 4.

Berger, Peter L., Brigitte Berger, and Hansfried Kellner. 1973. *The Homeless Mind: Modernization and Consciousness*. New York: Random House.

Berger, Peter L., and Hansfried Kellner. 1981. *Sociology Interpreted: An Essay On Method and Vocation*. Garden City, NY: Doubleday Anchor.

Berger, Peter L., and Thomas Luckmann. 1967. *The Social Construction of Reality*. New York: Doubleday Anchor.

Berger, Peter L., and Samuel P. Huntington. eds. 2002. *Many Globalizations: Cultural Diversity in the Contemporary World*. Oxford, UK: Oxford University Press.

Bergesen, Albert J. 2000. A linguistic model of art history. *Poetics* 28:73–90.

Bergesen, Albert J. 2004. Chomsky versus Mead. *Sociological Theory* 22:357–370.

Bergesen, Albert J. 2005. Culture and cognition. In *Blackwell Companion to the Sociology of Culture*, edited by Mark K. Jacobs and Nancy Weiss Hanrahan. Oxford, UK: Blackwell.

Berkovitz, Nitza. 1999. *From Motherhood to Citizenship*. Baltimore: Johns Hopkins University Press.

Berlin, Isaiah. ed. 1956. *The Age of Enlightenment: The 18th Century Philosophers*. New York: New American Library.

———. 2006. *Political Ideas in the Romantic Age: Their Rise and Influence on Modern Thought*. London: Chatto & Windus.

Berman, Harold J. 1983. *Law and Revolution: The Formation of the Western Legal Tradition*. Cambridge, MA: Harvard University Press.

Biggart, Nicole Woolsey, and Mauro F. Guillén. 1999. Developing difference: Social organization and the rise of the auto industries of South Korea, Taiwan, Spain, and Argentina. *American Sociological Review* 64:722–747.

Biggart, Nicole Woolsey, and Gary G. Hamilton. 1992. On the limits of a firm-based theory to explain business networks: The Western bias of neo-classical economics. In *Networks and Organizations: Structure, Form, and Action*, edited by Nitin Nohria and Robert G. Eccles (pp. 471–490). Boston: Harvard Business School Press.

Bijker, W. E., Thomas Hughes, and Trevor Pinch. eds. 1987. *The Social Construction of Technological Systems: New Directions in the Sociology and History of Technology*. Cambridge, MA: MIT Press.

Bill, James A., and Robert L. Hardgrave, Jr. 1981. *Comparative Politics: The Quest for Theory*. Washington, DC: Bell & Howell, University Press of America.

Blau, Peter M. 1955. *The Dynamics of Bureaucracy*. Chicago: University of Chicago Press.

Blau, Peter M., Cecilia McHugh Falbe, William McKinley, and Phelps K. Tracy. 1976. Technology and organization in manufacturing. *Administrative Science Quarterly* 21:20–40.

Blau, Peter M., and W. Richard Scott. 1962/2003. *Formal Organizations: A Comparative Approach*. San Francisco: Chandler, 1962; Stanford, CA: Stanford University Press, 2003.

Boas, Franz. 1982. *A Franz Boas Reader: The Shaping of American Anthropology, 1883/1911*, edited by George W. Stocking, Jr. Chicago: University of Chicago Press.

Boeker, Warren P. 1989. The development and institutionalization of subunit power in organizations. *Administrative Science Quarterly* 34:388–410.

Boli, John, and George M. Thomas. 1997. World culture in the world polity: A century of international non-governmental organization. *American Sociological Review* 62:171–190.

———, eds. 1999. *Constructing World Culture: International Nongovernmental Organizations Since 1875*. Stanford, CA: Stanford University Press.

Bourdieu, Pierre 1971. Systems of education and systems of thought. In *Knowledge and Control: New Directions for the Sociology of Education*, edited by M. K. D. Young (pp. 189–207). London: Collier Macmillan.

————. 1973. The three forms of theoretical knowledge. *Social Science Information* 12(1): 53–80.

————. 1977. *Outline of a Theory of Practice*. Cambridge: Cambridge University Press.

————. 1984. *Distinction: A Social Critique of the Judgment of Taste*. Cambridge: Cambridge University Press.

————. 1988. *Homo Academicus*. Stanford, CA: Stanford University Press.

Bourdieu, Pierre, and Loïc J. D. Wacquant. 1992. *An Invitation to Reflexive Sociology*. Chicago: University of Chicago Press.

Brint, Steven, and Jerome Karabel. 1991. Institutional origins and transformations: The case of American community colleges. In *The New Institutionalism in Organizational Analysis*, edited by Walter W. Powell and Paul J. DiMaggio (pp. 337–360). Chicago: University of Chicago Press.

Brinton, Mary C., and Victor Nee. eds. 1998. *The New Institutionalism in Sociology*. New York: Russell Sage Foundation.

Brown, John Seely, and Paul Duguid. 1991. Organizational learning and communities-of-practice: Toward a unified view of working, learning, and innovation. *Organization Science* 2:40–57.

————. 2000. *The Social Life of Information*. Boston: Harvard Business School Press.

Brown, Lawrence A. 1981. *Innovation Diffusion: A New Perspective*. London: Methuen.

Brunsson, Nils. 1989. *The Organization of Hypocrisy: Talk, Decisions and Actions in Organizations*. New York: John Wiley & Sons.

Brunsson, Nils, and Bengt Jacobsson. eds. 2000. *A World of Standards*. Oxford, UK: Oxford University Press.

Buchanan, James M., and Gordon Tullock. 1962. *The Calculus of Consent*. Ann Arbor: University of Michigan Press.

Buckley, Walter. 1967. *Sociology and Modern Systems Theory*. Englewood Cliffs, NJ: Prentice Hall.

Burdros, Art. 1997. The new capitalism and organizational rationality: The adoption of downsizing programs, 1979–1994. *Social Forces* 76:229–250.

Burawoy, Michael. 1979. *Manufacturing Consent: Changes in the Labor Process under Monopoly Capitalism*. Chicago: University of Chicago Press.

Burgess, John William. 1902. *Political Science and Comparative Constitutional Law*. Boston: Ginn.

Burke, Peter J., and Donald C. Reitzes. 1981. The link between identity and role performance. *Social Psychology Quarterly* 44:93–92.

Burns, Lawton R., and Douglas R. Wholey. 1993. Adoption and abandonment of matrix management programs: Effects of organizational characteristics and interorganizational networks. *Academy of Management Journal* 36:106–138.

Burrell, Gibson, and Gareth Morgan. 1979. *Sociological Paradigms and Organisational Analysis*. London: Heinemann.

Burt, Ronald S. 1987. Social contagion and innovation: Cohesion versus structural equivalence. *American Journal of Sociology* 92:1287–1335.

————. 1991. The problem of identity in collective action. In *Macro-Micro Linkages in Sociology*, edited by Joan Huber (pp. 51–75). Beverly Hills, CA: Sage.

————. 1992. *Structural Holes*. Cambridge, MA: Harvard University Press.

Calhoun, Craig. 1991. The problem with identity in collective action. In *Macro-Micro Linkages in Sociology*, edited by Joan Huber (pp. 51–75). Beverly Hills, CA: Sage Publications.

Camic, Charles. 1992. Reputation and predecessor selection: Parsons and the institutionalists. *American Sociological Review* 57:421–445.

Campbell, John L. 2004. *Institutional Change and Globalization*. Princeton, NJ: Princeton University Press.

————. 2005. Where do we stand? Common mechanisms in organizations and social movements research. In *Social Movements and Organization Theory*, edited by Gerald F. Davis, Doug McAdam, W. Richard Scott, and Mayer N. Zald (pp. 41–68). New York: Cambridge University Press.

Campbell, John L., J. Rogers Hollingsworth, and Leon N. Lindberg. eds. 1991. *Governance of the American Economy*. New York: Cambridge University Press.

Campbell, John L., and Leon N. Lindberg. 1990. Property rights and the organization of economic activity by the state. *American Sociological Review* 55:634–647.

————. 1991. The evolution of governance regimes. In *Governance of the American Economy*, edited by John L. Campbell, J. Rogers Hollingsworth, and Leon N. Lindberg (pp. 319–355). New York: Cambridge University Press.

Campbell, John L., and Ove K. Pedersen. eds. 2001. *The Rise of Neoliberalism and Institutional Analysis*. Princeton, NJ: Princeton University Press.

Caronna, Carol A. 2004. The misalignment of institutional "pillars": Consequences for the U.S. health field. *Journal of Health and Social Behavior* 45:45–58.

Carroll, Glenn R., Jacques Delacroix, and Jerry Goodstein. 1988. The political environments of organizations: An ecological view. In *Research in Organizational Behavior*, vol. 10, edited by Barry M. Staw and L. L. Cummings (pp. 359–392). Greenwich, CT: JAI Press.

Carroll, Glenn R., and Michael T. Hannan. 1989. Density dependence in the evolution of populations of newspaper organizations. *American Sociological Review* 54:524–548.

Casile, Maureen, and Alison Davis-Blake. 2002. When accreditation standards change: Factors affecting differential responsiveness of public and private organizations. *Academy of Management Journal* 45:180–195.

Caves, R. E. 2000. *Creative Industries: Contracts between Art and Commerce*. Cambridge, MA: Harvard University Press.

Cawson, Alan. ed. 1985. *Organized Interests and the State: Studies in Meso-Corporatism*. Beverly Hills, CA: Sage.

Chandler, Alfred D., Jr. 1962. *Strategy and Structure: Chapters in the History of the American Industrial Enterprise*. Cambridge, MA: M.I.T. Press.

————. 1977. *The Visible Hand: The Managerial Revolution in American Business*. Cambridge, MA: Belknap Press of Harvard University Press.

————. 1990. *Scale and Scope: The Dynamics of Industrial Capitalism*. Cambridge, MA: Belknap Press of the Harvard University Press.

Chomsky, Noam. 1986. *Knowledge of Language*. Westport, CT: Praeger.

Christensen, Søren, Peter Karnøe, Jesper Strangaard Pedersen, and Frank Dobbin. eds. 1997. Action in Institutions. *American Behavioral Scientist* 40:389–538.

Cicourel, Aaron V. 1968. *The Social Organization of Juvenile Justice*. New York: Wiley.

Clark, Burton R. 1960. *The Open Door College*. New York: McGraw-Hill.

————. 1970. *The Distinctive College: Antioch, Reed, and Swarthmore*. Chicago: Aldine.

Clemens, Elisabeth S. 1993. Organizational repertoires and institutional change: Women's groups and the transformation of U.S. politics, 1890–1920. *American Journal of Sociology* 98:755–798.

————. 1996. Organizational form as frame: Collective identity and political strategy in the American labor movement, 1880–1920. In *Comparative Perspectives on Social Movements: Political Opportunities, Mobilizing Structures, and Cultural Framings*, edited by Doug McAdam, John D. McCarthy, and Mayer N. Zald (pp. 205–226). Cambridge: Cambridge University Press.

————. 1997. *The People's Lobby: Organizational Innovation and the Rise of Interest Group Politics in the United States, 1890–1925*. Chicago: University of Chicago Press.

Coase, Ronald H. 1937. The Nature of the Firm. *Economica* N.S. 4:385–405.

————. 1972. Industrial organization: A proposal for research. In *Policy Issues and Research Opportunities in Industrial Organization*, edited by Victor R. Fuchs (pp. 59–73). New York: National Bureau of Economic Research.

————. 1983. The new institutional economics. *Journal of Institutional and Theoretical Economics* 140:229–231.

Coburn, Cynthia E. 2004. Beyond decoupling: Rethinking the relationship between the institutional environment and the classroom. *Sociology of Education* 77: 211–244.

Cohen, Michael D. 2007. Administrative behavior: Laying the foundation for Cyert and March. *Organization Science* 18: 503–506.

Cole, Robert E. 1979. *Work, Mobility, and Participation: A Comparative Study of American and Japanese Industry*. Berkeley: University of California Press.

————. 1989. *Strategies for Learning: Small-group Activities in American, Japanese, and Swedish Industry*. Berkeley: University of California Press.

————. 1999. *Managing Quality Fads: How American Business Learned to Play the Quality Game*. New York: Oxford University Press.

Cole, Robert E., and W. Richard Scott. eds. 2000. *The Quality Movement & Organization Theory*. Thousand Oaks, CA: Sage.

Coleman, James S. 1964. *Introduction to Mathematical Sociology*. New York: The Free Press.

————. 1974. *Power and the Structure of Society*. New York: W. W. Norton.

————. 1990. *Foundations of Social Theory*. Cambridge, MA: Belknap Press of Harvard University Press.

————. 1994. A rational choice perspective on economic sociology. In *The Handbook of Economic Sociology*, edited by Neil J. Smelser and Richard Swedberg (pp. 166–180). Princeton, NJ and New York: Princeton University Press and Russell Sage Foundation.

Collingwood, R. G. 1948. *The Idea of History*. Oxford, UK: Clarendon Press.

Commons, John R. 1924. *The Legal Foundations of Capitalism*. New York: Macmillan.

————. 1970. *The Economics of Collective Action*. Madison: University of Wisconsin Press. (Originally published in 1950)

Cooley, Charles Horton. 1902/1956. *Social Organization*. Glencoe, IL: Free Press.

Cooper, David J., Bob Hinings, Royston Greenwood, and John L. Brown. 1996. Sedimentation and transformation in organizational change: The case of Canadian law firms. *Organization Studies* 17:623–647.

Covaleski, Mark A., and Mark W. Dirsmith. 1988. An institutional perspective on the rise, social transformation and fall of a university budget category. *Administrative Science Quarterly* 33:562–587.

Cyert, Richard M., and James G. March. 1963. *A Behavioral Theory of the Firm*. Englewood Cliffs, NJ: Prentice Hall.

Czarniawska, Barbara, and Bernward Joerges. 1996. Travels of ideas. In *Translating Organizational Change*, edited by Barbara Czarniawska and Guji Sevón (pp. 13–48). Berlin: Walter de Gruyter.

Dacin, M. Tina. 1997. Isomorphism in context: The power and prescription of institutional norms. *Academy of Management Journal* 40:46–81.

Dacin, M. Tina, Marc J. Ventresca, and Brent D. Beal. 1999. The embeddedness of organizations: Dialogue and directions. *Journal of Management* 25:317–356.

Daft, Richard, and Karl E. Weick. 1984. Toward a model of organizations as interpretation systems. *Academy of Management Review* 9:284–295.

D'Andrade, Roy G. 1984. Cultural meaning systems. In *Culture Theory: Essays on Mind, Self, and Emotion*, edited by Richard A. Shweder and Robert A. LeVine (pp. 88–119). Cambridge: Cambridge University Press.

D'Aunno, Thomas, Robert I. Sutton, and Richard H. Price. 1991. Isomorphism and external support in conflicting institutional environments: A study of drug abuse treatment units. *Academy of Management Journal* 14:636–661.

David, Paul A. 1985. Clio and the economics of QWERTY. *American Economic Review* 75:332–337.

————. 1992. *Why are institutions the 'carriers of history'? Notes on path-dependence and the evolution of conventions, organizations and institutions*. Paper presented to the Stanford Institute for Theoretical Economics, Stanford University.

————. 2000. Path dependence, its critics, and the quest for "historical economics." In *Evolution and Path Dependence in Economic Ideas: Past and Present*, edited by P. Garrouste and S. Ionnides. Cheltenham, UK: Edward Elgar.

Davis, Gerald F., Kristina A. Diekmann, and Catherine H. Tinsley. 1994. The decline and fall of the conglomerate firm in the 1980s: The deinstitutionalization of an organizational form. *American Sociological Review* 59:547–570.

Davis, Gerald F., and Henrich R. Greve. 1997. Corporate elite networks and governance changes in the 1980s. *American Journal of Sociology* 103:1–37.

Davis, Gerald F., Doug McAdam, W. Richard Scott, and Mayer N. Zald. eds. 2005. *Social Movements and Organization Theory*. Cambridge: Cambridge University Press.

Davis, Kingsley. 1949. *Human Society*. New York: Macmillan.

de Tocqueville, Alexis. 1835-40/1969. *Democracy in America*, trans. George Lawrence, edited by J. P. Mayer. New York: Doubleday, Anchor Books.

Deephouse, David L. 1996. Does isomorphism legitimate? *Academy of Management Journal* 39:1024–1039.

Dezalay, Yves, and Bryant G. Garth. 1996. *Dealing in Virtue: International Commercial Arbitration and the Construction of a Transnational Legal Order*. Chicago: University of Chicago Press.

Dill, William R. 1958. Environment as an influence on managerial autonomy. *Administrative Science Quarterly* 2:409–443.

DiMaggio, Paul J. 1979. Review essay: On Pierre Bourdieu. *American Journal of Sociology* 84:1460–1474.

———. 1986. Structural analysis of organizational fields: A block model approach. In *Research in Organization Behavior*, vol. 8, edited by Barry M. Staw and L. L. Cummings (pp. 355–370). Greenwich, CT: JAI Press.

———. 1988. Interest and agency in institutional theory. In *Institutional Patterns and Organizations: Culture and Environment*, edited by Lynne G. Zucker (p. 21). Cambridge, MA: Ballinger.

———. 1990. Cultural aspects of economic organization and behavior. In *Beyond the Marketplace: Rethinking Economy and Society*, edited by Roger Friedland and A. F. Robertson (pp. 113–136). New York: Aldine de Gruyter.

———. 1991. Constructing an organizational field as a professional project: U.S. art museums, 1920–1940. In *The New Institutionalism in Organizational Analysis*, edited by Walter W. Powell and Paul J. DiMaggio (pp. 267–292). Chicago: University of Chicago Press.

———. 1994. Culture and economy. In *Handbook of Economic Sociology,* edited by Neil J. Smelser and Richard Swedberg (pp. 27–57). Princeton, NJ and New York: Princeton University Press and Russell Sage Foundation.

———. 1997. Culture and cognition: An interdisciplinary review. *Annual Review of Sociology* 23:263–287.

DiMaggio, Paul J., and Walter W. Powell. 1983. The iron cage revisited: Institutional isomorphism and collective rationality in organizational fields. *American Sociological Review* 48:147–160.

———. 1991. Introduction. In *The New Institutionalism in Organizational Analysis*, edited by Walter W. Powell and Paul J. DiMaggio (pp. 1–38). Chicago: University of Chicago Press.

Djelic, Marie-Laure. 1998. *Exporting the American Model*. Oxford: Oxford University Press.

Djelic, Marie-Laure, and Kerstin Sahlin-Andersson. eds. 2006. *Transnational Governance: Institutional Dynamics of Regulation*. Cambridge: Cambridge University Press.

Djelic, Marie-Laure, and Sigrid Quack. 2003a. Conclusion: Globalization as a double process of institutional change and institution building. In *Globalization and Institutions: Redefining the Rules of the Economic Game*, edited by Marie-Laure Djelic and Sigrid Quack (pp. 302–333). Cheltenham, UK: Edward Elgar.

Djelic, Marie-Laure, and Sigrid Quack. eds. 2003b. *Globalization and Institutions: Redefining the Rules of the Economic Game*. Cheltenham, UK: Edward Elgar.

Djelic, Marie-Laure, and Sigrid Quack. 2003c. Introduction: Governing globalization—bringing institutions back in. In *Globalization and Institutions: Redefining the Rules of the Economic Game*, edited by Marie-Laure Djelic and Sigrid Quack (pp. 1–14). Cheltenham, UK: Edward Elgar.

Dobbin, Frank R. 1994a. Cultural models of organization: The social construction of rational organizing principles. In *The Sociology of Culture: Emerging Theoretical Perspectives*, edited by Diana Crane (pp. 117–141). Oxford, UK: Blackwell.

———. 1994b. *Forging Industrial Policy: The United States, Britain, and France in the Railway Age*. New York: Cambridge University Press.

Dobbin, Frank R., Lauren B. Edelman, John W. Meyer, W. Richard Scott, and Ann Swidler. 1988. The expansion of due process in organizations. In *Institutional Patterns and Organizations: Culture and Environment*, edited by Lynne G. Zucker (pp. 71–100). Cambridge, MA: Ballinger.

Dobbin, Frank R., and John R. Sutton. 1998. The strength of a weak state: The rights revolution and the rise of human resources management divisions. *American Journal of Sociology* 104:441–476.

Dobbin, Frank R., John R. Sutton, John W. Meyer, and W. Richard Scott. 1993. Equal opportunity law and the construction of internal labor markets. *American Journal of Sociology* 99:396–427.

Donald, Merlin 1991. *Origins of the Modern Mind: Three Stages in the Evolution of Culture and Cognition*. Cambridge, MA: Harvard University Press.

Dore, Ronald 1973. *British Factory, Japanese Factory: The Origins of National Diversity in Industrial Relations*. Berkeley: University of California Press.

Dornbusch, Sanford M., and W. Richard Scott, with the assistance of Bruce C. Busching and James D. Laing. 1975. *Evaluation and the Exercise of Authority*. San Francisco: Jossey-Bass.

Douglas, Mary. 1982. The effects of modernization on religious change. *Daedalus* (Winter):1–19.

———. 1986. *How Institutions Think*. Syracuse, NY: Syracuse University Press.

Dowling, John, and Jeffrey Pfeffer. 1975. Organizational legitimacy: Social values and organizational behavior. *Pacific Sociological Review* 18:122–136.

Drori, Gili S., John W. Meyer, and Hokyu Hwang, eds. 2006. *Globalization and Organization: World Society and Organizational Change*. Oxford, UK: Oxford University Press.

Dupri, Louis. 2004. *The Enlightenment and the Intellectual Foundations of Modern Culture*. New Haven, CT: Yale University Press.

Durkheim, Emile. 1893/1949. *The Division of Labor in Society.* Glencoe, IL: Free Press.

———. 1901/1950. *The Rules of Sociological Method.* Glencoe, IL: Free Press.

———. 1912/1961. *The Elementary Forms of Religious Life.* New York: Collier Books.

Dutton, Jane E., and Janet M. Dukerrich. 1991. Keeping an eye on the mirror: Image and identity in organizational adaptation. *Administrative Science Quarterly* 34:517–554.

Easton, David. 1965. *A Framework for Political Analysis.* Englewood Cliffs, NJ: Prentice Hall.

Eckstein, Harry. 1963. A perspective on comparative politics: Past and present. In *Comparative Politics,* edited by Harry Eckstein and David E. Apter (pp. 3–32). New York: The Free Press.

Edelman, Lauren B. 1992. Legal ambiguity and symbolic structures: Organizational mediation of civil rights law. *American Journal of Sociology* 97:1531–1576.

Edelman, Lauren B., Christopher Uggen, and Howard S. Erlanger. 1999. The endogeneity of legal regulation: Grievance procedures as rational myth. *American Journal of Sociology* 105:406–454.

Edelman, Lauren B., and Mark C. Suchman. 1997. The legal environment of organizations. *Annual Review of Sociology* 23:479–515.

Ellul, Jacques. 1954/1964. *The Technological Society.* New York: Knopf.

Elsbach, Kimberly D. 1994. Managing organizational legitimacy in the California cattle industry: The construction and effectiveness of verbal accounts. *Administrative Science Quarterly* 39:57–88.

———. 2002. Intraorganizational institutions. In *Blackwell Companion to Organizations,* edited by Joel A. C. Baum (pp. 37–57). Oxford, UK: Blackwell.

Elsbach, Kimberly D., and Robert I. Sutton. 1992. Acquiring organizational legitimacy through illegitimate actions: A marriage of institutional and impression management theories. *Academy of Management Journal* 35:699–738.

Elster, Jon. 1983. *Explaining Technical Change: A Case Study in the Philosophy of Science.* Cambridge: Cambridge University Press.

———. 1989. *Nuts and Bolts for the Social Sciences.* Chicago: University of Chicago Press.

Emery, Fred E., and E. L. Trist. 1967. The causal texture of organizational environments. *Human Relations* 18:21–32.

Emirbayer, Mustafa, and Ann Mische. 1998. What is agency? *American Journal of Sociology* 103:962–1023.

Ertman, Thomas. 1997. *Birth of the Leviathan: Building States and Regimes in Medieval and Early Modern Europe.* Cambridge: Cambridge University Press.

Espeland, Wendy Nelson, and Mitchell L. Stevens. 1998. Commensuration as a social process. *Annual Review of Sociology* 24:313–343.

Evans, Peter B., Dietrich Rusechemeyer, and Theda Skocpol. eds. 1985. *Bringing the State Back In.* Cambridge: Cambridge University Press.

Feldman, Martha S., and Brian T. Pentland. 2003. Reconceptualizing organizational routines as a source of flexibility and change. *Administrative Science Quarterly* 48: 94–118.

Ferejohn, John, and Morris Fiorina. 1975. Purposive models of legislative behavior. *American Economic Review, Papers and Proceedings* 65:407–415.

Fine, Gary Alan, and Lori J. Ducharme. 1995. The ethnographic present: Images of institutional control in second-school research. In *A Second Chicago School? The Development of a Postwar American Sociology*, edited by Gary Allan Fine (pp. 108–135). Chicago: University of Chicago Press.

Finnemore, Martha. 1993. International organizations as teachers of norms: The United Nations Educational, Scientific, and Cultural Organization and Science Policy. *International Organizations* 47:567–597.

Fligstein, Neil. 1985. The spread of the multidivisional form among large firms, 1919–1979. *American Sociological Review* 50:377–391.

———. 1987. The intraorganizational power struggle: The rise of finance presidents in large corporations, 1919–1979. *American Sociological Review* 52:44–58.

———. 1990. *The Transformation of Corporate Control.* Cambridge, MA: Harvard University Press.

———. 1991. The structural transformation of American industry: An institutional account of the causes of diversification in the largest firms, 1919–1979. In *The New Institutionalism in Organizational Analysis*, edited by Walter W. Powell and Paul J. DiMaggio (pp. 311–336). Chicago: University of Chicago Press.

———. 2001a. *The Architecture of Markets: An Economic Sociology of Twenty-First-Century Capitalist Societies.* Princeton, NJ: Princeton University Press.

———. 2001b. Social skill and the theory of fields. *Sociological Theory* 19:105–125.

Frank, David John, Ann Hironaka, and Evan Schofer. 2000. The nation-state and the natural environment over the twentieth century. *American Sociological Review* 65: 96–110.

Freidson, Eliot. 1970. *Profession of Medicine.* New York: Dodd, Mead.

Friedman, Thomas L. 2005. *The World is Flat: A Brief History of the Twenty-First Century.* New York: Farrar, Straus and Giroux.

Friedland, Roger, and Robert R. Alford. 1991. Bringing society back In: Symbols, practices, and institutional contradictions. In *The New Institutionalism in Organizational Analysis*, edited by Walter W. Powell and Paul J. DiMaggio (pp. 232–263). Chicago: University of Chicago Press.

Frost, Peter J., Larry F. Moore, Meryl Reis Louis, Craig C. Lundberg, and Joanne Martin. eds. 1985. *Organizational Culture.* Beverly Hills, CA: Sage.

Gagliardi, Pasquale. 1990. Artifacts as pathways and remains of organizational life. *In Symbols and Artifacts: Views of the Corporate Landscape*, edited by Pasquale Gagliardi (pp. 3–38). New York: Walter de Gruyter.

Galaskiewicz, Joseph, and Wolfgang Bielefeld. 1998. *Nonprofit Organizations in an Age of Uncertainty: A Study of Organizational Change.* New York: Aldine De Gruyter.

Galaskiewicz, Joseph, and Ronald S. Burt. 1991. Interorganizational contagion in corporate philanthropy. *Administrative Science Quarterly* 36:88–105.

Garfinkel, Harold. 1967. *Studies in Ethnomethodology.* Englewood Cliffs, NJ: Prentice Hall.

———. 1974. The origins of the term "ethnomethodogy." In *Ethnomethodology: Selected Readings,* edited by Roy Turner (pp. 15–18). Harmondworth, UK: Penguin Books.

Geertz, Clifford. 1971. *Islam Observed: Religious Development in Morocco and Indonesia.* Chicago: University of Chicago Press.

———. 1973. *The Interpretation of Cultures.* New York: Basic Books.

Georgopoulos, Basil S. 1972. The hospital as an organization and problem-solving system. In *Organization Research on Health Institutions,* edited by Basil S. Georgopoulos (pp. 9–48). Ann Arbor: Institute for Social Research, University of Michigan.

Gergen, Kenneth J., and Keith E. Davis. eds. 1985. *The Social Construction of the Person.* New York: Springer-Verlag.

Gereffi, Gary. 1994. The international economy and economic development. In *Handbook of Economic Sociology,* edited by Neil J. Smelser and Richard Swedberg (pp. 206–233). Princeton and New York: Princeton University Press and Russell Sage Foundation.

Ghoshal, Sumantra, and D. Eleanor Westney. eds. 1993. *Organization Theory and the Multinational Corporation.* New York: St. Martin's Press.

Giddens, Anthony. 1979. *Central Problems in Social Theory: Action, Structure and Contradiction in Social Analysis.* Berkeley: University of California.

———. 1984. *The Constitution of Society.* Berkeley: University of California Press.

Glassman, Robert. 1973. Persistence and loose coupling in living systems. *Behavioral Science* 18:83–98.

Goffman, Erving. 1961. *Asylums.* Garden City, NY: Doubleday, Anchor Books.

———. 1974. *Frame Analysis.* Cambridge, MA: Harvard University Press.

———. 1983. The interaction order. *American Sociological Review* 48:1–17.

Goodrick, Elizabeth, and Gerald R. Salancik. 1996. Organizational discretion in responding to institutional practices: Hospitals and Cesarean births. *Administrative Science Quarterly* 41:1–28.

Gopnik, A., A. N. Melzoff, and P. K. Kuhl. 1999. *The Scientist in the Crib: Minds, Brains and How Children Learn.* New York: Morrow.

Gouldner, Alvin W. 1954. *Patterns of Industrial Bureaucracy.* Glencoe, IL: Free Press.

Granovetter, Mark. 1973. The strength of weak ties. *American Journal of Sociology* 78:1360–1380.

———. 1985. Economic action and social structure: The problem of embeddedness. *American Journal of Sociology* 91:481–510.

Gray, John. 2005, August 11. The world is round: Review of "The World Is Flat: A Brief History of the Twenty-First Century" by Thomas L. Friedman. *The New York Review of Books* 52, no. 13.

Greening, Daniel W., and Barbara Gray. 1994. Testing a model of organizational response to social and political issues. *Academy of Management Journal* 37:467–498.

Greenwood, Royston, and C. R. Hinings. 1993. Understanding strategic change: The contribution of archetypes. *Academy of Management Journal* 36:1052–1081.

———. 1996. Understanding radical organizational change: Bringing together the old and the new institutionalism. *Academy of Management Review* 21:1022–1054.

Greenwood, Royston, Roy Suddaby, and C. R. Hinings. 2002. Theorizing change: The role of professional association in the transformation of institutional fields. *Academy of Management Journal* 45:58–80.

Greif, Avner. 2006. *Institutions and the Path to the Modern Economy: Lessons from Medieval Trade.* Cambridge: Cambridge University Press.

Greve, Henrich R. 1995. Jumping ship: The diffusion of strategy abandonment. *Administrative Science Quarterly* 40:444–473.

———. 1998. Managerial cognition and the mimetic adoption of market positions: What you see is what you do. *Strategic Management Journal* 19:967–988.

Griswold, Wendy. 1992. Recent developments in the sociology of culture: Four good arguments (and one bad one). *Acta Sociologica* 35:323–328.

Guillén, Mauro F. 1994. *Models of Management: Work, Authority, and Organization in a Comparative Perspective.* Chicago: University of Chicago Press.

———. 2001a. Introduction to the transaction edition. In *Reinhold Bendix, Work and Authority in Industry* (pp. xvii–lxv). New Brunswick, NJ: Transaction Publishers.

———. 2001b. *The Limits of Convergence: Globalization and Organizational Change in Argentina, South Korea, and Spain.* Princeton, NJ: Princeton University Press.

Gulick, Luther, and L. Urwick. eds. 1937. *Papers in the Science of Administration.* New York: Institute of Public Administration, Columbia University.

Gusfield, Joseph R. 1955. Social structure and moral reform: A study of the Women's Christian Temperance Union. *American Journal of Sociology* 61:221–232.

Hall, Peter A. 1986. *Governing the Economy: The Politics of State Intervention in Britain and France.* Cambridge: Polity Press.

Hall, Peter A., and David Soskice. 2001a. An introduction to varieties of capitalism. In *Varieties of Capitalism: The Institutional Foundation of Comparative Advantage,* edited by Peter A. Hall and David Soskice (pp. 1–68). Oxford, UK: Oxford University Press.

———. ed. 2001b. *Varieties of Capitalism: The Institutional Foundations of Comparative Advantage.* New York: Oxford University Press.

Hall, Peter A., and Rosemary C. R. Taylor. 1996. Political science and the three new institutionalisms. *Political Studies* 44:936–957.

Hall, Richard H. 1992. Taking things a bit too far: Some problems with emergent institutional theory. In *Issues, Theory and Research in Industrial Organizational Psychology,* edited by Kathryn Kelley (pp. 71–87). Amsterdam: Elsevier.

Hallett, Tim, and Marc J. Ventresca. 2006. Inhabited institutions: Social inter-actions and organizational forms in Gouldner's Patterns of Industrial Bureaucracy. *Theory and Society* 35: 213-236.

Halliday, Terence C., Michael J. Powell, and Mark W. Granfors. 1993. After minimalism: Transformation of state bar associations from market depen-dence to state reliance, 1918 to 1950. *American Sociological Review* 58:515–535.

Hanks, William F. 1991. "Foreword" to *Situated Learning: Legitimate Peripheral Participation* by Jean Lave and Etienne Wenger (pp. 13–26). Cambridge: Cambridge University Press.

Hannan, Michael T., and Glenn R. Carroll. 1987. The ecology of organizational founding: American labor unions, 1836–1985. *American Journal of Sociology* 92:910–943.

Hannan, Michael T., Glenn R. Carroll, Elizabeth A. Dundon, and John Charles Torres. 1995. Organizational evolution in a multinational context: Entries of automobile manufacturers in Belgium, Britain, France, Germany, and Italy. *American Sociological Review* 60:509–528.

Hannan, Michael T., and John Freeman. 1977. The population ecology of orga-nizations. *American Journal of Sociology* 82:929–964.

———. 1984. Structural inertia and organizational change. *American Socio-logical Review* 49:149–164.

———. 1989. *Organizational Ecology*. Cambridge, MA: Harvard University Press.

Hasenclever, A., P. Mayer, and V. Rittberger. 1997. *Theories of International Regimes*. Cambridge: Cambridge University Press.

Haunschild, Pamela R. 1993. Interorganizational imitation: The impact of inter-locks on corporate acquisition activity. *Administrative Science Quarterly* 38:564–592.

Haunschild, Pamela R., and Christine M. Beckman. 1998. When do interlocks matter? Alternative sources of information and interlock influence. *Administrative Science Quarterly* 43:815–844.

Haunschild, Pamela R., and Anne S. Miner. 1997. Modes of interorganizational imitation: The effects of outcome salience and uncertainty. *Administrative Science Quarterly* 42:472–500.

Haveman, Heather A. 1993. Follow the leader: Mimetic isomorphism and entry into new markets. *Administrative Science Quarterly* 38:593–627.

Haveman, Heather A., and Hayagreeva Rao. 1997. Structuring a theory of moral sentiments: Institutional and organizational coevolution in the early thrift industry. *American Journal of Sociology* 102:1606–1651.

Hawley, Amos. 1950. *Human Ecology*. New York: Ronald Press.

———. 1968. *Human Ecology: A Theoretical Essay*. Chicago: University of Chicago Press.

Hay, Peter. 1993. Royal treatment. *Performing Arts* (March) : 70.

Hayek, Friedrich A. 1948. *Individualism and Economic Order*. Chicago: University of Chicago Press.

Hechter, Michael. 1987. *Principles of Group Solidarity*. Berkeley: University of California Press.

Hechter, Michael, Karl-Dieter Opp, and Reinhard Wippler. eds. 1990. *Social Institutions: Their Emergence, Maintenance and Effects*. New York: Aldine de Gruyter.

Hegel, G. W. F. 1807/1967. *The Phenomenology of Mind*. New York: Harper & Row.

Heilbroner, Robert L. 1985. *The Nature and Logic of Capitalism*. New York: W. W. Norton.

Heimer, Carol A. 1999. Competing institutions: Law, medicine, and family in neonatal intensive care. *Law and Society Review* 33:17–66.

Heise, David R. 1979. *Understanding Events: Affect and the Construction of Social Action*. Cambridge: Cambridge University Press.

Helper, Susan, John Paul MacDuffie, and Charles Sabel. 2000. Pragmatic collaborations: Advancing knowledge while controlling opportunism. Unpublished paper, Wharton School, University of Pennsylvania.

Hemenway, David. 1975. *Industrywide Voluntary Product Standards*. Cambridge, MA: Ballinger.

Hernes, Gudmund. 1998. Real virtuality. In *Social Mechanisms: An Analytical Approach to Social Theory*, edited by Peter Hedström and Richard Swedberg (pp. 74–101). New York: Cambridge University Press.

Hirsch, Paul M. 1972. Processing fads and fashions: An organization-set analysis of cultural industry systems. *American Sociological Review* 77:639–659.

———. 1985. The study of industries. In *Research in the Sociology of Organizations*, vol. 4, edited by Sam B. Bacharach and S. M. Mitchell (pp. 271–309). Greenwich, CT: JAI Press.

———. 1997. Review essay: Sociology without social structure: Neoinstitutional theory meets brave new world. *American Journal of Sociology* 102:1702–1723.

Hirsch, Paul M., and Michael D. Lounsbury. 1996. Rediscovering volition: The institutional economics of Douglass C. North. *Academy of Management Review* 21:872–884.

Hirschman, Albert O. 1991. *The Rhetoric of Reaction*. Cambridge, MA: Belknap Press of Harvard University Press.

———. 1996. *The Passions and the Interests: Political Arguments for Capitalism Before its Triumph*. Princeton, NJ: Princeton University Press.

Hodgson, Geoffrey M. 1996. Institutional economic theory: The old versus the new. In *After Marx and Sraffa: Essays in Political Economy*, edited by Geoffrey M. Hodgson (pp. 194–213). New York: St. Martin's Press.

———. ed. 1993. *The Economics of Institutions*. Aldershot: Edward Elgar.

———. 1994. The return of institutional economics. In *The Handbook of Economic Sociology*, edited by Neil J. Smelser and Richard Swedberg (pp. 58–76). Princeton, NJ and New York: Princeton University Press and Russell Sage Foundation.

Hoffman, Andrew W. 1997. *From Heresy to Dogma: An Institutional History of Corporate Environmentalism*. San Francisco: New Lexington Press.

———. 1999. Institutional evolution and change: Environmentalism and the U.S. chemical industry. *Academy of Management Journal* 42:351–71.

———. 2001. Linking organizational and field level analysis. *Organization & Environment* 14:133–156.

Hoffman, Andrew J., and Marc J. Ventresca. eds. 2002. *Organizations, Policy, and the Natural Environment: Institutional and Strategic Perspectives*. Stanford, CA: Stanford University Press.

Hofstede, Geert. 1991. *Culture and Organizations: Software of the Mind*. New York: McGraw-Hill.

Hollingsworth, J. Rogers, and Robert Boyer. eds. 1997. *Contemporary Capitalism: The Embeddedness of Institutions*. Cambridge: Cambridge University Press.

Holm, Petter. 1995. The dynamics of institutionalization: Transformation processes in Norwegian fisheries. *Administrative Science Quarterly* 40:398–422.

Hopwood, Anthony, and Peter Miller. 1994. *Accounting as a Social and Institutional Practice*. Cambridge: Cambridge University Press.

Hughes, Everett C. 1936. The ecological aspect of institutions. *American Sociological Review* 1:180–189.

———. 1939. Institutions. In *An Outline of the Principles of Sociology*, edited by Robert E. Park (pp. 218–330). New York: Barnes & Noble.

———. 1958. *Men and their Work*. Glencoe, IL: Free Press. (Collected essays dating from 1928)

Hybels, Ralph C., and Alan R. Ryan. 1996. The legitimation of commercial biotechnology through the business press, 1974–1989. Presented at the annual meetings of the Academy of Management, Cincinnati, Ohio.

Ingram, Paul. 2002. Interorganizational learning. In *The Blackwell Companion to Organizations*, edited by Joel A. C. Baum (pp. 642–663). Oxford, UK: Blackwell Publishers.

Innis, Harold A. 1972. *Empire and Communications*. Toronto: University of Toronto Press.

———. 1995. *Staples, Markets, and Cultural Change: Selected Essays*, edited by Daniel Drache. Montreal: McGill-Queen University Press.

Jaccoby, Sanford M. 1990. The new institutionalism: What can it learn from the old? *Industrial Relations* 29:316–359.

Jensen, Michael C., and William H. Meckling. 1976. Theory of the firm: Managerial behavior, agency costs, and ownership structure. *Journal of Financial Economics* 3:305–360.

Jepperson, Ronald L. 1991. Institutions, institutional effects, and institutionalization. In *The New Institutionalism in Organizational Analysis*, edited by Walter W. Powell and Paul J. DiMaggio (pp. 143–163). Chicago: University of Chicago Press.

Jepperson, Ronald L., and John W. Meyer. 1991. The public order and the construction of formal organizations. In *The New Institutionalism in Organizational Analysis*, edited by Walter W. Powell and Paul J. DiMaggio (pp. 204–231). Chicago: University of Chicago Press.

Jepperson, Ronald L., and Ann Swidler. 1994. What properties of culture should we measure? *Poetics* 22:359–371.

Kahn, Robert L., and Mayer N. Zald. eds. 1990. *Organizations and Nation-States: New Perspectives on Conflict and Cooperation*. San Francisco: Jossey-Bass.

Kalleberg, Arne L., David Knoke, Peter V. Marsden, and Joe L. Spaeth. 1996. *Organizations in America: Analyzing Their Structures and Human Resource Practices*. Thousand Oaks, CA: Sage.

Kaplan, Marilyn R., and J. Richard Harrison. 1993. Defusing the director liability crisis: The strategic management of legal threats. *Organization Science* 4:412–432.

Karl, Terry Lynn. 1997. *The Paradox of Plenty: Oil Booms and Petro-States*. Berkeley: University of California Press.

Katz, Daniel, and Robert L. Kahn. (1966). *The Social Psychology of Organizations*. New York: Wiley.

Katz, M. L., and C. Shapiro. 1985. Network externalities, competition, and compatibility. *American Economic Review* 75:424–440.

Keohane, Robert O. ed. 1989. *International Institutions and State Power: Essays in International Relations Theory*. Boulder, CO: Westview Press.

Kerr, Clark, John T. Dunlop, Frederick Harbison, and Charles A. Myers. 1964. *Industrialism and Industrial Man*, 2nd ed. New York: Oxford University Press.

Kilduff, Martin. 1993. The reproduction of inertia in multinational corporations. In *Organization Theory and the Multinational Corporation,* edited by Sumantra Ghoshal and D. Eleanor Westney (pp. 259–274). New York: St. Martin's Press.

Kimberly, John R. 1975. Environmental constraints and organizational structure: A comparative analysis of rehabilitation organizations. *Administrative Science Quarterly* 20:1–9.

Knorr-Certina, Karin. 1999. *Epistemic Cultures: How the Sciences Make Knowledge.* Cambridge, MA: Harvard University Press.

Knudsen, Christian. 1993. Modelling rationality: Institutions and processes in economic theory. In *Rationality, Institutions and Economic Methodology,* edited by Uskali Mäki, Bo Gustafsson, and Christian Knudsen (pp. 265–299). London: Routledge.

———. 1995a. The competence view of the firm: What can modern economists learn from Philip Selznick's sociological theory of leadership? In *The Institutional Construction of Organizations: International and Longitudinal Studies,* edited by W. Richard Scott and Søren Christensen (pp. 135–163). Thousand Oaks, CA: Sage.

———. 1995b. Theories of the firm, strategic management, and leadership. In *Resource-Based and Evolutionary Theories of the Firm: Toward a Synthesis,* edited by Cynthia A. Montgomery (pp. 179–217). Boston: Kluwer.

Kraatz, Matthew S. 1998. Learning by association? Interorganizational networks and adaptation to environmental change. *Academy of Management Journal* 41:621–643.

Kraatz, Matthew S., and Edward J. Zajac. 1996. Exploring the limits of the new institutionalism: The causes and consequences of illegitimate organizational change. *American Sociological Review* 61:812–836.

Krasner, Stephen D. ed. 1983. *International Regimes.* Ithaca, NY: Cornell University Press.

———. 1988. Sovereignty: An institutional perspective. *Comparative Political Studies* 21:66–94.

———. 1993. Westphalia. In *Ideas and Foreign Policy,* edited by Judith Goldstein and Robert Keohane. Ithaca, NY: Cornell University Press.

Kroeber, Alfred L., and Clyde Kluckhohn. 1952. Culture: A critical review of concepts and definitions. *Peabody Museum Papers* 47. Harvard University Press.

Kroeber, Alfred L., and Talcott Parsons. 1958. The concepts of culture and of social systems. *American Sociological Review* 23:582–583.

Kuhn, Thomas. 1970. *The Structure of Scientific Revolutions* 2nd ed. Chicago: University of Chicago Press.

Kunda, Gideon. 1992. *Engineering Culture: Control and Commitment in a High-Tech Corporation.* Philadelphia: Temple University Press.

Lampel, Joseph, Jamal Shamsie, and Theresa K. Lant. eds. 2006. *The Business of Culture: Strategic Perspectives on Entertainment and Media.* Mahwah, NJ: Lawrence Erlbaum.

Landy, M., M. Roberts, and S. Thomas. 1990. *The Environmental Protection Agency: Asking the Wrong Questions.* New York: Oxford University Press.

Langlois, Richard N. 1986a. The new institutional economics: An introductory essay. In *Economics as a Process: Essays in the New Institutional Economics,* edited by Richard N. Langlois (pp. 1–25). New York: Cambridge University Press.

———. 1986b. Rationality, institutions and explanations. In *Economics as a Process: Essays in the New Institutional Economics,* edited by Richard N. Langlois (pp. 225–255). New York: Cambridge University Press.

Lasswell, Harold. 1936. *Politics: Who Gets What, When, How?* New York: Whittlesey House.

Latour, Bruno. 1986. The powers of association. In *Power, Action, and Belief,* edited by John Law (pp. 164–180). London: Routledge and Kegan Paul.

Laumann, Edward O., Joseph Galaskiewicz, and Peter V. Marsden. 1978. Community structure as interorganizational linkage. *Annual Review of Sociology* 4:455–484.

Laumann, Edward O., and David Knoke. 1987. *The Organizational State: Social Choice in National Policy Domains.* Madison: University of Wisconsin Press.

Lave, Jean, and Etienne Wenger. 1991. *Situated Learning: Legitimate Peripheral Participation.* Cambridge: Cambridge University Press.

Lawrence, Paul R., and Jay W. Lorsch. 1967. *Organization and Environment: Managing Differentiation and Integration.* Boston: Graduate School of Business Administration, Harvard University.

Leblebici, Husayin, Gerald R. Salancik, Anne Copay, and Tom King. 1991. Institutional change and the transformation of interorganizational fields: An organizational history of the U.S. radio broadcasting industry. *Administrative Science Quarterly* 36:333–363.

Levitt, Barbara, and James G. March. 1988. Organization learning. *Annual Review of Sociology* 14:319–340.

Levi-Strauss, Claude. 1966. *The Savage Mind.* Chicago: University of Chicago Press.

Lewin, Kurt. 1951. *Field Theory in Social Psychology.* New York: Harper.

Lindblom, Charles E. 1977. Politics and Markets: *The World's Political-Economic Systems.* New York: Basic Books.

Lipset, Seymour Martin, Martin A. Trow, and James S. Coleman. 1956. *Union Democracy.* Glencoe, IL: Free Press.

Lipsky, Martin. 1980. *Street-Level Bureaucracy.* New York: Russell Sage Foundation.

Lounsbury, Michael, Marc J. Ventresca, and Paul M. Hirsch. 2003. Social movements, field frames, and industry emergence: A cultural-political perspective on recycling. *Socio-Economic Review* 1: 70-104.

Loya, Thomas A., and John Boli. 1999. Standardization in the world polity: Technical rationality over power. In *Constructing World Culture: International Nongovernmental Organizations since 1875,* edited by John Boli and George M. Thomas (pp. 169–197). Stanford, CA: Stanford University Press.

Macaulay, Stewart. 1963. Non-contractual relations in business. *American Sociological Review*, 28:55–70.

Maines, David R. 1977. Social organization and social structure in symbolic interactionist thought. *Annual Review of Sociology* 3:235–259.

Mäki, Uskali, Bo Gustafsson, and Christian Knudsen. eds. 1993. *Rationality, Institutions and Economic Methodology.* London: Routledge.

March, James G. ed. 1965. *Handbook of Organizations.* Chicago: Rand McNally.

———. 1981. Decisions in organizations and theories of choice. In *Perspectives on Organization Design and Behavior,* edited by Andrew H. Van de Ven and William F. Joyce (pp. 205–244). New York: John Wiley, Wiley-Interscience.

———. 1994. *A Primer on Decision Making: How Decisions Happen.* New York: The Free Press.

March, James G., and Johan P. Olsen. 1984. The new institutionalism: Organizational factors in political life. *American Political Science Review* 78:734–749.

———. 1989. *Rediscovering Institutions: The Organizational Basis of Politics.* New York: The Free Press.

March, James G., and Herbert A. Simon. 1958. *Organizations.* New York: Wiley.

Mares, David R., and Walter W. Powell. 1990. Cooperative security regimes: Preventing international conflicts. In *Organizations and Nation-States: New Perspectives on Conflict and Cooperation,* edited by Robert L. Kahn and Mayer N. Zald (pp. 55–94). San Francisco: Jossey-Bass.

Markus, Hazel, and R. B. Zajonc. 1985. The cognitive perspective in social psychology. In *Handbook of Social Psychology,* vol. 1, 3rd ed., edited by Gardner Lindzey and Elliot Aronson (pp. 137–230). New York: Random House.

Martin, Joanne. 1992. *Cultures in Organizations: Three Perspectives.* New York: Oxford University Press.

———. 1994. The organization of exclusion: The institutionalization of sex inequality, gendered faculty jobs, and gendered knowledge in organizational theory and research. *Organizations* 1:401–431.

Marx, Karl. 1844/1972. Economic and philosophic manuscripts of 1944: Selections. In *The Marx-Engels Reader*, edited by Robert C. Tucker (pp. 52–106). New York: W. W. Norton.

———. 1845–1846/1972. The German ideology: Part I. In *The Marx-Engels Reader*, edited by Robert C. Tucker (pp. 110–164). New York: W. W. Norton.

Masten, Scott E. 1986. The economic institutions of capitalism: A review article. *Journal of Institutional and Theoretical Economics* 142:445–451.

———. 1994. Culture and social movements. In *New Social Movements*, edited by E. Laraña, H. Johnson, and Joseph R. Gusfield (pp. 36–57). Philadelphia, PA: Temple University Press.

McAdam, Doug, John D. McCarthy, and Mayer N. Zald. 1996. Introduction: Opportunities, mobilizing structures, and framing processes—Toward a synthetic, comparative perspective on social movements. In *Comparative Perspectives on Social Movements: Political Opportunities, Mobilizing Structures, and Cultural Framings*, edited by Doug McAdam, John D. McCarthy, and Mayer N. Zald (pp. 1–22). Cambridge: Cambridge University Press.

McAdam, Doug, and W. Richard Scott. 2005. Organizations and movements. In *Social Movements and Organization Theory*, edited by Gerald F. Davis, Doug McAdam, W. Richard Scott, and Mayer N. Zald (pp. 4–40). Cambridge: Cambridge University Press.

McAdam, Doug, Sidney Tarrow, and Charles Tilly. 2001. *Dynamics of Contention.* Cambridge: Cambridge University Press.

McCarthy, John D., and Mayer N. Zald. 1977. Resource mobilization and social movements: A partial theory. *American Journal of Sociology* 82:1212–1241.

McDonough, Patricia M., Marc J. Ventresca, and Charles Outcalt. 2000. Field of dreams: Organization field approaches to understanding the transformation of college access, 1965–1995. In *Higher Education: Handbook of Theory and Research*, vol. 15 (pp. 371–405). New York: Agathon Press.

McKelvey, Bill. 1982. *Organizational Systematics.* Berkeley: University of California Press.

McKenzie, Richard B., and Dwight R. Lee. 1991. *Quicksilver Capital.* New York: The Free Press.

McLaughlin, Milbrey W. 1975. *Evaluation and Reform: The Elementary and Secondary Education Act of 1965.* Cambridge, MA: Ballinger.

McLaughlin, Milbrey W., W. Richard Scott, Sarah Deschenes, Kathryn Hopkins, and Anne Newman. Forthcoming. *Between Movement and Establishment: Organizations Advocating for Youth.*

Mead, George Herbert. 1934. *Mind, Self and Society.* Chicago: University of Chicago Press.

Mehler, J., and E. Dupoux. 1994. *What Infants Know: The New Cognitive Science of Early Development.* Oxford, UK: Blackwell.

Melnick, R. Shep. *Regulation and the Courts: The Case of the Clean Air Act.* Washington, DC: Brookings Institution.

Menand, Louis. 2001. *The Metaphysical Club: A Story of Ideas in America.* New York: Farrar, Straus and Giroux.

Menger, Carl. 1883/1963. *Problems of Economics and Sociology,* edited by Louis Schneider. Urbana: University of Illinois Press.

Merton, Robert K. 1936. The unanticipated consequences of purposive social action. *American Sociological Review* 1:894–904.

———. 1940/1957. Bureaucratic structure and personality. In *Social Theory and Social Structure* 2nd ed., edited by Robert K. Merton (pp. 195–206). Glencoe, IL: Free Press.

Merton, Robert K., Ailsa P. Gray, Barbara Hockey, and Hanan C. Selvin. eds. 1952. *Reader in Bureaucracy.* Glencoe, IL: Free Press.

Meyer, John W. 1983. Conclusion: Institutionalization and the rationality of formal organizational structure. In *Organizational Environments: Ritual and Rationality,* edited by John W. Meyer and W. Richard Scott (pp. 261–282). Beverly Hills, CA: Sage.

———. 1994. Rationalized environments. In *Institutional Environments and Organizations: Structural Complexity and Individualism,* edited by W. Richard Scott and John W. Meyer (pp. 28–54). Thousand Oaks, CA: Sage.

Meyer, John W., John Boli, and George M. Thomas. 1987. Ontology and rationalization in the Western cultural account. In *Institutional Structure: Constituting State, Society, and the Individual,* edited by George M. Thomas, John W. Meyer, Francisco O. Ramirez, and John Boli (pp. 12–37). Newbury Park, CA: Sage.

Meyer, John W., John Boli, George M. Thomas, and Francisco O. Ramirez. 1997. World society and the nation state. *American Journal of Sociology* 103:144–181.

Meyer, John W., Gili S. Drori, and Hokyu Hwang. 2006. World society and the proliferation of formal organization. In *Globalization and Organization: World Society and Organizational Change,* edited by Gili S. Drori, John W. Meyer, and Hokyu Hwang (pp. 25–49). Oxford, UK: Oxford University Press.

Meyer, John W., and Brian Rowan. 1977. Institutionalized organizations: Formal structure as myth and ceremony. *American Journal of Sociology* 83:340–363.

Meyer, John W., and W. Richard Scott. 1983a. Centralization and the legitimacy problems of local government. In *Organizational Environments: Ritual and Rationality,* edited by John W. Meyer and W. Richard Scott (pp. 199–215). Beverly Hills, CA: Sage.

Meyer, John W., and W. Richard Scott, with the assistance of Brian Rowan and Terrence E. Deal. 1983b. *Organizational Environments: Ritual and Rationality.* Beverly Hills, CA: Sage. (Updated edition in 1992)

Meyer, John W., W. Richard Scott, and David Strang. 1987. Centralization, fragmentation, and school district complexity. *Administrative Science Quarterly* 32:186–201.

Meyer, John W., W. Richard Scott, David Strang, and Andrew L. Creighton. 1988. Bureaucratization without centralization: Changes in the organizational system of U.S. public education, 1940–80. In *Institutional Patterns and Organizations: Culture and Environment,* edited by Lynne G. Zucker (pp. 139–168). Cambridge, MA: Ballinger.

Mezias, Stephen J. 1990. An institutional model of organizational practice: Financial reporting at the Fortune 200. *Administrative Science Quarterly* 35:431–457.

———. Using institutional theory to understand for-profit sectors: The case of financial reporting standards. In *The Institutional Construction of Organizations: International and Longitudinal Studies,* edited by W. Richard Scott and Soren Christensen (pp. 164–196). London: Sage Publications.

Michels, Robert. 1915/1949. *Political Parties.* Trans. by Eden and Cedar Paul. Glencoe, IL: Free Press.

Micklethwait, John, and Adrian Wooldridge. 2003. *The Company: A Short History of a Revolutionary Idea.* New York: Modern Library, Random House.

Miles, Robert H. 1982. *Coffin Nails and Corporate Strategy.* Englewood Cliffs, NJ: Prentice Hall.

Milgrom, Paul, and John Roberts. 1992. *Economics, Organization and Management.* Englewood Cliffs, NJ: Prentice Hall.

Miller, Jon. 1994. *The Social Control of Religious Zeal: A Study of Organizational Contradictions.* New Brunswick, NJ: Rutgers University Press.

Miner, Anne S. 1991. The social ecology of jobs. *American Sociological Review* 56:772–785.

Moe, Terry M. 1984. The new economics of organization. *American Journal of Political Science* 28:739–777.

———. 1989. The politics of bureaucratic structure. In *Can the Government Govern?,* edited by John Chubb and Paul Peterson (pp. 267–329). Washington, DC: Brookings.

———. 1990a. Political institutions: The neglected side of the story. *Journal of Law, Economics and Organizations* 6:213–253.

———. 1990b. The politics of structural choice: Toward a theory of public bureaucracy. In *Organization Theory: From Chester Barnard to the Present and Beyond,* edited by Oliver E. Williamson (pp. 116–153). New York: Oxford University Press.

Mohr, John W. 1994. Soldiers, mothers, tramps and others: Discourse roles in the 1907 New York City Charity Directory. *Poetics* 22:327–357.

———. Forthcoming. Implicit terrains: Meaning, measurement, and spatial metaphors in organization theory. In *Constructing Industries and Markets,* edited by Joseph Porac and Marc Ventresca. New York: Elsevier.

Mohr, John W., and Francesca Guerra-Pearson. Forthcoming. The differentiation of institutional space: Organizational forms in the New York social welfare sector, 1888–1917. In *How Institutions Change,* edited by Walter W. Powell and Daniel L. Jones. Chicago: University of Chicago Press.

Mohr, Lawrence B. 1982. *Explaining Organizational Behavior.* San Francisco: Jossey-Bass.

Morrill, Calvin. Forthcoming. Institutional change through interstitial emergence: The growth of alternative dispute resolution in American law, 1965–1995. In *How Institutions Change*, edited by Walter W. Powell and Daniel L. Jones. Chicago: University of Chicago Press.

National Commission on Excellence in Education. 1983. *A Nation at Risk: The Imperative for Educational Reform*. Washington, DC: Government Printing Office.

Nee, Victor. 1998. Sources of the new institutionalism. In *The New Institutionalism in Sociology*, edited by Mary C. Brinton and Victor Nee (pp. 1–16). New York: Russell Sage Foundation.

Nelson, Richard R., and Sidney G. Winter. 1982. *An Evolutionary Theory of Economic Change*. Cambridge, MA: Belknap Press of Harvard University Press.

Nisbett, Richard, and Lee Ross. 1980. *Human Inference: Strategies and Shortcomings of Social Judgment*. Englewood Cliffs, NJ: Prentice Hall.

Nohria, Nitin, and Robert G. Eccles. eds. 1992. *Networks and Organizations: Structure, Form, and Action*. Boston: Harvard Business School Press.

Noll, Roger T. ed. 1985. *Regulatory Policy and the Social Sciences*. Berkeley: University of California Press.

North, Douglass C. 1989. Institutional change and economic history. *Journal of Institutional and Theoretical Economics* 145:238–245.

———. 1990. *Institutions, Institutional Change and Economic Performance*. Cambridge: Cambridge University Press.

———. 2005. *Understanding the Process of Economic Change*. Princeton, NJ: Princeton University Press.

North, Douglass C., and Robert Paul Thomas. 1973. *The Rise of the Western World: A New Economic History*. Cambridge: Cambridge University Press.

Oliver, Christine. 1991. Strategic responses to institutional processes. *Academy of Management Review* 16:145–179.

———. 1992. The antecedents of deinstitutionalization. *Organization Studies* 13:563–588.

Ó Riain, Seán. 2000. States and markets in an era of globalization. *Annual Review of Sociology* 26:187–213.

Orlikowski, Wanda J. 1992. The duality of technology: Rethinking the concept of technology in organizations. *Organization Science* 3:398–427.

Orr, Ryan J., and W. Richard Scott. Forthcoming. Confronting institutional exceptions on global projects: A process model. *Journal of International Business Studies*.

Orren, Karen, and Stephen Skowronek. 1994. Beyond the iconography of order: Notes for "new" institutionalism. In *The Dynamics of American Politics*, edited by L. D. Dodd and C. Jillson (pp. 311–332). Boulder, CO: Westview.

Orton, J. Douglas, and Karl E. Weick. 1990. Loosely coupled systems: A reconceptualization. *Academy of Management Review* 15:203–223.

Ouchi, William G. 1981. *Theory Z: How American Business Can Meet the Japanese Challenge*. New York: Addison-Wesley.

Owen-Smith, Jason. Forthcoming. *Structural components of institutional change: Science and commerce in academe.* Unpublished paper, University of Michigan.

Oxley, J. E. 1999. Institutional environment and the mechanisms of governance: The impact of intellectual property protection on the structure of inter-firm alliances. *Journal of Economic Behavior & Organization* 38:283–309.

Pagett, John F., and Christopher K. Ansell. 1993. Robust action and the rise of the Medici, 1400–1434. *American Journal of Sociology* 98:1259–1318.

Palmer, Donald A., P. Devereaux Jennings, and Xueguang Zhou. 1993. Late adoption of the multidivisional form by large U.S. corporations: Institutional, political, and economic accounts. *Administrative Science Quarterly* 38:100–131.

Parsons, Talcott. 1937. *The Structure of Social Action.* New York: McGraw-Hill.

———. 1951. *The Social System.* New York: The Free Press.

———. 1953. A revised analytical approach to the theory of social stratification. In *Class, Status and Power: A Reader in Social Stratification,* edited by Reinhard Bendix and Seymour Martin Lipset (pp. 92–129). Glencoe, IL: Free Press.

———. 1960a. A sociological approach to the theory of organizations. In *Structure and Process in Modern Societies,* edited by Talcott Parsons (pp. 16–58). Glencoe, IL: Free Press. (Originally published in 1956)

———. 1960b. Some ingredients of a general theory of formal organization. In *Structure and Process in Modern Societies,* edited by Talcott Parsons (pp. 59–96). Glencoe, IL: Free Press. (Originally published in 1956)

———. 1934/1990. Prolegomena to a theory of social institutions. *American Sociological Review* 55:319–339.

Parsons, Talcott, Robert F. Bales, and Edward A. Shils. 1953. *Working Papers in the Theory of Action.* Glencoe, IL: Free Press.

Pedersen, Jesper Standgaard, and Frank Dobbin. 1997. The social invention of collective actors: On the rise of the organization. *American Behavioral Scientist* 40:431–443.

Perrow, Charles. 1961. The analysis of goals in complex organizations. *American Sociological Review* 26:854–866.

———. 1985. Review essay: Overboard with myth and symbols. *American Journal of Sociology* 91:151–155.

———. 1986. *Complex Organizations: A Critical Essay,* 3rd ed. New York: Random House.

Peters, B. Guy. 1999. *Institutional Theory in Political Science: The "New Institutionalism."* London: Pinter.

Peterson, Paul E., Barry G. Rabe, and Kenneth K. Wong. 1986. *When Federalism Works.* Washington, DC: Brookings Institution.

Pfeffer, Jeffrey. 1981. Management as symbolic action: The creation and maintenance of organizational paradigms. In *Research in Organizational Behavior,* vol 13, edited by Barry M. Staw and L. L. Cummings (pp. 1–52). Greenwich, CT: JAI Press.

——. 1992. *Managing with Power: Politics and Influence in Organizations.* Boston: Harvard Business School Press.

Pfeffer, Jeffrey, and Yinon Cohen. 1984. Determinants of internal labor markets in organizations. *Administrative Science Quarterly* 29:550–572.

Pfeffer, Jeffrey, and Gerald Salancik. 1978. *The External Control of Organizations.* New York: Harper & Row.

Pierson, Paul. 2004. *Politics in Time: History, Institutions, and Social Analysis.* Princeton, NJ: Princeton University Press.

Podolny, Joel M. 1993. A status-based model of market competition. *American Journal of Sociology* 98:829–872.

Porac, Joseph F., James B. Wade, and Timothy G. Pollock. 1999. Industry categories and the politics of the comparable firm in CEO compensation. *Administrative Science Quarterly* 44:112–144.

Powell, Walter W. 1988. Institutional effects on organizational structure and performance. In *Institutional Patterns and Organizations: Culture and Environment*, edited by Lynne G. Zucker (pp. 115–136). Cambridge, MA: Ballinger.

——. 1990. Neither market nor hierarchy: Network forms of organization. In *Research in Organizational Behavior*, vol. 12, edited by Barry M. Staw and L. L. Cummings (pp. 295–336). Greenwich, CT: JAI Press.

——. 1991. Expanding the scope of institutional analysis. In *The New Institutionalism in Organizational Analysis*, edited by Walter W. Powell and Paul J. DiMaggio (pp. 183–203). Chicago: University of Chicago Press.

——. 1998. The social construction of an organizational field: The case of biotechnology. *International Journal of Technology Management.*

Powell, Walter W., and Paul J. DiMaggio. eds. 1991. *The New Institutionalism in Organizational Analysis.* Chicago: University of Chicago Press.

Pratt, John W., and Richard J. Zeckhauser. eds. 1985. *Principals and Agents: The Structure of Business.* Boston, MA: Harvard Business School Press.

President's Research Committee on Social Trends. 1934. *Recent Social Trends in the United States.* New York: McGraw-Hill.

Rao, Hayagreeva. 1998. Caveat emptor: The construction of nonprofit consumer watchdog organizations. *American Journal of Sociology* 103:912–961.

Rao, Hayagreeva, Philippe Monin, and Rodolphe Durand. 2003. Institutional change in Toque Ville: Nouvelle cuisine as an identity movement in French gastronomy. *American Journal of Sociology* 108:795–843.

Rao, Havagreeva, and Kumar Sivakumar. 1999. Institutional sources of boundary-spanning structures: The establishment of investor relations departments in the Fortune 500 industrials. *Organization Science* 10:27–42.

Reed, Michael. 1985. *Redirections in Organizational Analysis.* London: Tavistock Publications.

Reddy, Michael. 1979. The conduit metaphor. In *Metaphor and Thought*, edited by Andrew Ortney (pp. 284–324). New York: Cambridge University Press.

Ridley, Matt. 2003. *Nature via Nurture: Genes, Experience & What Makes Us Human.* New York: HarperCollins.

Riker, William. 1980. Implications from the disequilibrium of majority rules for the study of institutions. *American Political Science Review* 74:432–447.

Rittberger, V. 1993. *Regime Theory and International Relations.* Oxford: Clarendon Press.

Robinson, Paul. 1985. *Opera and Ideas: From Mozart to Strauss.* Ithaca, NY: Cornell University Press.

Roethlisberger, Fritz J., and William J. Dickson. 1939. *Management and the Worker.* Cambridge, MA: Harvard University Press.

Rogers, Everett. 1995. *Diffusion of Innovation.* 4th ed. New York: The Free Press.

Rorty, Richard. 1989. *Contingency, Irony and Solidarity.* New York: Cambridge University Press.

Rosenberg, Morris. 1979. *Conceiving the Self.* New York: Basic Books.

Rosenberg, Nathan, and L. E. Birdzell, Jr. 1986. *How the West Grew Rich: The Economic Transformation of the Industrial World.* New York: Basic Books.

Rowan, Brian. 1982. Organizational structure and the institutional environment: The case of public schools. *Administrative Science Quarterly* 27:259–279.

Roy, Donald. 1952. Quota restriction and goldbricking in a machine shop. *American Journal of Sociology* 57:427–442.

Roy, William G. 1997. *Socializing Capital: The Rise of the Large Industrial Corporation in America.* Princeton, NJ: Princeton University Press.

Ruef, Martin, and W. Richard Scott. 1998. A multidimensional model of organizational legitimacy: Hospital survival in changing institutional environments. *Administrative Science Quarterly* 43:877–904.

Sahlin-Andersson, Kerstin 1996. Imitating by editing success: The construction of organization fields. In *Translating Organizational Change,* edited by Barbara Czarniawska and Bernward Joerges (pp. 69–92). New York: Walter de Gruyter.

Sahlin-Andersson, Kerstin, and Lars Engwall. eds. 2002. *The Expansion of Management Knowledge: Carriers, Flows and Sources.* Stanford, CA: Stanford University Press.

Salaman, Graeme. 1978. Toward a sociology of organisational structure. *The Sociological Review* 26:519–554.

Saxenian, Annalee. 1994. *Regional Advantage: Culture and Competition in Silicon Valley and Route 128.* Cambridge, MA: Harvard University Press.

Scharpf, Fritz W. 1997. *Games Real Actors Play.* Boulder, CO: Westview.

Schmitter, Philippe. 1990. Sectors in modern capitalism: Models of governance and variations in performance. In *Labour Relations and Economic Performance,* edited by Renato Brunetta and Carlo Dell'Aringa (pp. 3–39). Houndmills, UK: Macmillan.

Schmitter, Philippe C., and Gerhard Lehmbruch. eds. 1979. *Trends toward Corporatist Intermediation.* Beverly Hills, CA: Sage.

Schmoller, Gustav von. 1900–1904. *Grundriss der Allgemeinen Volkswirtschaftslehre.* Leipzig: Duncker & Humbolt.

Schotter, Andrew 1986. The evolution of rules. In *Economics as a Process: Essays in the New Institutional Economics,* edited by Richard N. Langlois (pp. 117–134). New York: Cambridge University Press.

Schneiberg, Marc. 2002. Organizational heterogeneity and the production of new forms: Politics, social movements and mutual companies in American fire insurance, 1900–1930. In *Social Structure and Organizations Revisited: Research in the Sociology of Organizations,* vol. 19 (pp. 39–89). Amsterdam: Elsevier.

Schneiberg, Marc, and Sarah Soule. 2005. Institutionalization as a contested multilevel process. In *Social Movements and Organization Theory,* edited by Gerald F. Davis, Doug McAdam, W. Richard Scott, and Mayer N. Zald (pp. 122–160). Cambridge: Cambridge University Press.

Schrödinger, Erwin. 1945. *What Is Life?* New York: Cambridge University Press.

Schrumpeter, Joseph A. 1926/1961. *The Theory of Economic Development.* New York: Oxford University Press.

———. 1942/1975. *Capitalism, Socialism and Democracy,* 2nd ed. New York: Harper and Row.

Schutz, Alfred. 1932/1967. *The Phenomenology of the Social World.* Trans. by George Walsh and Frederick Lehnert. Evanston, IL: Northwestern University Press.

Scott, W. Richard. 1987. The adolescence of institutional theory. *Administrative Science Quarterly* 32:493–511.

———. 1992. *Organizations: Rational, Natural, and Open Systems,* 3rd ed. Englewood Cliffs, NJ: Prentice Hall.

———. 1994a. Conceptualizing organizational fields: Linking organizations and societal systems. In *Systemrationalität und Partialinteresse* [Systems Rationality and Partial Interests], edited by Hans-Ulrich Derlien, Uta Gerhardt, and Fritz W. Scharpf (pp. 203–221). Baden-Baden, Germany: Nomos Verlagsgesellschaft.

———. 1994b. Institutions and organizations: Toward a theoretical synthesis. In *Institutional Environments and Organizations: Structural Complexity and Individualism,* edited by W. Richard Scott and John W. Meyer (pp. 55–80). Thousand Oaks, CA: Sage.

———. 1994c. Law and organizations. In *The Legalistic Organization,* edited by Sim B. Sitkin and Robert J. Bies (pp. 3–18). Thousand Oaks, CA: Sage.

———. 2003a. Institutional carriers: Reviewing modes of transporting ideas over time and space and considering their consequences. *Industrial and Corporate Change* 12:879–894.

———. 2003b. *Organizations: Rational, Natural and Open Systems,* 5th ed. Upper Saddle River, NJ: Prentice Hall.

———. 2005a. Evolving professions: An institutional field approach. In *Organization und Profession,* edited by Thomas Klatetzki and Veronika Tacke (pp. 119–141). Weisbaden: Verlag für Sozialwissenschaften.

———. 2005b. Institutional theory: Contributing to a theoretical research program. In *Great Minds in Management: The Process of Theory Development,* edited by Ken G. Smith and Michael A. Hitt (pp. 460–484). Oxford: Oxford University Press.

———. Forthcoming-a. Approaching adulthood: The maturing of institutional theory. *Theory and Society.*

————. Forthcoming-b. Lords of the dance: Professions as institutional agents. *Organization Studies.*

Scott, W. Richard, and Elaine V. Backman. 1990. Institutional theory and the medical care sector. In *Innovations in Health Care Delivery: Insights for Organization Theory,* edited by Stephen S. Mick (pp. 20–52). San Francisco: Jossey-Bass.

Scott, W. Richard, and Søren Christensen. eds. 1995. *The Institutional Construction of Organizations: International and Longitudinal Studies.* Thousand Oaks, CA: Sage.

Scott, W. Richard, and Gerald F. Davis. 2007. *Organizations and Organizing: Rational, Natural and Open System Perspectives.* Upper Saddle River, NJ: Pierson Prentice Hall.

Scott, W. Richard, Peter J. Mendel, and Seth Pollack. Forthcoming. Environments and fields: Studying the evolution of a field of medical care organizations. In *How Institutions Change,* edited by Walter W. Powell and Daniel L. Jones. Chicago: University of Chicago Press.

Scott, W. Richard, and John W. Meyer. 1983. The organization of societal sectors. In *Organizational Environments: Ritual and Rationality,* edited by John W. Meyer and W. Richard Scott (pp. 129–153). [Revised version in *The New Institutionalism in Organizational Analysis,* edited by Walter W. Powell and Paul J. DiMaggio (pp. 108–140). Chicago: University of Chicago Press, 1991.]

————. ed. 1994. *Institutional Environments and Organizations: Structural Complexity and Individualism.* Thousand Oaks, CA: Sage.

Scott, W. Richard, Martin Ruef, Peter J. Mendel, and Carol A. Caronna. 2000. *Institutional Change and Healthcare Organizations: From Professional Dominance to Managed Care.* Chicago: University of Chicago Press.

Searle, John R. 1995. *The Construction of Social Reality.* New York: The Free Press.

Seavoy, Ronald E. 1982. *The Origins of the American Business Corporation, 1784–1855: Broadening the Concept of Public Service during Industrialization.* Westport, CT: Greenwood Press.

Selznick, Philip. 1948. Foundations of the theory of organization. *American Sociological Review* 13:25–35.

————. 1949. *TVA and the Grass Roots.* Berkeley: University of California Press.

———— 1957. *Leadership in Administration.* New York: Harper & Row.

————. 1969. *Law, Society, and Industrial Justice.* New York: Russell Sage Foundation.

————. 1992. *The Moral Commonwealth: Social Theory and the Promise of Community.* Berkeley: University of California Press.

————. 1996. Institutionalism "Old" and "New." *Administrative Science Quarterly* 41:270–277.

Sewell, William H., Jr. 1992. A theory of structure: Duality, agency, and transformation. *American Journal of Sociology* 98:1–29.

Shenhav, Yehouda. 1995. From chaos to systems: The engineering foundations of organizational theory, 1879–1932. *Administrative Science Quarterly* 40:557–586.

————. 1999. *Manufacturing Rationality: The Engineering Foundations of the Managerial Revolution.* Oxford: Oxford University Press.

Shepsle, Kenneth A. 1989. Studying institutions: Lessons from the rational choice approach. *Journal of Theoretical Politics* 1:131–147.

Shepsle, Kenneth A., and Barry Weingast. 1987. The institutional foundations of committee power. *American Political Science Review* 81:85–104.

Sherif, Muzafer. 1935. A study of some social factors in perception. *Archives of Psychology,* no. 187.

Shonfield, Alfred. 1965. *Modern Capitalism.* London: Oxford University Press.

Silverman, Brian S. 2002. Organizational economics. In *The Blackwell Companion to Organizations,* edited by Joel A. C. Baum (pp. 477–493). Oxford: Blackwell.

Silverman, David. 1971. *The Theory of Organisations: A Sociological Framework.* New York: Basic Books.

———. 1972. Some neglected questions about social reality. In *New Directions in Sociological Theory,* edited by Paul Filmer, Michael Phillipson, David Silverman, and David Walsh (pp. 165–182). Cambridge, MA: MIT Press.

Silverman, David, and J. Jones. 1976. *Organizational Work: The Language of Grading and the Grading of Language.* London: Macmillan.

Simon, Herbert A. 1945/1997. *Administrative Behavior: A Study of Decision-Making Processes in Administrative Organization.* New York: Macmillan, 1945; New York: The Free Press, 1997.

———. 1991. *Models of My Life.* New York: Basic Books.

Simonde de Sismondi, J.C.L. 1837. *Études sur L'économie Politique,* vol. 1. Paris: Treuttel et Würtz.

Simons, Tal, and Paul Ingram. 1997. Organization and ideology: Kibbutzim and hired labor, 1951–1965. *Administrative Science Quarterly* 42:784–813.

Sine, Wesley D., and Pamela S. Tolbert. 2006. *Institutions in action: Tenure systems and faculty employment in colleges and universities.* Unpublished paper, Cornell University, Ithaca, NY.

Singh, Jitendra V., David J. Tucker, and Robert J. House. 1986. Organizational legitimacy and the liability of newness. *Administrative Science Quarterly* 31:171–193.

Sitkin, Sim B., and Robert J. Bies. eds. 1994. *The Legalistic Organization.* Thousand Oaks, CA: Sage.

Sjöstrand, Sven-Erik. 1995. Toward a theory of institutional change. In *On Economic Institutions: Theory and Applications,* edited by John Groenewegen, Christos Pitelis, and Sven-Erik Sjöstrand (pp. 19–44). Aldershot, UK: Edward Elgar.

Skocpol, Theda. 1979. *States and Social Revolutions.* Cambridge: Cambridge University Press.

———. 1985. Bringing the state back in: Strategies of analysis in current research. In *Bringing the State Back In,* edited by Peter B. Evans, Dietrich Rueschemeyer, and Theda Skocpol (pp. 3–37). Cambridge: Cambridge University Press.

Skowronek, Stephen. 1982. *Building a New American State: The Expansion of National Administrative Capacities, 1877–1920.* Cambridge: Cambridge University Press.

Smelser, Neil J., and Richard Swedberg. eds. 1994. *The Handbook of Economic Sociology.* New York: Princeton University Press and Russell Sage Foundation.

————. ed. 2005. *The Handbook of Economic Sociology*, 2nd ed. New York: Princeton University Press and Russell Sage Foundation.

Smith-Doerr, Laurel, and Walter W. Powell. 2005. Networks and economic life. In *The Handbook of Economic Sociology*, edited by Neil J. Smelser and Richard Swedberg (pp. 379–402). New York: Princeton University Press and Russell Sage Foundation.

Snow, David A., and Robert D. Benford. 1992. Master frames and cycles of protest. In *Frontiers in Social Movement Theory*, edited by Aldon Morris and Carol McClurg Mueller (pp. 133-155). New Haven, CT: Yale University Press.

Snow, David A., E. Burke Rochford, Jr., Steven K. Worden, and Robert D. Benford. 1986. Frame alignment processes, micromobilization, and movement participation. *American Sociological Review* 51:464–481.

Somers, Ann R. 1969. *Hospital Regulation: The Dilemma of Public Policy*. Princeton, NJ: Industrial Relations Section.

Somers, Margaret R., and Gloria Gibson. 1994. Reclaiming the epistemological "other": Narrative and the social constitution of identity. In *Social Theory and the Politics of Identity*, edited by Craig Calhoun (pp. 37–99). Oxford: Basil Blackwell.

Spencer, Herbert. 1876, 1896, 1910. *The Principles of Sociology*, 3 vols. London: Appleton-Century-Crofts.

Stark, David. 1996. Recombinant property in East European capitalism. *American Journal of Sociology* 101:993–1027.

Starr, Paul. 1982. *The Social Transformation of American Medicine*. New York: Basic Books.

Stern, Robert N. 1979. The development of an interorganizational control network: The case of intercollegiate athletics. *Administrative Science Quarterly* 24:242–266.

Stigler, George J. 1968. *The Organization of Industry*. Homewood, IL: Richard D. Irwin.

Stinchcombe, Arthur L. 1965. Social structure and organizations. In *Handbook of Organizations*, edited by James G. March (pp. 142–193). Chicago: Rand McNally.

————. 1968. *Constructing Social Theories*. Chicago: University of Chicago Press.

————. 1997. On the virtues of the old institutionalism. *Annual Review of Sociology* 23:1–18.

Strang, David, and John W. Meyer. 1993. Institutional conditions for diffusion. *Theory and Society* 22:487–511.

Strang, David, and Wesley D. Sine. 2002. Interorganizational institutions. In *The Blackwell Companion to Organizations*, edited by Joel A. C. Baum (pp. 497–519). Oxford, UK: Blackwell.

Strang, David, and Sarah A. Soule. 1998. Diffusion in organizations and social movements: From hybrid corn to poison pills. *Annual Review of Sociology* 24:265–290.

Strauss, Anselm. 1993. *Continual Permutations of Action*. New York: Aldine de Gruyter.

Streeck, Wolfgang, and Philippe C. Schmitter. 1985. Community, market, state—and associations? The prospective contribution of interest governance to social order. In *Private Interest Government: Beyond Market and State*, edited by Wolfgang Streeck and Philippe C. Schmitter (pp. 1–29). Beverly Hills, CA: Sage.

Stryker, Robin. 1994. Rules, resources and legitimacy processes: Some implications for social conflict, order, and change. *American Journal of Sociology* 99:847–910.

———. 2000. Legitimacy processes as institutional politics: Implications for theory and research in the sociology of organizations. In *Research in the Sociology of Organizations*, vol. 17, edited by Samuel B. Bacharach (pp. 179–223). Greenwich, CT: JAI Press.

Stryker, Sheldon. 1980. *Symbolic Interactionism: A Social Structural Version.* Menlo Park, CA: Cummings.

Suchman, Mark C. 1995a. Localism and globalism in institutional analysis: The emergence of contractual norms in venture finance. In *The Institutional Construction of Organizations: International and Longitudinal Studies*, edited by W. Richard Scott and Søren Christensen (pp. 39–63). Thousand Oaks, CA: Sage.

———. 1995b. Managing legitimacy: Strategic and institutional approaches. *Academy of Management Review* 20:571–610.

———. 2003. The contract as social artifact. *Law & Society Review* 37:91–142.

———. Forthcoming. Constructed ecologies: Reproduction and structuration in emerging organizational communities. In *How Institutions Change*, edited by Walter W. Powell and Daniel L. Jones. Chicago: University of Chicago Press.

Suchman, Mark C., and Mia L. Cahill. 1996. The hired-gun as facilitator: The case of lawyers in Silicon Valley. *Law and Social Inquiry* 21:837–874.

Suchman, Mark C., and Lauren B. Edelman. 1997. Legal rational myths: The new institutionalism and the law and society tradition. *Law and Social Inquiry* 21:903–941.

Suchman, Mark C., Daniel J. Steward, and Clifford A. Westfall. 2001. The legal environment of entrepreneurship: Observations on the legitimation of venture finance in Silicon Valley. In *The Entrepreneurship Dynamic: Origins of Entrepreneurship and the Evolution of Industries*, edited by Claudia Bird Schoonhoven and Elaine Romanelli (pp. 349–382). Stanford, CA: Stanford University Press.

Sumner, William Graham. 1906. *Folkways.* Boston: Ginn & Co.

Sutton, John R., Frank R. Dobbin, John W. Meyer, and W. Richard Scott. 1994. The legalization of the workplace. *American Journal of Sociology* 99:944–971.

Swedberg, Richard. 1991. Major traditions of economic sociology. *Annual Review of Sociology* 17:251–276.

———. 1998. *Max Weber and the Idea of Economic Sociology.* Princeton, NJ: Princeton University Press.

Swidler, Ann. 1986. Culture in action: Symbols and strategies. *American Sociological Review* 51:273–286.

Tate, Jay, 2001. National varieties of standardization. In *Varieties of Capitalism*, edited by Peter A. Hall and David Soskice (pp. 442–473). Oxford: Oxford University Press.

Taylor, Frederick Winslow. 1911. *The Principles of Scientific Management*. New York: Harper.

Taylor, Serge. 1984. *Making Bureaucracies Think: The Environment Impact Statement Strategy of Administrative Reform*. Stanford, CA: Stanford University Press.

Taylor, Verta, and Nancy Whitter. 1992. Collective identity in social movement communities: Lesbian feminist mobilization. In *Frontiers in Social Movement Theory*, edited by Aldon Morris and Carol McClurg Mueller (pp. 104–130). New Haven, CT: Yale University Press.

Teece, David J. 1981. Internal organization and economic performance: An empirical study of the profitability of principal firms. *Journal of Industrial Economics* 30:173–200.

Thelen, Kathleen. 1999. Historical institutionalism in comparative politics. *American Review of Political Science* 2:369–404.

Thelen, Kathleen, and Sven Steinmo. 1992. Historical institutionalism in comparative politics. In *Structuring Politics: Historical Institutionalism in Comparative* Analysis, edited by Sven Steinmo, Kathleen Thelen, and Frank Longstreth (pp. 1–32). Cambridge: Cambridge University Press.

Thoits, Peggy A. 1989. The sociology of emotions. *Annual Review of Sociology* 15:317–342.

Thomas, George M., John W. Meyer, Francisco O. Ramirez, and John Boli. eds. 1987. *Institutional Structure: Constituting State, Society, and the Individual*. Newbury Park, CA: Sage.

Thompson, James D. 1967/2003. *Organizations in Action*. New York: McGraw-Hill. [Reprinted, New Brunswick, NJ: Transaction Publishers, 2003.]

Thornton, Patricia H. 2004. *Markets from Culture: Institutional Logics and Organizational Decisions in Higher Education Publishing*. Stanford, CA: Stanford University Press.

Thornton, Patricia H., and William Ocasio. 1999. Institutional logics and the historical contingency of power in organizations: Executive succession in the higher education publishing industry, 1958–1990. *American Journal of Sociology* 105:801–843.

Tilly, Charles. 1978. *From Mobilization to Revolution*. Reading, MA: Addison-Wesley.

Tolbert, Pamela S. 1988. Institutional sources of organizational culture in major law firms. In *Institutional Patterns and Organizations: Culture and Environment*, edited by Lynne G. Zucker (pp. 101–113). Cambridge, MA: Ballinger.

Tolbert, Pamela S., and Lynne G. Zucker. 1983. Institutional sources of change in the formal structure of organizations: The diffusion of civil service reform, 1880–1935. *Administrative Science Quarterly* 30:22–39.

———. 1996. The institutionalization of institutional theory. In *Handbook of Organization Studies,* edited by Stewart R. Clegg, Cynthia Hardy, and Walter R. Nord (pp. 175–190). London: Sage.

Trice, Harrison M., and Janice M. Beyer. 1993. *The Cultures of Work Organizations.* Englewood Cliffs, NJ: Prentice Hall.

Tucker, Robert C. 1972. Introduction: The writings of Marx and Engels. In *The Marx-Engels Reader* (pp. xv–xxiv), edited by Robert C. Tucker. New York: Norton.

Tullock, Gordon. 1976. *The Vote Motive.* London: Institute for Economic Affairs.

Turner, Roy. ed. 1974. *Ethnomethodology: Selected Readings.* Harmondsworth, UK: Penguin.

Tushman, Michael L., and Philip Anderson. 1986. Technological discontinuities and organizational environments. *Administrative Science Quarterly,* 31:439–465.

Tversky, Amos, and Donald Kahneman. 1974. Judgment under uncertainty. *Science* 185:1124–1131.

Uzzi, Brian D. 1996. The sources and consequences of embeddedness for the economic performance of organizations: The network effect. *American Sociological Review* 61:674–698.

Vanberg, Viktor. 1989. Carl Menger's evolutionary and John R. Commons' collective action approach to institutions: A comparison. *Review of Political Economy* 1:334–360.

Van de Ven, Andrew H. 1993. The institutional theory of John R. Commons: A review and commentary. *Academy of Management Review* 18:129–152.

Van de Ven, Andrew H., and Robert Drazin 1985. The concept of fit in contingency theory. In *Research in Organizational Behavior,* edited by L. L. Cummings and Barry M. Staw, vol. 7 (pp. 171–222). Greenwich, CT: JAI Press.

Van de Ven, Andrew H., and Raghu Garud. 1994. The coevolution of technical and institutional events in the development of an innovation. In *Evolutionary Dynamics of Organizations,* edited by Joel A. C. Baum and Jitendra Singh (pp. 425–443). New York: Oxford University Press.

Van de Ven, Andrew H., and George P. Huber. eds. 1990. Longitudinal field research methods for studying processes of organizational change. *Organization Science* 1(3):213–335 and (4):375–439. (Special Issues)

Vaughn, Diane. 1996. *The Challenger Launch Decision: Risky Technology, Culture, and Deviance at NASA.* Chicago: University of Chicago Press.

———. 1999. The dark side of organizations: Mistakes, misconduct, and disaster. *Annual Review of Sociology* 25:271–305.

Veblen, Thorstein B. 1898. Why is economics not an evolutionary science? *Quarterly Journal of Economics* 12:373–397.

———. 1909. The limitations of marginal utility. *Journal of Political Economy* 17:235–245.

———. 1919. *The Place of Science in Modern Civilization and Other Essays.* New York: Huebsch.

Ventresca, Marc J., and John W. Mohr. 2002. Archival research methods. In *The Blackwell Companion to Organizations*, edited by Joel A. C. Baum (pp. 805–828). Oxford, UK: Blackwell.

Ventresca, Marc J., Dara Szliowicz, and M. Tina Dacin. 2003. Innovations in governance: Global structuring and the field of public exchange-traded markets. *In Globalization and Institutions: Redefining the Rules of the Economic Game,* edited by Marie-Laure Djelic and Sigrid Quack (pp. 243–277). Cheltenham, UK: Edward Elgar.

Vogus, Timothy J., and Gerald F. Davis. 2005. Elite mobilization for anti-takeover legislation, 1982–1990. In *Social Movements and Organization Theory*, edited by Gerald F. Davis, Doug McAdam, W. Richard Scott, and Mayer N. Zald (pp. 96–121). New York: Cambridge University Press.

Walker, Gordon, and David Weber. 1984. A transaction cost approach to make-or-buy decisions. *Administrative Science Quarterly* 29:373–391.

Wallerstein, Immanuel. 1979. From feudalism to capitalism: Transition or transitions. In *The Capitalist World-Economy: Essays by Immanuel Wallerstein* (pp. 138–151). Cambridge: Cambridge University Press.

Warren, Roland L. 1967. The interorganizational field as a focus for investigation. *Administrative Science Quarterly* 12:396–419.

———. 1972. *The Community in America.* Chicago: Rand McNally.

Warren, Roland L., Stephen M. Rose, and Ann F. Bergunder. 1974. *The Structure of Urban Reform: Community Decision Organizations in Stability and Change.* Lexington, MA: Lexington Books.

Weber, Max. 1906–1924/1946. From *Max Weber: Essays in Sociology.* Translated and edited by Hans H. Gerth and C. Wright Mills. New York: Oxford University Press.

———. 1924/1947. *The Theory of Social and Economic Organization.* Translated and edited by A. M. Henderson and Talcott Parsons. New York: Oxford University Press.

———. 1904–1918/1949. *The Methodology of the Social Sciences.* Translated and edited by Edward A. Shils and Henry A. Finch. Glencoe, IL: Free Press.

———. 1924/1968. *Economy and Society: An Interpretive Sociology,* 3 vols, edited by Guenther Roth and Claus Wittich. New York: Bedminister Press.

Weick, Karl E. 1976. Educational organizations as loosely coupled systems. *Administrative Science Quarterly* 21:1–19.

———. 1979. *The Social Psychology of Organizing,* 2nd ed. Reading, MA: Addison-Wesley.

———. 1995. *Sensemaking in Organizations.* Thousand Oaks, CA: Sage.

———. 2000. Quality improvement: A sensemaking perspective. In *The Quality Movement & Organization Theory*, edited by Robert E. Cole and W. Richard Scott (pp. 155–172). Thousand Oaks, CA: Sage.

Weingast, Barry R. 1989. The political institutions of representative government. *Working Papers in Political Science P-89-14.* Hoover Institution, Stanford University.

———. 2002. Rational choice institutionalism. In *The State of the Discipline,* edited by Ira Katznelson and Helen Milner (pp. 660–692). New York: W. W. Norton.

Westney, D. Eleanor. 1987. *Imitation and Innovation: The Transfer of Western Organizational Patterns to Meiji Japan.* Cambridge, MA: Harvard University Press.

Westphal, James D., Ranjay Gulati, and Stephen M. Shortell. 1997. Customization or conformity? An institutional and network perspective on the content and consequences of TQM adoption. *Administrative Science Quarterly* 42:366–394.

Westphal, James D., and Edward J. Zajac. 1994. Substance and symbolism in CEOs' long-term incentives plans. *Administrative Science Quarterly* 39:367–390.

———. 1998. The symbolic management of stockholders: Corporate governance reforms and shareholder reactions. *Administrative Science Quarterly* 43:127–153.

Whetten, David A., and Paul C. Godfrey. eds. 1999. *Identity in Organizations: Building Theory Through Conversations.* Thousand Oaks, CA: Sage.

White, William D. 1982. The American hospital industry since 1900: A short history. In *Advances in Health Economics and Health Services Research,* edited by Richard M. Scheffler, vol. 3 (pp. 143–170). Greenwich, CT: JAI Press.

Whitley, Richard D. 1987. Taking firms seriously as economic actors: Toward a sociology of firm behaviour. *Organisation Studies* 8:125–147.

———. 1992a. *Business Systems in East Asia: Firms, Markets, and Societies.* London: Sage Publications.

———. 1992b. The social construction of organizations and markets: The comparative analysis of business recipes. In *Rethinking Organizations: New Directions in Organization Theory and Analysis,* edited by Michael Reed and Michael Hughes (pp. 120–143). Newbury Park, CA: Sage.

———. 1992c. Societies, firms, and markets: The social structuring of business systems. In *European Business Systems: Firms and Markets in Their National Contexts,* edited by Richard Whitley (pp. 5–44). London: Sage Publications.

Wiley, Mary Glenn, and Mayer N. Zald. 1968. The growth and transformation of educational accrediting agencies: An exploratory study in social control of institutions. *Sociology of Education* 41:36–56.

Williamson, Oliver E. 1975. *Markets and Hierarchies: Analysis and Antitrust Implications.* New York: The Free Press.

———. 1981. The economics of organization: The transaction cost approach. *American Journal of Sociology* 87: 548–577.

———. 1985. *The Economic Institutions of Capitalism.* New York: The Free Press.

———. 1991. Comparative economic organization: The analysis of discrete structural alternatives. *Administrative Science Quarterly* 36:269–296.

———. 1994. Transaction cost economics and organization theory. In *The Handbook of Economic Sociology,* edited by Neil J. Smelser and Richard Swedberg (pp. 77–107). Princeton, NJ: Princeton University Press and Russell Sage Foundation.

———. 2005. Transaction cost economics: The process of theory development. In *Great Minds in Management: The Process of Theory Development,* edited by

Ken G. Smith and Michael A. Hitt (pp. 485–508). Oxford: Oxford University Press.

Willoughby, Westel Woodbury. 1896. *An Examination of the Nature of the State.* New York: Macmillan.

———. 1904. *The American Constitutional System.* New York: Century.

Wilson, James Q. ed. 1980. *The Politics of Regulation.* New York: Basic Books.

Wilson, Woodrow. 1889. *The State and Federal Governments of the United States.* Boston: D.C. Heath.

Winter, Sidney F. 1964. Economic "natural selection" and the theory of the firm. *Yale Economic Essays* 4:225–272.

———. 1990. Survival, selection, and inheritance in evolutionary theories of organization. In *Organizational Evolution: New Directions,* edited by Jitndra V. Singh (pp. 269–297). Newbury Park, CA: Sage.

———. 2005. Developing evolutionary theory for economics and management. In *Great Minds in Management: The Process of Theory Development,* edited by Ken G. Smith and Michael A. Hitt (pp. 509–546). Oxford: Oxford University Press.

Womack, James P., Daniel T. Jones, and Daniel Roos. 1991. *The Machine that Changed the World: The Story of Lean Production.* New York: HarperCollins (Harper Perennial).

Woodward, Joan. 1958. *Management and Technology.* London: H.M.S.O.

Wuthnow, Robert. 1987. *Meaning and Moral Order: Explorations in Cultural Analysis.* Berkeley: University of California Press.

Wuthnow, Robert, James Dividson Hunter, Albert J. Bergesen, and Edith Kurzwell. 1984. *Cultural Analysis: The Work of Peter L. Berger, Mary Douglas, Michel Foucault, and Jurgen Habermas.* Boston: Routledge & Kegan Paul.

Zajac, Edward J., and James D. Westphal. 2002. Intraorganizational economics. In *The Blackwell Companion to Organizations,* edited by Joel A. C. Baum (pp. 233–255). Oxford: Blackwell.

Zald, Mayer N. 1996. Culture, ideology and strategic framing. In *Comparative Perspectives on Social Movements,* edited by Doug McAdam, John D. McCarthy, and Mayer N. Zald (pp. 261–274). Cambridge: Cambridge University Press.

Zald, Mayer N., and Roberta Ash. 1966. Social movement organizations: Growth, decay, and change. *Social Forces* 44:327–340.

Zald, Mayer N., and Patricia Denton. 1963. From evangelism to general service: The transformation of the YMCA. *Administrative Science Quarterly* 8:214–234.

Zilber, Tammar B. 2002. Institutionalization as an interplay between actions, meanings, and actors: The case of a rape crisis center in Israel. *Academy of Management Journal* 45:234–254.

Zimmerman, Donald H. 1969. Record-keeping and the intake process in a public welfare agency. In *On Record: Files and Dossiers in American Life,* edited by Stanton Wheeler (pp. 319–354). New York: Russell Sage Foundation.

Znaniecki, Florian. 1945. Social organization and institutions. In *Twentieth Century Society,* edited by Gerges Gurvitch and Wilbert E. Moore (pp. 172–217). New York: The Philosophical Library.

Zuboff, Shoshana. 1985. Technologies that informate: Implications for human resource management in the computerized industrial workplace. In *Human Resources, Management Trends and Challenges,* edited by Richard E. Walton and Raul R. Lawrence (pp. 103–139). Boston: Harvard Business School Press.

———. 1988. *In the Age of the Smart Machine.* New York: Basic Books.

Zucker, Lynne G. 1977. The role of institutionalization in cultural persistence. *American Sociological Review* 42:726–743.

———. 1983. Organizations as institutions. In *Research in the Sociology of Organizations,* edited by Samuel B. Bacharach, vol. 2 (pp. 1–47). Greenwich, CT: JAI Press.

———. ed. 1988a. *Institutional Patterns and Organizations: Culture and Environment.* Cambridge, MA: Ballinger.

———. 1988b. Where do institutional patterns come from? Organizations as actors in social systems. In *Institutional Patterns and Organizations: Culture and Environment,* edited by Lynne G. Zucker (pp. 23–49). Cambridge, MA: Ballinger.

———. 1989. Combining institutional theory and population ecology: No legitimacy, no history (Comment on Carroll and Hannan, 1989). *American Sociological Review* 54:542–545.

———. 1991. Postscript: Microfoundations of institutional thought. In *The New Institutionalism in Organizational Analysis,* edited by Walter W. Powell and Paul J. DiMaggio (pp. 103–106). Chicago: University of Chicago Press.

Zuckerman, Ezra W. 1999. The categorical imperative: Securities analysts and the illegitimacy discount. *American Journal of Sociology* 104:1398–1438.

Zysman, John. 1983. *Governments, Markets and Growth: Finance and the Politics of Industrial Change.* Ithaca, NY: Cornell University.

Index

Actors and action:
    collective 74–75, 189–190
    social construction of,
        15, 64–66, 74–76
    theory of organization, 42
Affect. *See* Emotion
Agency and agents:
    and institutional change, 94–105,
        108–109, 118–119
    and institutional construction,
        94–103
    types of, 97–103
Artifacts:
    as carriers of institutional
        elements, 83–85, 145
Associations:
    as institutional agents, 100–101
Authority, 13, 53, 60
    types of, 13

Basel Mission, 131–132
Bureaucracy:
    Columbia School approach to,
        20–23
    design of, 104–105, 114–115

Carnegie School, 25–26
Carriers. *See* Institution, carriers
Coercive processes, 52–55
    and legitimacy, 53
    and normative processes, 53, 136
    and the state, 34, 98–99
Cognitive, 16, 25–26, 36–37
    aspects of diffusion, 57, 137–138
    and classification of
        cultures, 38–39

limitations of individuals, 37
    theory, 36–37
    See also Cultural-cognitive
        elements and processes
Columbia School, 20–23
Community, interorganization,
    183–184
Constitutive processes, 64–65,
    74–75, 100, 111–112, 125–128,
    140–141, 194
Contracts, relational, 124–125
Corporations, 75, 113, 137, 143,
    153–154, 162, 200–202
    and charitable
        contributions, 163
    and interlocking boards, 143
    and liability of boards, 175
    governance structures in, 29–30,
        113, 162, 200–202
    multidivisional structures in
        113, 162, 200–202
    takeover defenses in, 102, 143
Cultural-cognitive elements and
    processes, 15–16, 40–41, 43,
    56–59, 61, 64–66, 74–76, 80, 88,
    96–97, 100, 110–111, 125–128,
    130, 140–141, 186–189, 197
    and constitutive rules, 64–65,
        74–75, 100, 111–112, 125–128,
        140–141, 194
    and construction of institutions,
        64–66, 74–75, 96–97, 100
    and diffusion of innovations,
        140–142
    and framing processes,
        141–142, 187–188

and legitimacy, 59–61, 138,
    154–155, 158–159
and levels of analysis, 85–90
and maintenance of institutions,
    129–130
and organization fields, 186–189
and professionals, 100
carriers of, 79–85
Culture, 15, 23–24, 37–40, 56–59
and behavior, 41, 49
and social structure, 39
as "tool kit," 40
material, 83–84
semiotic functions, 38, 57
See also Cultural-cognitive
    elements and processes

Decision making, 25, 167
Deinstitutionalization, 195–208
and faculty tenure systems,
    198–199
of permanent employment
    policies, 199–200
of French haut cuisine, 207–208
of U.S. corporations, 201–202
of the U.S. health care field,
    202–205
sources of, 196–198
See also Institutionalization
Diffusion, 79–85, 132–145
and carriers, 141–145
and cultural-cognitive
    processes, 140–142
and early vs. late adopters,
    161–196
and editing processes, 80
and normative processes, 135–137
and regulative processes, 134–135
and organizational attributes,
    163–164
and organizational linkages,
    164–165
and reference groups, 166
and theorization, 140–141
demand-side vs. supply-side
    explanations, 133
mechanisms of, 133, 140–145
of CEO inventive plans, 137
of civil service reforms,
    134–135, 161–162

of employment practices, 99, 161,
of innovative group activities,
    139–140
of managerial ideologies and
    practices, 139, 143
of multidivisional structures,
    162, 200–202
of norms regarding corporate
    contributions, 165
of state bar associations, 176–177
of total quality management
    (TQM) in hospitals, 163
of TQM in manufacturing firms,
    139–140
of Western models of
    organization, 135

Ecology, population, 86–87,
    88–89, 109–112
Economics:
and early institutional theory, 2–5
and neoinstitutional theory, 26–31
and regulative elements, 52, 90
Austrian School of, 2, 17(n1)
evolutional theory in 3, 30–33
neoclassical, 4–5, 29
Emotion, 39, 54, 56, 59
Entrepreneur, institutional, 97–98
defined, 98
Ethnomethodology, 40–41
Entropy, 128
Environment:
technical vs. institutional, x, 43
institutional complexity of, 159–60

Field, organization, 16, 44, 86–90, 99,
    108–109, 152, 181–208, 212
and cultural frames, 187–188
and institutional logics, 186–187,
    201, 203–204
and relational systems 185–186
core vs. peripheral actors, 102
defined, 86, 184
governance systems,
    185–186, 204–205,
key components, 185–90
of alternative dispute resolution,
    102–103
of art museums, 108–109
of consumer protection, 109

of health care, 202–205
of largest U.S. corporations, 200–202
of international commercial
    arbitration, 108
of state bar associations, 176–177
structuration processes, 190–195
varying location in, 161

Governance structures:
in organizational fields, 185–186
of large corporations
    113, 162, 200–202
organizations as, 29, 112–114
political institutions as, 33, 35, 53,
    98–99, 114–115

Habitus, 42–43

Identity:
organizational, 116, 125
politics, 207
theory, 37
Ideal type, 14
Ideas, 127, 212–213
Incentive, 52–53, 122–123
Institution:
agents, 94–103
and agency, 76–77, 94–105,
    108–109, 118–119
and emotion, 39, 54, 56, 59
and ideas, 127, 212–213
and performance, 123, 152, 197
and power, 23, 49, 61, 95, 98–99,
    197, 200–201
and levels of analysis,
    85–90, 106–119
as a level or organization, 24
as functional arena, 8–9
as property and process 50, 121
as symbolic systems, 12–13, 14–16,
    39–40, 48–70, 79–81, 100
background vs. proximate,
    112–113
carriers of, 79–85, 140–145
collective organizational response
    to, 175–177
conflicting, 61–62, 102–103,
    153–157, 159–160
consistency of support for,
    58–60, 62

construction of, 93–119
content of, 73–76
cultural-cognitive elements and
    processes in, 15–16, 40–41, 43,
    56–59, 61, 64–66, 74–76, 80,
    88, 96–97, 100, 110–111,
    125–128, 130, 140–141,
    186–189, 197
defined, 3, 9, 10, 12, 14,
    16, 22, 23, 48
diffusion of, 79–85, 132–145
elements (pillars) of, 47–70
functional explanation of,
    29, 113–114
indicators of, 50–59
individual organizational
    responses to, 151–153,
    169–175
integrated conception of, 50–51
intraorganizational, 116–117
maintenance of, 128–132
microfoundations of, 15, 43,
    49–50, 76–79
normative elements and processes
    in, 14, 24, 54–56, 61, 68, 74,
    87–88, 96, 100–101, 123–125,
    130–131, 135–137, 154, 157,
    174, 197, 208
perceived objectivity of, 11, 42,
    57, 66, 125–128
regulative elements and processes
    in, 50–54, 63–66, 76, 87,
    96–97, 98–99, 131, 134–135,
    153, 154, 156, 157, 173, 176,
    197–198, 201
shaping of technical
    processes, 83–84
stability of, 48–49, 128–132
theorization of, 100, 126, 140–141
transnational, 106–107
Institutionalization, 15, 17, 21–23,
    40–41, 70–79, 85, 93–120,
    122–128, 132, 190–193, 195–208
and deinstitutionalization,
    128, 195–208
and increasing commitments,
    21–22, 123–125
and increasing objectification,
    125–128
and increasing returns, 122–123

and power, 23, 49, 61, 77, 95, 131
defined, 14, 16, 21–22
demand- vs. supply-side
    explanations 104–105
mechanisms, 121–128
phases of, 40–41, 144–145
top-down and bottom-up
    processes, 77–78, 136,
    166–169, 173–177, 190–193
Institutional change, 79–85, 93–119,
    190–208
and agency, 94–103
and bricolage, 142
and social movements, 103, 194
convergent vs. divergent, 132–133,
    151–153, 177
Institutional effects and
    processes, 121–146
and organization fields, 181–208
and organization populations,
    109–112
and organization strategies,
    169–177
and societal systems, 107–108,
    205–207
depth vs. shallowness, 134
naturalistic vs. agent-based
    accounts, 94–97
sources of divergence in, 177
top down and bottom-up
    processes, 77–78, 136,
    166–169, 173–177, 190–193
translation, 133
Institutional logics, 68, 186–187,
    200, 201, 204
as conceptions of control, 200–202
as business recipes, 187
defined, 186
Institutional theory:
conservative bias of, 219–220
distinctive features, 211–214
maturation of, 215–219
old vs. new, 16, 26–44
Interests (preferences),
    4, 12, 32–35, 52, 66
endogenous vs. exogenous, 4
International:
organizations, 101
relations, 34
Isomorphism, 151–157

Law and society theory, 54, 167–169
Legal systems, 6, 12–13, 52–54,
    59–62, 74, 98–99, 134–136,
    153–154, 156–157, 161–162, 173,
    175–177, 185–186, 197–198,
    200–202, 204
Legitimacy, 24, 29–62, 108,
    151–158, 173, 207
and accreditation, 60, 155, 157
and authority systems, 13, 53, 60
and cultural-cognitive elements,
    59–61, 138, 154–155, 158–159
and embeddedness, 138
and goals, 24, 151–152
and impression management, 155
and isomorphism, 151–157
and legal sanctions, 156
and media, 156
and normative elements, 59–61,
    154–156
and organization population
    density, 89, 138
and organization structure, 152–153
and regulative elements, 61–62,
    153–156
bases of, 19–61, 153–156
defined, 59
Levels of analysis, 85–90

Markets, 28, 123
as governance structures, 28
social construction of, 75
Mechanisms, 43, 121–22, 140–145
Media, 80–81, 141

Nation. *See* State
National Aeronautics and Space
    Administration (NASA), 116
Network measures, 142–142
Normative elements and processes,
    14, 24, 54–56, 61, 68, 74, 87–88,
    96, 100–101, 123–125, 130–131,
    135–137, 154, 157, 174, 197, 208
and coercive processes, 53, 136
and institutional stability, 130–131
and legitimacy, 59–61, 154–156
and levels of analysis, 85–90
and sociologists, 55
carriers of, 79–85
Norms, defined, 54–55

Objectification, 40–41, 125–128
    defined, 125
Open system theory, x
Organization:
    archetypes (forms), 75, 109–110,
        188–189
    as area of study, 19–20
    as game player, 150
    as information system, 167
    as institution, 150
    as level of analysis, 85–80
    and public policy, 166–169
    complexity of administrative
        structure, 159–160
    decoupling in, 144, 156, 171–173
    field, 16, 44, 86–90, 99, 108–109,
        152, 181–208
    formal and informal
        structures in, 153
    founding of, 158–159
    genetics, 111
    goals, 24, 151–152
    hybrid, 160
    identity, 116
    imprinting of, 109, 158–159
    inertia of, 109, 128
    international, 34, 101
    network forms, 125
    population, 86–90, 109–112, 182
    response to institutional
        pressures, 163–169
    set, 182
    subtypes, 75
Ontology, 63–66

Path-dependence, 122–123
Personnel systems, 99,134–136,
        159, 161–162, 167–168, 193–194,
        198, 199–200
Phenomenology, 40–41
Political science:
    and early institutional theory, 5–8
    and historical institutionalism,
        31–32, 35
    and neoinstitutional theory, 31–35
    behavioralist approaches in, 7
    rational choice approaches in,
        7, 32–35, 95–96, 114
Population, organization,
        86–90, 109–112, 182

defined, 86–87
    density, 89, 138
Power, 23, 49, 61, 77, 95,
        131, 200–202
    and legitimacy, 53, 61
    See also Agency and agents
Pragmatism, 4, 69–70
Professions, 10, 61, 75, 99–100
    and cultural cognitive
        elements, 108
    and the state, 98,100
    as institutional agents, 99–100
    in fine arts, 108–109
    legal, 100, 111–112
    personnel, 99, 134–135, 159,
        161–162, 167–168,
        193–194, 198
    medical, 198, 202–205
Property rights, 34, 98
    defined 98

Rational, 2–4, 14
    choice, 7, 29, 32–36, 112–115
    man, 2–4
Rationality, 43, 66–70
    and social context, 69
    bounded, 25, 28, 67
    collective, 217–218
    modes of, 67–68
Rationalization, 43, 74–75, 150–151
    defined, 74
Regulative elements and
        processes, 50–54, 63–66, 76,
        87, 96–97, 98–99, 131, 134–135,
        153, 154, 156, 157, 173, 176,
        197–198, 201
    and constitutive processes, 64–65
    and diffusion of institutions,
        134–135
    and institutional stability, 131–132
    and legitimacy, 61, 153–154
    and levels of analysis, 85–90
    and the natural environment, 176
    and the tobacco industry, 176
    carriers of, 79–85
    costs of, 53–54
Relational systems:
    as carrier of institutional
        elements, 81–82, 142–144
Resource dependence theory, 59, 169

Roles, 55, 59–59
    defined, 55
    intermediary, 144
Routines, 30–31
    as carrier of institutional
        elements, 82–83, 144–145

Schools:
    administrative complexity in,
        159–160
    and retention of innovations, 131
    tenure systems in, 198–199
Scientific continuum, 63–64
Sense making, 167, 192–93
Silicon Valley, 111–112
Social construction, 11–12, 15–16, 32,
        64–66, 74–75, 125–128, 140–141
    of actors, 15, 32, 64–65, 74–75
    of collective actors, 74–75
    of markets, 75
    of technology, 84
    of truth vs. reality, 64–65
    See also, Constitutive processes
Social movements, 103, 194–195
    as institutional agent, 103
Social science:
    and natural science, 13, 64
Social structure:
    and action, 49–50
    and material resources, 49
    duality of, 50
Society:
    as level of analysis, 85–90, 107–108
Sociology:
    and early institutional theory, 8–16
    and neoinstitutional theory, 36–44
    and normative elements, 55–56, 90
    and rational choice theory, 44
State, 34, 53–54, 98–99
    and personnel systems, 99
    and regulative processes,
        98–99, 134
    autonomy of, 53
    weak, 136

Strategies, organization, 169–177
    institutional shaping of, 169–170
    of individual organizations,
        169–177
    of collections of organizations,
        175–177
Structural:
    equivalence, 165, 185
    holes, 102
Structuration, 49–50, 77–79, 84–85,
        99, 195–208
    and destructuration, 195–208
    Giddens' theory of, 49–50, 77–79
    of French *haut cuisine*, 207–208
    of health care field, 202–205
    indicators of, 190–191
    of routines, 144–145
    of organization fields, 195–208
    of technology, 83–84
Symbolic systems, 12–13, 15–16,
        39–40, 48–70, 79–81, 100
    and behavior, 49–50
    as carrier of institutional
        elements, 140–142
    See also Cultural-cognitive
        elements and processes

Technology:
    information and
        communication, 81
    social construction of, 83–84
    structuration of, 84–85
Tennessee Valley Authority (TVA),
        22–23, 115–116
Transaction cost, 3, 27–30, 112–114

Values:
    defined, 54
    stratification of, 24

World system, 97–90
    and construction of institutions,
        106–107
    as level of analysis, 85–90

About the Author

W. Richard (Dick) Scott (Ph.D., University of Chicago) is Professor Emeritus in the Department of Sociology with courtesy appointments in the Graduate School of Business, School of Education, and School of Medicine, Stanford University. He has spent his entire professional career at Stanford, serving as Director of the NIMH Training Program on Organizations and Mental Health from 1972 to 1989 and as Director of the Stanford Center for Organizations Research from 1988 to 1996. He is the author or editor of more than 20 books and 125 articles and book chapters. His books include two widely used texts in organizations: an early book with Peter M. Blau, *Formal Organizations: A Comparative Approach,* published in 1962 and reprinted as a Stanford Business Classic in 2003 by Stanford University Press; and his book, *Organizations: Rational, Natural and Open Systems,* first published in 1981, with the 5th edition appearing in 2003. A successor volume, coauthored with Gerald F. Davis, *Organizations and Organizing: Rational, Natural and Open System Perspectives,* was published in 2007. His most recent research monographs are *Institutional Change and Healthcare Organizations: From Professional Dominance to Managed Care* (with Martin Ruef, Peter J. Mendel, and Carol A. Caronna), 2000; and *Between Movement and Establishment: Organizations Advocating for Youth* (with Milbrey McLaughlin, Sarah Deschenes, Kathryn Hopkins, and Anne Newman), forthcoming.

Dick is a past fellow of the Center for Advanced Study in the Behavioral Sciences and of the Bellagio Study and Conference Center, and in 1988 he was the recipient of the Distinguished Scholar Award from the Management and Organization Theory Division of the Academy of Management. In 1996, he received the Richard D. Irwin Award for Scholarly Contributions to Management from the Academy of Management. In 2000, the Section on Organization, Occupations and

Work of the American Sociological Association created the W. Richard Scott award to annually recognize an outstanding article-length contribution to the field. He was elected to membership in the Institute of Medicine, National Academy of Sciences in 1975. He received an Honorary Doctorate from the Copenhagen Business School in 2000 and from the Helsinki School of Economics and Business in 2001. From 2006 to 2007, he served as President of the Sociological Research Association.

Dick and his wife, Joy, celebrated their 50th anniversary in 2005 and have three children and five grandchildren (and three grand-dogs and a cat).